International Examples of Lean in Healthcare

Typically entrenched and systemic, healthcare problems require the sort of comprehensive solutions that can only be addressed by a change in culture and a shift in thinking. Organizations around the world are using Lean to redesign care and improve processes in a way that achieves and sustains meaningful results for patients, staff, physicians, and health systems. This book demonstrates how honest appraisal, intelligent planning, and vigilant follow-up have led to dramatic improvements in a variety of healthcare settings across the world. It teaches us how innovative organizations can find sustainable solutions to seemingly intractable problems by following a path guided by Lean Thinking. Lean methods may not solve every healthcare problem, but as these cases prove, changing a culture rather than personnel results in more effective sustainable change.

This multi-authored book provides expert descriptions of Lean methods and their application in healthcare, written by the people who developed and tested the methods in healthcare settings. Each chapter brings together a description of the technique or approach, with examples of application in practice from the author's own practice. Authors use an engaging approach to their narrative, with examples from their personal experience or engagement being described to illustrate the practical application of theoretic approaches. In painting a picture of the environment in which these tools and techniques have been applied, readers will understand the transferability to their own workplace environment. This will be an opportunity to tell real stories of the application of Lean in healthcare and give readers the opportunity to learn from people from across the world, about subjects on which they are acknowledged topic experts, based on day-to-day Lean practice.

International Examples of
Lean in Healthcare

Case Studies of Best Practices

Elaine Mead, Cameron Stark, and Maimie Thompson

Routledge
Taylor & Francis Group

A PRODUCTIVITY PRESS BOOK

First published 2023
by Routledge
605 Third Avenue, New York, NY 10158

and by Routledge
4 Park Square, Milton Park, Abingdon, Oxon, OX14 4RN

Routledge is an imprint of the Taylor & Francis Group, an informa business

ISBN: 9780367344696 (hbk)
ISBN: 9781032398464 (pbk)
ISBN: 9780429346958 (ebk)

DOI: 10.4324/9780429346958

Typeset in Garamond
by Deanta Global Publishing Services, Chennai, India

Dedicated to the memory of our friend and colleague Murdina Campbell

1971–2022

Contents

Foreword

I was talking to a group of surgeons recently, and they had issues with access to theatres, a backlog of work after COVID-19, various problems with ineffective meetings, and a powerful sense that their work could be more equitably and efficiently organised. A short exercise in thinking about improvements generated a stream of good ideas – as you might expect from a group of energised, effective, and moderately competitive individuals – and a clear set of priority actions for what might be done next quickly emerged. Simultaneously, however, they were pessimistic about the possibilities of success, doubtful if anything would change, and startlingly unwilling to commit to the first steps.

How could this be? How had they learned to be so negative? They worked for a highly effective and externally validated organisation that had an excellent reputation with patients and professionals alike for the quality of their services. Experience, nonetheless, had taught the surgeons that their ideas would be buried in interdepartmental disagreements and enervating discussions about budgets and time and middle-management worries about unknowable, unforeseeable consequences. As any bright and motivated people would, they could see many possibilities, but they were also naturally conservative about any change that was not within the clinical research model. They also doubted they had "permission" to try.

Yet the leaders of their organisation were publicly encouraging a continuous improvement effort, supporting the wider and deeper learning of improvement science through Lean tools, clearly wanting to support staff in their efforts to improve processes and thus improve both staff and patient experience. They absolutely thought they had given everyone permission! What was wrong? Why was there such a disconnect between intent and outcome?

Not long after this discussion, I was high up in the French Alps. I am an experienced alpinist and together with my friend and guide Yves, we climbed up to our goal, high up on a remote glacier, near the summit of Mont Blanc, Europe's highest mountain. We were watching some other climbers following in our tracks. My guide was not impressed. We were using very technical equipment and techniques including very specialised touring skis and we had climbed the high glacier roped together – it was a notorious spot for hidden crevasses, accidents were likely, and indeed climbers regularly died there or thereabouts. Our followers were attempting the route without skis, and they were not roped together. We thought it likely they were heading for a famous rock climb nearby. We had a brief discussion about the annual death toll on Mont Blanc. Often a complex mixture of bad luck, rapid changes in weather, and inexperience led to tragic situations and many near misses. More rarely the cause was foolhardiness – itself usually just a lack of experience, combined with inadequate technique, dressed up in over-confidence.

Yves was strong on metaphor. "People," he said, nodding towards the other climbers, "need to realise that Mont Blanc is like the ocean. Learning to swim in pool, sail dinghies on reservoir, kayak on a gentle river, these things do not prepare you to cross the ocean." He sighed and briefly reflected with me on several mountain rescue callouts he had had to join over the years: in terrible weather; in the dark; at bad times of the season. He didn't mind helping – indeed he felt a moral duty to help – but he always wondered why, on so many occasions, people thought the ocean was just a bigger version of the gentle waters they had come from and learned in, and thus, almost inevitably, they had lacked the humility to see the real task they had given themselves.

This book is both a guide and a map, a description of the territory and its joys plus a helpful sharing of experience.

After nearly 20 years of working on the implementation of Lean in healthcare, in organisations I led and whilst trying to help others to cross the same ocean, climb the same mountain, there is one thing I am certain of: we all need a guide by our sides. With us and beside us. However sure we are, experienced we are, and enthusiastically we approach the task, we will need help.

In many texts and from many trainers, consultants, and other Lean leaders, what you first get is a reductive account of Lean tools and promises of easy wins (not always sustained!). This introduction may lead us to mistake the ocean for a balmy lido. Here, however, in this book, the authors have brought together a full set of experiences to help develop a range of skills. Of course, the technique is important and discipline with tools and methods must be learned. But, as a counterpoint to the reductive (and indeed seductive) approach, here we learn about context and leadership and timescale and performance demands – and, of course, the patients – all combining to create a huge, complex challenge. Here the authors help us to see what they have learned and where their experience can translate into general principles. And, crucially, help is outlined for how to find the right guide, the right strategic partner.

So often, the attitudes and engagement (or otherwise) of the senior doctors is a massive reveal in the progress that organisations are making by implementing Lean. Junior doctors may join with the nurses, managers, other colleagues, and patients to make huge progress on individual point and service line improvements, engineering great gains in time, mistake proofing, and other process benefits that often feel transformational in a healthcare setting. This is climbing into the scenic and sunny foothills, seeing the incredible views from a new perspective for the first time. The local mountains can then be scaled by leaders who see that context, behaviour, and crucially their visible leadership, all add to the creation of a culture where continuous improvement, driven by Lean skills, can thrive. But the biggest mountains of all require even more effort, more time, and more support. I am certain, from their own training and experience in clinical care, the senior doctors know this huge challenge is there and prefer the safe ground of what they already know. The view from the foothills may be sufficient for some Lean leaders, but for all staff, including the senior doctors, to genuinely feel valued, engaged, trusted, respected, and happy – and for every patient consistently to receive timely, value-adding care – this is the mountain we want to be on, the real ocean we long to venture into. The surgeons I spoke to were not without ideas, enthusiasm, and knowledge. Their managers hoped to engage their effort but so far had yet to penetrate their protective cloak of realistic cynicism. They are making progress, nonetheless. They understand their goal and they know there is climbing still to be done.

Faced with obvious difficulties and hidden traps and dangers created by a change in the weather, we can all become guides; we can all coach each other and learn together. Partly this is a new leadership ethos to learn with curiosity and humility – and partly this progress is possible because others have already learned and stand ready at our side.

Here, the authors set out to share their learning, stand with us, beside us, and guide us from the gentle shallows into the great and fabulous ocean.

Dr Stephen Singleton
Cumbria, UK
July 2022

Acknowledgements

We thank the organisations that we have worked with and learned from. Many clinicians, managers, and quality improvement experts have shared their time and expertise with us and although not all are represented in this book, they have all influenced its contents.

The book commenced a few months before the onset of the COVID-19 pandemic which inevitably directed all the contributors into other work in their own services. We are grateful to them for their perseverance with their chapters in these extraordinary circumstances. Kris Mednansky at Taylor & Francis was an unflagging guide and support in the process of producing this book.

Cameron Stark would like to thank Marilyn for her encouragement and support.

Editors

Elaine Mead is an executive director of Improvement, Care and Compassion, IC&C, an organisation committed to supporting leaders on their improvement journey across the UK and Europe. She has worked as Executive Sensei for National Health Service (NHS) Improvement in England and is a Leadership Faculty member of the Institute of Health Improvement. Elaine is a founding member of the Catalysis European CEO Forum and continues to connect and support colleagues from across Europe, from her base in Scotland. She is a certified Lean Leader from Tees, Esk and Wear Valley NHS Foundation Trust having had a close association with the Virginia Mason Institute. Elaine is also a Fellow of, and tutor for, the Institute of Quality and Safety (ISQua). Prior to establishing IC&C Elaine was chief executive for NHS Highland for eight years where she led the development of the Highland Quality Approach to improve the quality of care based on increasing value. She has over 30 years of experience of working in the NHS including as a clinician and in executive roles.

Cameron Stark, MB ChB, MPH, MSc (Dist), MRCPsych, FFPH, is an Honorary Reader and Part-time Lecturer at the University of the Highlands and Islands (UHI) Outer Hebrides. Stark leads the UHI postgraduate module on the application of Lean in healthcare. After graduating from the University of Glasgow, he trained in psychiatry and public health and worked as an NHS Public Health Doctor for over 30 years. Stark was the quality improvement science lead for NHS Highland and trained as a Lean leader with Tees, Esk and Wear Valley NHS Foundation Trust. He has published over 60 papers in peer-reviewed journals and has written or edited 5 previous textbooks.

Maimie Thompson is an engagement and communication specialist currently working in healthcare planning and the use of digital technologies in the public sector. She has contributed to a range of publications including as a co-author of a chapter for the *International Handbook on Integrated Care* (second edition) about Scotland. Maimie is a certified Lean leader and a former recipient of NHS Scotland's manager of the year award for her work on unscheduled care.

Contributors

Todd L. Allen, FACEP, serves as the senior vice-president and chief quality officer at the Queen's Health System based in Honolulu, Hawaii. He has overall responsibility for regulatory reporting and certifications, quality, safety, infection prevention and control, and the function of performance improvement. He previously served at Intermountain Healthcare in Salt Lake City, UT, as the assistant chief quality officer and as the senior executive medical director for the Healthcare Delivery Institute. His research has been supported by the National Heart, Lung and Blood Institute (NHLBI), and he has authored or co-authored over 45 peer-reviewed publications. Todd also serves as an invited lecturer on quality, Lean methods, and improvement in healthcare for systems throughout the United States and Europe.

Salah Arafa is an interventional cardiologist at the Heart Hospital of Hamad Medical Corporation, Doha. He graduated from Tripoli University Libya and completed his post-graduation in the UK. He has more than 30 years of clinical experience. In addition, he is the director of performance improvement and has experience in quality improvement and risk management leading many initiatives at the facility level. He is a key member of many patient safety committees at the facility and corporate levels. Salah has many research, posters, and presentations under his name.

Kim Barnas is a recognized authority in creating fully integrated management systems in hospitals around the world. She is the current chief executive of Catalysis, a former hospital president, author of *Beyond Heroes: A Lean Management System for Healthcare* (winner of the 2014 Shingo Prize for Research) and co-author of *Becoming the Change: Leadership Behavior Strategies for Continuous Improvement in Healthcare*.

Steven Bartley is the associate director of Improvement and Design at Tees, Esk and Wear Valleys NHS Foundation Trust (TEWV). Steven has over 25 years of experience in quality improvement, first in the automotive sector and then in the public sector. He has worked across healthcare and Local Authority service provision. He was head of TEWV's External Kaizen Promotion Office, providing training and coaching across many organisations. Steven was the head of quality improvement at TEWV before taking up his current post.

Murdina Campbell was a senior quality improvement lead in the Programme Management Office at NHS Highland. Murdina trained as a midwife and was a ward sister at Raigmore Hospital in Inverness leading a combined day-patient and in-patient unit. She trained in Lean with NHS Highland's Kaizen Promotion Office (KPO). Murdina later became deputy head of the KPO, where she taught Lean methods and coached staff training to lead Rapid Process Improvement

Workshops. Murdina also led work on rapid adaptions to NHS Highland services during the COVID-19 pandemic and supported an organisational improvement programme on out-patient service delivery in NHS Highland's Programme Management Office.

Graham Canning, BEng (Hons), MSc, is the managing director of consultancy firm Lean FSL Associates, and a partner in the training company People-Centered Excellence. He has worked in improvement consultancy roles for 17 years across many sectors including healthcare. His experience is built on 15 years of working in the manufacturing sector for companies such as Toyota, Black & Decker, and Pilkington Glass. He recently presented a paper on Toyota Kata at the European Lean Educators Conference in Portugal and is certified to Level 3b in Cardiff University's Lean Competency System (LCS). Graham is an experienced Kata coach and a founding member of the Kata School, UK. He lectures part time on the Executive MBA programme at Cardiff Business School and leads a research workstream for the Lean Enterprise Research Council (LERC) on the successful use of Kata to grow scientific thinking in organisations.

Nathan Clifford is the expert by experience lead for Southern Health NHS Foundation Trust in England. His role involves using his own lived experience to affect change within the Trust. He is a strong advocate to ensure that patients' voices are heard in a meaningful and effective manner as part of quality improvement in healthcare. He has also undergone quality improvement methodology training.

Kay Cordiner joined the Institute for Healthcare Improvement in 2018 as Faculty. She supports the spread of the methodology across other health systems including Hamad Medical Corporation in Doha, Northwell Hospital in New York and Western Health and Social Care Trust in Northern Ireland as well as in Scotland. She is also faculty for the Royal College of Physicians on Quality Improvement and has published on Value Management in the *Harvard Business Review* and *British Medical Journal*.

Sarah Curtis is the expert by experience lead for NHS Hampshire, Southampton and Isle of White Clinical Commissioning Group.

Poonam Gupta, MBBS, MScPH, CPHQ, CMQ/OE, is a physician and currently head of quality improvement at the Heart Hospital of Hamad Medical Corporation, Doha, Qatar. Gupta is trained as an improvement advisor and patient safety executive with the Institute for Healthcare Improvement, Boston, and trained in Lean for healthcare at the University of Tennessee Knoxville, Haslam College of Business. As program director for value improvement in Heart Hospital, her work has been highly successful and has gained local and international attention. She is a faculty and improvement advisor for Institute for Healthcare Improvement, Boston. Gupta is the author of many published papers and abstracts in international peer-reviewed journals and teaching resources. She has earned more than 15 awards for several Quality Improvement and Patient Safety (QIPS) initiatives and has been a local and international speaker at various patient safety forums. Additionally, she collaborates with the Ministry of Public Health, Qatar, as healthcare facilities licensing inspector.

Ann Hill is a certified Kata coach, and her Lean experience has been predominantly within healthcare across several different settings. She specialises in leadership development and executive coaching. Ann has led national, regional, and organisational programmes and worked as an international consultant. Her improvement journey began as a biomedical scientist, combining the operational delivery of five services into one.

Fiona Keogan, BSc, MSc Physiotherapy, Post Grad Dip Stats, is the director of Lean transformation at St James's Hospital Dublin where she led the Older Person's Value Stream in Ireland East Hospital Group from 2017 to 2021. After graduating from Trinity College Dublin, she trained in musculoskeletal physiotherapy and worked as an advanced practice clinician and manager for almost 20 years. Fiona was hospital lead for the development of frailty intervention services in her role as Clinical Services manager 2015–2017 (the first service of its type in Ireland) and trained in Lean methodology with Cardiff University. She led multiple improvement projects in Ireland East Hospital Group, and her work on frailty won three Irish Healthcare awards and first prize at the Stanford Lean Transformation Conference in 2020.

Anne-Marie Keown, BSc Physiotherapy, MSc, and PhD candidate, University College Dublin Health Systems, is executive lead for Regional Integration and service redesign. Prior to this, she was the director of transformation and chief operating officer in the Ireland East Hospital Group. She has been a Lean practitioner for 18 years and has a proven track record in delivering large-scale improvement and transformation of services. Her work with the National Acute Medicine programme in the implementation of a National Early Warning Score received the Taoiseach's award. Ann-Marie's career spans 30 years, and she has worked in Ireland, the United Kingdom, Canada, and the Middle East.

Karl Marlowe, FRCPsych, is a consultant psychiatrist and currently the chief medical officer at Oxford Health NHS Foundation Trust. He has extensive training and experience in Quality Improvement methodologies (e.g., Improvement Science in Action; Lean) having led Quality Improvement projects in England: at East London NHS and Southern Health NHS Foundation Trusts. He holds post-graduate qualifications from University College London, Kings College London, and Oxford's Said Business School.

Páll Matthíasson, MD, PhD, MRCPsych, FRCP, FRCPEdin, is a consultant psychiatrist, and immediate past chief executive of LandspítalI – The National University Hospital of Iceland. Matthiasson currently leads work for the Icelandic government on a 2030 strategy and action plan in mental health. Following graduation in medicine from the University of Iceland, he trained in psychiatry at Bethlem and Maudsley Hospitals and completed a PhD in Neuropsychopharmacology at the Institute of Psychiatry. He worked as a consultant psychiatrist and quality lead within the NHS and independent hospitals in London before taking up the post of clinical director and then executive director for mental health in Iceland. From 2013 to 2021, Marthiasson was chief executive of Landspítali The National University Hospital of Iceland, a 700-bed, 6,000-staff hospital. Throughout his time as chief executive, he brought the health service on a quality and improvement drive, to reduce harm and improve outcomes. He has been an honorary senior lecturer at the University of Iceland and has in recent years a particular research interest in the user/patient experience and equal access.

Jens Normand has a MA in Economy and Leadership. For over a decade, together with the chief executive, he is responsible for the development of a culture of continuous quality improvement at the Mental Health Services of Greater Copenhagen. Before that, he worked as a senior consultant in other hospitals, helping and coaching leadership in quality improvement work. For six years,

Jens was also the chief development leader in Danske Bank. He has published two books about leadership and management in Improvement cultures.

Benedikt Olgeirsson is an engineer from the University of Iceland with a MA in Construction Engineering and Project Management from the University of Washington at Seattle. Benedikt has worked in several industries such as construction, transportation, logistics, and investments. He was the deputy chief executive of Landspítali from 2010 to 2015 and then the executive director of development until 2021. He currently works as a consultant and is the chairman of Vordur Insurance. In all of his management positions, Benedikt has focused on building a clear strategy for the organisation with a strong emphasis on continuous improvement.

Louise Roig, MA in History and Minority Studies, is a trained Lean facilitator and coach. She has contributed to the Lean journey at the Mental Health Services of Greater Copenhagen for over a decade with her co-author Jens Normand. During the last five years, she has been responsible for leadership training supporting the hospital's senior management team with their strategic work and policy deployment.

Gudrun Björg Sigurbjörnsdottir is a registered midwife, with a BSc in Nursing from the University of Iceland, and an MPH from the Nordic School of Public Health. Gudrun has worked at Landspitali – the University Hospital of Iceland for a long time, first as a midwife in the labor ward and ultrasound clinic, later as a manager and director in the Women's and Children's clinic and in the economic department of the hospital. She has been a manager for the Project Office or KPO (Kaizen Promotion Office) of Landspítali since 2009. As a manager of the KPO, Gudrun has been leading the implementation of Lean in the hospital and the improvement school. The focus has been on quality, patient safety, and the participation of patients in continuous improvements in the hospital.

Iain Smith, PhD, PGC, BSc, is an Associate Researcher at the Newcastle University Business School. With over 25 years of experience in England's National Health Service, Iain has worked in local, regional, and national roles as a quality improvement leader. He has trained in quality improvement methods with the Institute for Healthcare Improvement and trained as a Lean leader with Virginia Mason Medical Centre. Iain has applied these methods across many sectors of healthcare including in acute hospitals, primary care, and mental health services. As a mathematics graduate, he also holds postgraduate qualifications in innovation and transformational change and a PhD in the application of Lean thinking to design healthcare facilities and service systems.

Marc Rouppe van der Voort, MSc, studied Business Administration at Erasmus University Rotterdam and performed his PhD research at Maastricht University. He currently leads a transformation process in St Antonius Hospital to free up capacity by improving the way care is delivered and developing digitally supported healthcare. He has also led nationwide hospital programs on improving flow and reducing waiting and has worked in several management consulting roles. He has published three books on the application of Lean thinking in Dutch Healthcare. Van der Voort has led the Dutch Network for Lean in Healthcare (Lidz) for eight years and is currently on the advisory board of Lidz.

Frits van Merode, MSc, MA, BSc, BA, PhD, studied economics and philosophy at Erasmus University in Rotterdam and technical mathematics at the Eindhoven University of Technology.

Since 2001, he has been a full professor of Logistics and Operations Management in Healthcare at the Care and Public Health Research Institute (CAPHRI) of Maastricht University and Maastricht University Medical Centre+. Van Merode was dean of the Faculty of Health Sciences (2004–2006), dean of the Faculty of Sciences (2011–2015), and a member of the Executive Board (2008–2018) of the Maastricht University Medical Centre+. His main research projects are directed to the design of the layout of hospital buildings, intelligent operations management systems for healthcare, and real-time scheduling systems both for patients and for staff.

Anna Roos Vijverberg, MSc, studied medicine at Leiden University. Since 2018, she has been a PhD student at the Care and Public Health Research Institute (CAPHRI) of Maastricht University and the Department of Lean and Health Logistics at the St Antonius Hospital. Her research focuses on the Lean philosophy and the concept of value-based healthcare. More specifically, she investigates whether changes in the process design of the colorectal cancer care chain can lead to an improvement in quality of care, clinical outcomes, and flow.

Chapter 1

Using Lean in Healthcare

Cameron Stark, Elaine Mead, and Maimie Thompson

Contents

Aims

This chapter aims to:

- Describe the context of Lean in healthcare.
- Present examples and information on its effectiveness.
- Note the range of experiences of Lean application in healthcare, including circumstances where Lean implementations fail or do not deliver their desired results.
- Discuss the importance of context in Lean.
- Outline the chapters in the book to help the reader to navigate the volume.

Introduction

Lean is an organization-wide socio-technical performance improvement system.

(Marsilio et al., 2022, p. 3)

DOI: 10.4324/9780429346958-1

Implementing Lean in healthcare organisations is difficult. Anecdotal reports of either success or failure predominated in the literature for many years making it difficult for the reader to come to overall conclusions (Moraros et al., 2016). Systematic reviews have begun to appear (Tlapa et al., 2020). These provide evidence for the impact of Lean on service delivery in healthcare but also show that many Lean implementations, both in healthcare and in other organisations, do not always spread within organisations or are not sustained (Secchi & Camuffo, 2019).

The literature on Lean in healthcare has begun to move from discussions of methods alone to efforts to understand what affects its use in day-to-day healthcare practice (Sloan et al., 2014). The management of change is complex and response to change depends on both the organisational context and how individual staff members perceive the change (Oreg et al., 2011; Stark & Hookway, 2019). The views and responses of doctors have proved particularly important in Lean implementations in healthcare (Fournier et al., 2021).

Marsilio and Pissara reviewed socio-technical components of Lean implementations and concluded that strategic management; organisational structure including the role of Human resources departments and the existence of multi-skilled teams; organisational culture and the Lean tools themselves all affect the likelihood of successful introductions of Lean into a healthcare organisation (Marsilio & Pisarra, 2021). This is a similar list to the 'readiness factors' proposed by other researchers for consideration when introducing Lean into a healthcare organisation, and it indicates that good Lean expertise, management and strategic alignment are essential for a successful implementation. (Narayanamurthy et al., 2018). In the UK, Matthias and Brown (p. 1435) noted that 'significant operational and cultural hurdles (that) must be overcome for the full strategic benefits of Lean to be realised': the international literature demonstrates that this is a common challenge across the world, rather than one unique to the publicly funded health services (Lorden et al., 2014; Matthias & Brown, 2016).

This book provides a series of case studies that allow the reader to review practical applications of Lean in healthcare organisations. The chapters discuss the role of the application of methods, wider change across departments and organisations, the standardisation of Lean applications, the role of management and leaders, the importance of purpose and the use of data. The intent of all the chapters is to share practical learning, both what worked and what was less helpful. Context has proven to be of fundamental importance, and so case reports from a range of organisations on different continents are included. Different case examples cover both publicly and privately funded organisations and both hospital and community services.

History and Principles

Lean is a term coined to describe the application of techniques for quality improvement that were refined in Japan and popularised through work at Toyota (Teich & Faddoul, 2013). Lean has an inherent attraction to healthcare organisations as it developed 'as a reaction to the failures and weaknesses of mass-production … and the inherent challenges around maintaining quality at volume, as well as the potential inability to adequately reflect customer need' (Bateman et al., 2018a, p. 2). The tension of delivering high quality personalised care at volume is felt by all health and social care organisations so the resonance that this description of Lean has for care providers, and the hope it offers them, is apparent.

Lean has the added attraction that it acknowledges both capacity and demand; includes methods that can be applied to manage variations in demand; seeks to reduce errors and pays explicit attention to waste – a factor at the forefront of minds in systems that invariably operate with some degree of resource constraint. Maximising the value of the system to the patients who use it and minimising waste that does not take them closer to their goals has obvious appeal to healthcare managers and funders.

Core principles of Lean are summarised in Box 1.1. To this summary, we would add the importance of respect for staff and co-production with service users and funders, which are underpinning components of a Lean approach. Respect for staff lends itself to the kind of expert-driven systems that usually exist in healthcare settings. Lean can disrupt traditional organisational hierarchies by seeking to listen to the voice of all staff and patients. This can be a tension, however, in Lean implementations in systems where some clinical experts may expect very senior staff to have the final – and sometimes only – word on decisions relating to any aspect of care delivery.

While Lean is widely used in healthcare, it is challenging to use at sufficient scale to produce major organisational change (Marsilio et al., 2022). Hopp comments (p. 299) that 'most lean adopters achieve localised operational improvements without major strategic impact' (Hopp, 2018, p. 399). For many organisations, 'localised operational improvement' may be precisely what they seek, so this may be less of a concern than it appears. Many organisations do seek to increase the role of Lean approaches after initial successes. The challenges in moving from individual Lean-informed improvement projects to service line or organisation-wide improvement are significant, and some of the contributors to this book discuss their work on scaling Lean within their organisation.

There is also a tension in accounts of Lean between tools-based approaches that only focus on methods and those that argue that whole system change and attention to the adopting organisation's underlying philosophy is required (Andersson et al., 2020). Applications that apply a range of tools in depth to one or more specific areas of an organisation are sometimes described as 'pillar' implementations, while applications of a smaller range of tools over larger geographical or service areas can be described as 'platform' implementations (Bateman et al., 2018a).

This book deliberately includes examples that span the spectrum from local application of Lean tools to the organisation-wide spread of Lean. As we discuss in the final chapter, this is not a binary choice where one must choose either tool-only application or complete organisational immersion. This is a dynamic choice that can be reviewed over time and the degree of application and organisational alignment adapted to meet the current needs of an organisation and the situation in which it finds itself located. The case studies described illustrate the range of use of Lean that is possible within the broad rubric of healthcare.

FIVE CORE PRINCIPLES OF LEAN IN HEALTHCARE (WESTWOOD ET AL., 2007)

Value – understanding value from the customer's perspective (usually the patient).

Value streams – identifying all the steps (both helpful and unhelpful) in the pathways of care that patients experience as they move through the system.

Flow – working along care pathways to align healthcare processes to facilitate the smooth flow of patients and information.

Pull – creating processes that direct value towards the patient such that every step in the patient journey pulls people, skills, materials and information towards it, as needed.

Perfection – an ideal to be pursued through the ongoing continuous improvement of processes.

Lean in Healthcare

> The value of the service is co-created with the customer (or end user); patients are not customers at the end of a production process but right in the middle of it throughout their pathways of care.
>
> **(Smith et al., 2020, p. 2)**

The Smith et al. quote illustrates a key difference in healthcare from many other sectors that apply Lean. In manufacturing and retail services, the purchaser of the service generally arrives at the end of the process and makes a purchasing decision for an already formed product. In healthcare, the care delivered to the patient, and their experience of it, *is* the product. Patients have much less individual agency than retail purchasers. The clinicians have the knowledge and expertise, and they almost always must decide on diagnoses, interpret test results and recommend treatments based on their expertise. Although some people with long-term conditions do become experts on their own condition, most people must rely completely on the specialists involved in their care other than in selecting between treatment options presented to them by their healthcare professionals. They do not usually have control over the options that are offered, as these depend on established protocols and the judgement of the professionals involved. Many people ask the professional for their advice on the option they should choose, meaning that trust is important in the healthcare professional/patient relationship.

These considerations make the context of the application of Lean in healthcare different from many other settings. The professionals in healthcare have considerable autonomy because the choice of treatment is not always straightforward. Many people who need healthcare have more than one condition, and they may have had previous treatment, or be on existing medication, that further complicates the choice. Social circumstances may be important, such as the distance people must travel for a particular treatment or their work or family commitments which may affect what treatments are acceptable to them. In private healthcare systems, there may be treatments that are not included in the person's coverage. In public systems, some less common options may not be provided. These factors come together to produce different patient pathways for apparently similar conditions.

This is not as alien an environment for Lean as it might first seem. There are often several choices for treatment of a condition, but these options are not limitless. Research results will have identified preferred options, and specialist groups will often have produced guidelines for clinicians on the best choice of treatment. Even when there is a distinct choice, the pathways may include similar components. For example, in cancer treatment the surgery may be the same, but the type of chemotherapy offered may vary by patient. When different chemotherapies are provided, the same booking arrangements, pharmacy resources, drug administration location and nurses may deliver the care. In mental health services, discussed in this volume, different conditions treated as out-patients may share a booking system; assessment process; diary management for the clinicians and some aspects of information giving. This means that different treatment options may still share large portions of their pathway, and these are processes that can be improved by the application of Lean.

Radnor and colleagues noted that in much of healthcare it can be difficult or impossible to influence demand (Radnor et al., 2012). Lean offers much in responding to variation in demand. In some instances, demand can be levelled, such as in out-patient services where an accurate demand calculation will mean that the same number of appointments can be fed into the system each week without causing undue delay for patients.

In other instances, such as emergency care, the demand is unpredictable and will vary hour to hour, day to day, week to week and sometimes seasonally. Lean also offers approaches to cope with this, often by understanding the range of demand and identifying means of flexing capacity to cope. In some circumstances buffers may be added in the form of temporary additional capacity that then feed patients into the rest of the system at a manageable rate without disrupting their journey. Error reduction techniques are broadly applicable in healthcare, and the evidence-based approach of applying Plan-Do-Study-Act cycles to predict the change, measure the impact and adjust as required fits well with the scientific approach familiar to most healthcare staff. This has resulted in the adoption of Lean approaches in many healthcare systems.

A survey conducted in 2017 in the USA found that just under 70% of the hospitals responding used 'Lean or related Lean plus Six Sigma or Robust Process Improvement approaches' (Shortell et al., 2018). The response rate to the survey was under 30%, and as hospitals using these methods would be more likely to reply, this will overestimate the true proportion of use, but it does demonstrate significant application of Quality Improvement methods in US healthcare. There is other useful information in the survey: hospitals which reported using these methods were more likely to be in urban areas and to be part of larger hospital groups. Only 12% of the hospitals using these methods reported that they were using them system-wide. The time they had been using the system, leadership commitment, use of daily management and training were all associated with a greater likelihood of the organisation reporting positive outcomes on performance.

A second study, using the same method, surveyed Italian public hospitals (Marsilio et al., 2022). Surveyed in 2019, 35% of the 91 hospitals that responded reported that they were using Lean methods. Comparing the Italian hospitals with the earlier US sample, most hospitals reported starting with a 'model cell' – a single site in which techniques were used first. The majority in both systems also stated that they applied a 'true north' vision. This is a statement of what the organisation is about and how the values it wants to apply help it achieve its aims (Hirano & Furuya, 2006). The importance of 'true north' is described in several of the chapters in this book. Other factors, including the use of external experts, described by some in the book as 'Sensei' or technical partners, and the creation of a specialist internal team varied both between hospitals and between the two healthcare systems.

This use of the same survey in two different countries on two continents gives persuasive evidence of the spread of the use of Lean in healthcare and the importance of sharing experience across services and systems and indeed countries. This volume is intended to contribute to this shared learning.

Evidence of Impact

Systematic reviews use a pre-determined search strategy and set of assessment rules to identify, select and summarise research papers. Tlapa et al. undertook a systematic review of the impact of Lean interventions on Length of Stay (LOS) in ambulatory care with most settings being Emergency Departments. Waiting times to be seen reduced in 24 of the 26 studies in which it was measured. The proportion of patients leaving without being seen by a doctor decreased in 9 out of 12 studies. LOS decreased in 19 of the 22 studies in which this information was reported (Tlapa et al., 2020). Souza and colleagues also looked at papers on the use of Lean in Emergency Departments (Souza et al., 2021). They identified improvements in flow, waiting times, efficiency and patient safety.

Detailed accounts of Lean applications in individual healthcare systems offer further support. AOU Senese, a public hospital in Siena (Italy), reported that it released 5,417,395 euros for reinvestment in a four-year period. Its approach included a Lean management system 'fully embedded in the organization's corporate strategy' (Barnabè et al., 2019, p. 506).

Impact on staff is of obvious importance. One systematic review attempted to identify all peer-reviewed English and French language studies of Lean in healthcare which included reviews of the impact on staff (Mahmoud et al., 2021). See Table 1.1 for details.

In 17 eligible studies the authors found positive outcomes related to teamwork, communication and coordination: learning, innovation and personal development, morale, motivation and job satisfaction. A significant group of studies also reported negative outcomes linked to more intensive work with less downtime, and increased job strain, anxiety and stress. This emphasises the importance of staff engagement and paying careful attention to *muri* – unreasonableness in work procedures and work hours (Toussaint & Adams, 2015) – one of Ohno's three broad categories of waste (Ohno, 1988).

Importance of Context

One of the issues that is difficult to describe in reviews is the impact of different contexts for Lean implementations. Organisational context is widely recognised as relevant to the use of Lean in healthcare. Bateman and colleagues suggest that it should be 'adapted not adopted' (Bateman et al., 2018b, p. 1), while others identify Lean in healthcare as 'an ongoing reinvention of Toyota's original concept' (Andersson et al., 2020, p. 2). These conclusions are echoed by many of the contributors in this volume.

Healthcare organisations are often complex that work across service and sector boundaries. Fournier and Jobin examined a large-scale Lean introduction in Canada and identified characteristics that made Lean use in healthcare particularly challenging (Fournier & Jobin, 2018). Their observations referred to publicly funded healthcare, but many of their points are relevant to wider healthcare delivery settings:

- The quality and control of healthcare services are inherently political.
- Reforms usually target short-term efficiency with fixed targets and a 'tyranny of efficiency' that makes it difficult for managers to devolve the power for experimentation.
- Innovation is not usually seen as a thing of intrinsic value and must be negotiated with stakeholders.
- Labour relations are complex in healthcare, and Trade Unions often play an important role.
- Managers are highly constrained by laws and policies making decision-making inflexible.
- Service boundaries are often fuzzy.
- Services aim for distributed leadership, but doctors often have major influence that can make decision-making by other groups and professions challenging.
- There is role ambiguity between professional and managerial roles that can make delegation of authority and accountability difficult.
- Healthcare is a highly dynamic environment with rapid technological change and fluctuating demand.

Table 1.1   Selected Systematic Reviews of the Implementation of Lean in Healthcare

Authors	Areas Covered	Description
Henrique and Godinho Filho, (2020)	Lean and Six Sigma in Healthcare Empirical papers, published in English, 2004–2017	Most reports were on single department/ward implementation, e.g. Emergency Departments, the single most common area. Most frequent techniques mentioned were Value Stream Mapping, Standard Work and Visual Management. 81% of publications did not discuss sustainability.
Mahmoud et al. (2021)	Lean management in healthcare Focus on impact on staff Papers published in English or French up to February 2020	17 papers identified that included information on staff impact. Mixed findings: in some implementations, Lean was associated with increased stress on staff and increased workload. Also reports of improved teamwork, increased job satisfaction and improved morale in other studies.
Ramori et al. (2021)	Lean business models in healthcare Papers published in English, 1997–2018	Narrative review with limited synthesis. Few of the reports identified had similar methods, but many noted the challenges of staff engagement.
Souza et al. (2021)	Application of Lean in Emergency Departments Papers published in English, 2013–2020	Reported general success from initiatives. Concluded that we need to develop a culture of continuous improvement; staff should be trained on Lean concepts and encouraged to propose and implement solutions; communication is important and implementation on one site can produce success that can be shared to encourage other work. Noted that low managerial interest and weak relationships between managers and doctors decreased the likelihood and rate of improvement.
Reponen et al. (2021)	Research on benchmarking in Lean healthcare Papers published in English, up to October 2019	US papers dominate, no papers identified before 2008. The lack of consensus on the definition of Lean and variable approaches made comparisons difficult. Emphasised the importance of context. Several of the papers reviewed mentioned the importance of organisational culture and issues such as continuous improvement and a 'no blame approach'. Makes the point that 'no consensus on the dimensions of performance measurement and benchmarking in Lean healthcare exists' (p. 15).

Leite and colleagues looked at barriers to Lean in detail using examples from Brazil. They also obtained views from staff, including Lean coaches working in healthcare (Leite et al., 2020). The usual list of candidate issues was identified, but using thematic analysis, the researchers concluded that there were underlying barriers that caused the implementation problems. Some of these barriers related to the context of the Brazilian healthcare system, but others included the influence of staff behaviour, patients' behaviour in the system, constraints in the resource management of staff and physician's behaviours where they 'can act as a restraining force affecting patients, staff and system, every time that they avoid process improvement across the patient's journey' (p. 13).

The implication of these findings in different international settings is that there is a predictable range of factors that can affect the impact and sustainability of Lean implementations in healthcare. These are very similar to a list of success factors identified by Lin and colleagues in a review of the evidence on Lean in general service industries (Lins et al., 2021). To this can be added factors specific to the organisation – contingencies (Donaldson, 2001) – which need to be considered in implementation. Local managers are best placed to be aware of these issues and to respond to them. Organisational history such as previous change processes and labour relations can play important roles. When taking all these things together, creating a continuous improvement culture in practice remains challenging (Henrique & Godinho Filho, 2020).

Examples of Lean in Healthcare

The authors of the chapters in this volume provide case studies of the application of Lean methods in practice in healthcare settings. Engaging staff can be challenging. Murdina Campbell discusses the Lean Tool 5S and argues for its value both as a core Lean tool and as a way of introducing staff to Lean principles. Staff engagement, she contends, is a prerequisite for progressing Lean both because staff know their processes best and because respect for staff is a core tenet of Lean. Using tools like 5S can give early experience of success and set the groundwork for a wider daily management system.

Data is essential in quality improvement, and Todd Allen discusses how Intermountain Healthcare in Utah leveraged information to drive improvement. As he describes, the theory of change and the understanding of the expected causal chain drive the selection of the data. Some measures are used to test understanding of change and may be set aside, while other data will be used in the longer term and are often delivered through dashboards. Theories of change are essential to allow systematic testing of change and identification of intermediate measures (Fawcett, 2014). The context of the intervention is important and can affect the choices made (Schierhout et al., 2013).

Flow is an important consideration in all healthcare systems. Marc Rouppe van der Voort, Anna Roos Vijverberg and Frits van Merode present approaches to flow in the Netherlands. They discuss levels of quality improvement action and offer examples of long-term work on both in-patient and out-patient flow. Coaching and supporting staff to make changes results in benefits for patients and increases confidence and satisfaction for staff. Avoiding silos and providing executive leadership were important success factors in their work.

Kay Cordiner, Poonam Gupta, Salah Arafa and Cameron Stark present an example of the combination of Lean tools and approaches with good data and improved access to financial information. They describe the use of Value Management in Oman and Scotland. As with other examples, they began with a model cell, and they discuss considerations for choosing a location for the first implementation; how to engage teams and involve clinicians, and the considerations when expanding the approach to ever larger areas of the organisation.

Much of the published work on Lean in healthcare discusses applications in departments or services. Fiona Keogan and Anne-Marie Keown take a different tack and describe work intended to support a patient group. The context was of a public/private hospital network with partner community delivery organisations meaning that there was more than one funding mechanism and multiple organisations with different management making engagement very important. They provide a case example of older people living with frailty. When the Ireland East Hospital Group decided to work on this theme, they rapidly confirmed the complexity of the area. Staff ideas included prevention as well as management, and crossed hospital and community boundaries. Their example gives good examples of the importance of strategic alignment, staff engagement and continuing focus with some impressive results. Their work includes the use of week-long Rapid Improvement Events as well as other methods and offers inspiration for readers who want to focus on a patient group or wider patient pathway.

Some areas of healthcare have less published work than others. Mental health services are one area that has not always featured in Lean implementations. Louis Roig from Region Hovedstadens Psykiatri, which provides mental health services in the capital of Denmark, helps to remedy this. The setting was of four services that had recently merged and, as in the chapter from Iceland, there was initially no single agreed way of addressing quality improvement. The new service decided to use Lean. There were staff concerns about this and a worry that a cookie-cutter approach would be imposed when it was not appropriate. Their chapter describes the use of Lean in this setting and the value gained by applying Lean techniques.

Combining techniques in the context of a full application of Lean can bring dividends even in situations with significant financial and demand challenges. Páll Matthíasson, Benedikt Olgeirsson, and Gudrun Björg Sigurbjörnsdottir at Landspítali, the National University Hospital in Reykjavík in Iceland, have worked with international partners in Sweden and the USA to apply Lean to their hospital system. Iceland, as with most healthcare systems, faces the challenges of an ageing population with an increase in long-term conditions. Combined with the impact of the 2008–2011 financial crash which was exceptionally large in Iceland, Landspítali introduced several layers of Lean activity including Plan-Do-Study-Act cycles and local projects; kaizen events; Rapid Process Improvement Workshops and Daily Management and Production, Preparation and Process (3P) events. They tied this together by making training widely available and by making senior leaders a core part of the Lean effort. They also took the innovative step of investing in a communications and social media team to help explain to the public and consolidate their improvement efforts to reduce attendance at Emergency Departments.

When Lean techniques are already embedded, there are enormous opportunities to apply the principles from the beginning of a process. Iain Smith and Steven Bartley offer a detailed case example of the use of 3P in the design of an assessment and treatment unit for adults with learning disabilities in the National Health Service (NHS) in England. Their work, the first of its kind in NHS England, was in the context of an NHS Trust which was three years into a collaboration with the Virginia Mason Medical Center. They had established a Kaizen Promotion Office to coordinate and support Lean work and had trained over 30 staff to lead Rapid Process Improvement Workshops including directors of the organisation and senior managers. This put them in a good position to apply the principles of Lean design from the beginning of their process and so link the final product to the design needs of the service. Smith and Bartley's example also provides evidence of a mature collaboration with clinical and non-clinical staff, service users and the building design and construction team. This demonstrates the application of core Lean values in a real-life situation involving the investment of millions of pounds sterling into the building construction. Producing a greater alignment between the clinical process and building design produced benefits as soon as the building began to be used.

For value to be seen from the perspective of the patient, the active inclusion of service users in improvement events is essential. Nathan Clifford, Sarah Curtis, and Karl Marlowe at Southern Health NHS Foundation Trust in England provide a thoughtful description of their use of co-production in Lean Quality Improvement. From tentative beginnings, they have moved to widespread involvement of service users, including both carers and patients. They explain the support needed to make this successful and give examples of the positive impact of involvement on both staff and patient/carer participants. To do this well at scale requires careful consideration of the support required for carers and patients to be able to participate meaningfully. Southern Health has altered their practice to make co-production of Lean quality improvement possible. Their practical experience and sound advice will help other services seeking to include user and carer views in Quality Improvement training and events.

The importance of context means that spreading Lean across a range of different organisations at one time is challenging. Leaders in the English NHS had seen the international benefits of Lean healthcare and had observed examples in England such as the 3P work described in Chapter 9 by Smith and Bartley. To accelerate spread, the English health service created a central unit to provide wider support. Chapter 11 describes the work of Ann Hill and Graham Canning and colleagues who worked with seven organisations in the 'Vital Signs' programme to learn how to embed Lean. They concluded that there was a significant risk of organisations focusing on quality improvement tools and losing sight of the reasons the tools were being applied. To counter this risk, the team engaged with Mike Rother and colleagues and put scientific thinking at the centre of their approach. They promoted the use of Toyota Kata, which are set ways of considering problems and coaching how people think about and tackle improvement. Their contribution describes their learning from this work. They conclude that Improvement Kata and Coaching Kata are good fits for both Lean implementations and other types of Quality Improvement applications in healthcare and can be delivered at scale. They point to the importance of organisational culture and senior engagement in its introduction and emphasise that these are skills that require purposive practice to have large-scale impact.

Kim Barnas expands on this theme in her discussion of the role of senior leaders. Barnas argues that their contribution is key to progress and the maintenance of progress. Her chapter provides a detailed discussion of the work required by system leaders if their service is to maximise the value of a Lean implementation. Context is a recurring theme in the contributions to the book, and Kim Barnas makes the notable point that management engagement, knowledge and skills are a vital part of the context required for successful use of Lean at scale.

In the concluding chapter, the editors draw some broad themes from the examples in the book, identifying key considerations for organisations embarking on their Lean journey, or intentions to scale up their efforts.

Conclusions

The principles of Lean are not always understood and Andersson argues for the mindset of Lean to be included in training and discussion lest it be understood only as the application of a set of quality improvement tools (Andersson et al., 2020). The examples in this book back this up and make it clear that Lean is more than a collection of improvement tools that can be applied like the blades of a knife. Organisations can have considerable success with individual tools but to make changes at scale, clarity in purpose, organisational engagement, senior support, clinical engagement, data and good training and coaching are needed. The chapters in the book offer examples that address all these points, and which provide valuable learning for people who work on, or who want to work on, the introduction and expansion of Lean in healthcare.

Learning Points

- Lean has made an increasingly successful transition from application in industry to application in healthcare.
- Many of the principles of Lean lend themselves to application in healthcare, including respect for staff; focus on value to users – patients, in this case; improved flow; reduced waste and error reduction.
- There are many examples of Lean in healthcare, and recent surveys report use in many hospitals and health systems, although these range from use of individual tools to wholesale adoption of Lean management systems.
- Researchers have identified good evidence for the value of Lean in healthcare, although not all implementations of Lean deliver the desired benefits, and some are abandoned.
- The context and manner of Lean implementations is important. Senior leadership involvement, investment over time and active engagement of clinical staff, use of data and clarity in purpose are all important.
- The case examples in this volume discuss the application of Lean to many healthcare settings, in both publicly and privately funded systems, and in in-patient, out-patient and community settings.

Bibliography

Andersson, G., Lynch, M. P. J., Johansen, F. R., Fineide, M. J., & Martin, D. (2020). Exploring perceptions of Lean in the public sector. *Public Money & Management*, 1–9. https://doi.org/10.1080/09540962.2020.1847454

Barnabè, F., Guercini, J., & Perna, M. D. (2019). Assessing performance and value-creation capabilities in Lean healthcare: insights from a case study. *Public Money & Management*, *39*(7), 503–511. https://doi.org/10.1080/09540962.2019.1598197

Bateman, N., Lethbridge, S., & Esain, A. (2018a). Pillar or platform: a taxonomy for process improvement activities in public services. *Public Money & Management*, *38*(1), 5–12. https://doi.org/10.1080/09540962.2018.1389487

Bateman, N., Radnor, Z., & Glennon, R. (2018b). Editorial: the landscape of lean across public services. *Public Money & Management*, *38*(1), 1–4. https://doi.org/10.1080/09540962.2018.1389482

Donaldson, L. (2001). *The Contingency Theory of Organizations*. Sage.

Fawcett, J. (2014). Thoughts about conceptual models, theories, and quality improvement projects. *Nursing Science Quarterly*, *27*(4), 336–339. https://doi.org/10.1177/0894318414546411

Fournier, P.-L., & Jobin, M.-H. (2018). Understanding before implementing: the context of Lean in public healthcare organizations. *Public Money & Management*, *38*(1), 37–44. https://doi.org/10.1080/09540962.2018.1389505

Fournier, P.-L., Chênevert, D., & Jobin, M.-H. (2021). The antecedents of physicians' behavioral support for lean in healthcare: the mediating role of commitment to organizational change. *International Journal of Production Economics*, *232*, 107961. Retrieved Mon Feb 01 00:00:00 GMT 2021, from

Henrique, D. B., & Godinho Filho, M. (2020). A systematic literature review of empirical research in Lean and Six Sigma in healthcare. *Total Quality Management & Business Excellence*, *31*(3/4), 429–449. https://doi.org/10.1080/14783363.2018.1429259

Hirano, H., & Furuya, M. (2006). *JIT is Flow: Practice and Principles of Lean Manufacturing.* Productivity Press.

Hopp, W. J. (2018). Positive lean: merging the science of efficiency with the psychology of work. *International Journal of Production Research, 56*(1/2), 398–413. https://doi.org/10.1080/00207543.2017.1387301

Leite, H., Bateman, N., & Radnor, Z. (2020). Beyond the ostensible: an exploration of barriers to lean implementation and sustainability in healthcare. *Production Planning & Control, 31*(1), 1–18. https://doi.org/10.1080/09537287.2019.1623426

Lins, M. G., Zotes, L. P., & Caiado, R. (2021). Critical factors for lean and innovation in services: from a systematic review to an empirical investigation. *Total Quality Management & Business Excellence, 32*(5/6), 606–631. https://doi.org/10.1080/14783363.2019.1624518

Lorden, A. L., Zhang, Y., Lin, S. H., & Côté, M. J. (2014). Measures of success: the role of human factors in lean implementation in healthcare [Article]. *Quality Management Journal, 21*(3), 26–37. https://doi.org/10.1080/10686967.2014.11918394

Mahmoud, Z., Angelé-Halgand, N., Churruca, K., Ellis, L. A., & Braithwaite, J. (2021). The impact of lean management on frontline healthcare professionals: a scoping review of the literature. *BMC Health Services Research, 21*(1), 1–11. https://doi.org/10.1186/s12913-021-06344-0

Marsilio, M., & Pisarra, M. (2021). Lean management in health care: a review of reviews of socio-technical components for effective impact. *Journal of Health Organization and Management, 35*(4), 475–491. https://doi.org/10.1108/JHOM-06-2020-0241

Marsilio, M., Pisarra, M., Rubio, K., & Shortell, S. (2022). Lean adoption, implementation, and outcomes in public hospitals: benchmarking the US and Italy health systems. *BMC Health Services Research, 22*(1), 1–10. https://doi.org/10.1186/s12913-022-07473-w

Matthias, O., & Brown, S. (2016). Implementing operations strategy through Lean processes within health care. *International Journal of Operations & Production Management, 36*(11), 1435–1457. https://doi.org/10.1108/IJOPM-04-2015-0194

Moraros, J., Lemstra, M., & Nwankwo, C. (2016). Lean interventions in healthcare: do they actually work? A systematic literature review. *International Journal for Quality in Health Care, 28*(2), 150–165. https://doi.org/10.1093/intqhc/mzv123

Narayanamurthy, G., Gurumurthy, A., Subramanian, N., & Moser, R. (2018). Assessing the readiness to implement lean in healthcare institutions: a case study. *International Journal of Production Economics, 197,* 123–142. https://doi.org/10.1016/j.ijpe.2017.12.028

Ohno, T. (1988). *Toyota Production System: Beyond Large-Scale Production.* CRC Press.

Oreg, S., Vakola, M., & Armenakis, A. (2011). Change recipients' reactions to organizational change: a 60-year review of quantitative studies. *The Journal of Applied Behavioral Science, 47*(4), 461–524. https://doi.org/10.1177/0021886310396550

Radnor, Z. J., Holweg, M., & Waring, J. (2012). Lean in healthcare: the unfilled promise? *Social Science & Medicine, 74*(3), 364–371. https://doi.org/10.1016/j.socscimed.2011.02.011

Ramori, K. A., Cudney, E. A., Elrod, C. C., & Antony, J. (2021). Lean business models in healthcare: a systematic review. *Total Quality Management & Business Excellence, 32*(5–6), 558–573. https://doi.org/10.1080/14783363.2019.1601995

Reponen, E., Rundallo, T. G., Shortell, S. M., Blodgett, J. C., Juarez, A., Jokela, R., Mäkijärvi, M., & Torkki, P. (2021). Benchmarking outcomes on multiple contextual levels in lean healthcare: a systematic review, development of a conceptual framework, and a research agenda. *BMC Health Services Research, 21*(1), 1–18. https://doi.org/10.1186/s12913-021-06160-6

Schierhout, G., Hains, J., Brands, J., Lonergan, K., Bailie, R., Si, D., Kwedza, R., Kennedy, C., Cox, R., O'Donoghue, L., Fittock, M., & Dowden, M. (2013). Evaluating the effectiveness of a multifaceted, multilevel continuous quality improvement program in primary health care: developing a realist theory of change. *Implementation Science, 8*(1), 119.

Secchi, R., & Camuffo, A. (2019). Lean implementation failures: the role of organizational ambidexterity. *International Journal of Production Economics, 210,* 145–154. https://doi.org/10.1016/j.ijpe.2019.01.007

Shortell, S. M., Blodgett, J. C., Rundall, T. G., & Kralovec, P. (2018). Use of lean and related transformational performance improvement systems in hospitals in the United States: results from a national survey. *The Joint Commission Journal on Quality and Patient Safety, 44*(10), 574–582. https://doi.org/10.1016/j.jcjq.2018.03.002

Sloan, T., Fitzgerald, A., Hayes, K. J., Radnor, Z., Robinson, S., & Sohal, A. (2014). Lean in healthcare – history and recent developments. *Journal of Health Organization and Management, 28*(2), 130–134. https://doi.org/10.1108/JHOM-04-2014-0064

Smith, I., Hicks, C., & McGovern, T. (2020). Adapting Lean methods to facilitate stakeholder engagement and co-design in healthcare. *BMJ, 368,* m35. https://doi.org/10.1136/bmj.m35

Souza, D. L., Korzenowski, A. L., Alvarado, M. M., Sperafico, J. H., Ackermann, A. E. F., Mareth, T., & Scavarda, A. J. (2021). A systematic review on lean applications' in emergency departments. *Healthcare, 9*(6), 763. https://www.mdpi.com/2227-9032/9/6/763

Stark, C., & Hookway, G. (2019). *Applying Lean in Health and Social Care Services.* Routledge.

Teich, S. T., & Faddoul, F. F. (2013). Lean management-the journey from Toyota to healthcare. *Rambam Maimonides medical journal, 4*(2), e0007. https://doi.org/10.5041/RMMJ.10107

Tlapa, D., Zepeda-Lugo, C. A., Tortorella, G. L., Baez-Lopez, Y. A., Limon-Romero, J., Alvarado-Iniesta, A., & Rodriguez-Borbon, M. I. (2020). Effects of lean healthcare on patient flow: a systematic review. *Value in Health, 23,* 260–273. https://doi.org/10.1016/j.jval.2019.11.002

Toussaint, J. S., & Adams, E. (2015). *Management on the Mend.* ThedaCare Center for Healthcare Value.

Westwood, N., James-Moore, M., & Cooke, M. (2007). *Going Lean in the NHS.* https://www.england.nhs.uk/improvement-hub/wp-content/uploads/sites/44/2017/11/Going-Lean-in-the-NHS.pdf

Cameron Stark, MB ChB, MPH, MSc (Dist), MRCPsych, FFPH, is an Honorary Reader and Part-time Lecturer at the University of the Highlands and Islands (UHI) Outer Hebrides. Stark leads the UHI postgraduate module on the application of Lean in healthcare. After graduating from the University of Glasgow, he trained in psychiatry and public health and worked as an NHS Public Health Doctor for over 30 years. Stark was the quality improvement science lead for NHS Highland and trained as a Lean leader with Tees, Esk and Wear Valley NHS Foundation Trust. He has published over 60 papers in peer-reviewed journals and has written or edited 5 previous textbooks.

Elaine Mead is an executive director of Improvement, Care and Compassion, IC&C, an organisation committed to supporting leaders on their improvement journey across the UK and Europe. She has worked as Executive Sensei for National Health Service (NHS) Improvement in England and is a Leadership Faculty member of the Institute of Health Improvement. Elaine is a founding member of the Catalysis European CEO Forum and continues to connect and support colleagues from across Europe, from her base in Scotland. She is a certified Lean Leader from Tees, Esk and Wear Valley NHS Foundation Trust having had a close association with the Virginia Mason Institute. Elaine is also a Fellow of, and tutor for, the Institute of Quality and Safety (ISQua). Prior to establishing IC&C Elaine was chief executive for NHS Highland for eight years where she led the development of the Highland Quality Approach to improve the quality of care based on increasing value. She has over 30 years of experience of working in the NHS including as a clinician and in executive roles.

Maimie Thompson is an engagement and communication specialist currently working in healthcare planning and the use of digital technologies in the public sector. She has contributed to a range of publications including as a co-author of a chapter for the *International Handbook on Integrated Care* (second edition) about Scotland. Maimie is a certified Lean leader and a former recipient of NHS Scotland's manager of the year award for her work on unscheduled care.

Chapter 2

Applying 5S in Healthcare

Murdina Campbell

Contents

DOI: 10.4324/9780429346958-2

Aims

- Describe the reasons for the use of 5S in healthcare.
- Explain the steps used in 5S.
- Appreciate the importance of teamwork and staff engagement.
- Identify the importance of process and local context.
- Locate 5S in the broad context of Lean transformation.

Introduction

5S is a core Lean technique and is a particularly good fit with healthcare settings. 5S was first described in industrial settings (Hirano, 1996, 2009) where it contributed to reduced waste, error proofing, and increased efficiency. There was an early recognition of its potential for application in healthcare (Hadfield, 2006) perhaps at least partly because of its focus on safety (Ikuma & Nahmens, 2014). The technique has been used in many healthcare settings including in laboratories (Jiménez et al., 2015), theatre supply chains (O'Mahony et al., 2021), primary care (Vedovatto Klein Kerschner et al., 2020), ambulatory care (Kanamori et al., 2016a; Rutledge et al., 2010), and outpatient clinics (Ishijima et al., 2016; Waldhausen et al., 2010). 5S has been used successfully in healthcare systems as diverse as the Russian Federation (Kurmangulov et al., 2019) and Uganda (Kanamori et al., 2016b; Take et al., 2015). 5S is often used in combination with other techniques such as the introduction of Standard Work and Visual Controls. 5S is acceptable to staff and can contribute to other aims such as increased cleanliness (Ching et al., 2020).

This chapter describes the use of Lean in NHS Highland. NHS Highland is part of the Scottish National Health Service (NHS). The NHS is a publicly funded health service that provides primary care, community care, and secondary care. Primary care is delivered through a network of General Practices which are independent businesses that contract with the NHS for the delivery of services. Hospitals and most community services are provided directly. NHS Highland Board covers a rural part of Scotland, and although it supplies services for around 40% of the land area of Scotland, only 300,000 people, about 5% of the Scottish population, live in the board area. There is one District General Hospital, Raigmore Hospital in the city of Inverness which includes services including High Dependency and Intensive Care, cancer treatment services, hospital paediatrics, obstetrics, medicine, and surgery. There are 3 Rural General Hospitals, a psychiatric hospital and 14 community hospitals (Mead et al., 2017). This chapter describes work on 5S at Raigmore Hospital.

CASE STUDY: PERSONAL INTRODUCTION TO 5S

The first time I heard about 5S was when I was working in Raigmore Hospital and told to attend a training session by my manager. She said it was 'something to do with waste'.

As a team leader in several clinical areas, I decided to take along some support staff and the cleaner to the training. When we arrived at the session, the room was full of portering and cleaning staff as most attendees thought they were there to be trained in waste disposal and recycling. The facilitators soon informed us that we were learning about organising the workplace using a Lean tool called 5S and the confusion continued. The lessons learned from this inauspicious beginning were:

■ The importance of clear and unambiguous communication with staff.
■ Delivering training on Lean tools in isolation and without context will not embed the methodology within an organisation and therefore not deliver improvements.

Fast forward 12 months and one of the clinical areas I was responsible for managing was suddenly reduced in size by 50% to allow the development of a new service. There was no longer the luxury of storing anything 'just in case' we needed it, nor could we over-order bulky items that took up space. I remembered the 5S training and how it could help in this situation. Applying the 5S process transformed the way we ordered supplies, organised the clinic space, where we stored things, and made the whole team proud of their exemplary workspace within the hospital.

5S

Although grounded in industrial practice (Jaca et al., 2014), 5S was popularised in healthcare by groups such as the Virginia Mason Institute (Kenney, 2011) and ThedaCare (Toussaint & Adams, 2015). The Japanese terms for 5S are rendered into English in various ways but often as shown in Table 2.1 (Stark & Hookway, 2019, p. 33).

Applying a sixth 'S' – 'Safety' to all stages of the method is good practice in any healthcare setting and can help to reassure staff that risks of harm are being considered.

This section discusses use of 5S, including safety, in practice and identifies challenges based on experience in numerous settings.

Getting Started

Starting any project that has the potential for significant changes can be daunting. However, there are a few ways to help ensure staff buy-in. This is crucial to the success of any 5S project. This means employees are open, willing, and committed to making contributions to make the plan a success. Some helpful ways to develop employee engagement include:

■ Providing examples and outlining what success would look like.

Table 2.1 5S Terms

Japanese	English	Meaning
Seiri	Sort	Remove anything unnecessary
Seiton	Set in Order	Give everything a place
Seiso	Sweep	Prevention and Maintenance
Seiketsu	Standardise	Develop a consistent process
Shitsuke	Sustain	Maintaining the work

- Allowing staff to openly discuss their concerns, including the pros and cons of the improvement project.
- Training in how to apply 5S in the workplace.

Throughout the employee buy-in process, many teams will show excitement and interest when it comes to discussing the pitfalls and barriers associated with the recent changes. As this is done, and details are worked through, the team lead or facilitator will gain greater insight and information on how to best work with the team in the future. When pitfalls and barriers are met with positivity from the team leader, even some of the most ambitious plans can come to fruition. It is important to remember that positivity at the top spreads throughout the team.

Thinking of 5S as part of work processes rather than something separate makes it more likely to be sustainable. It changes the way the workplace is organised, and in turn it can change the way work is performed.

The team involved in implementing the stages of 5S in the workplace should be people who work in the area. 5S cannot be done to anyone or any area without a good knowledge of the working environment and the teams' needs. For instance, it would not make sense to take a team of office employees into a ward area and expect them to know the equipment required in the clinical area. Therefore, the team working in the area should always be involved in the changes that are being made or considered for that specific area.

A Lean mindset should be established before even starting the processes of 5S. Accountability along with setting expectations is vital. Setting out what is expected, identifying the benefits, and specifying who will benefit from the changes are all useful disciplines. When creating a plan, it is helpful to start out with a reason for the changes to be made. For instance, the team may be frustrated by time wasted searching for supplies, there may be a general lack of organisation in the area, or there could be safety concerns.

It is important not to feel that it is essential to get the best Standard Work or Standard Operating Procedure (SOPs) immediately. It is also important not to impose SOPs on the teams. When employees are forced into doing something without being asked for input or thoughts, the natural reaction is to resist the change. Any manager or coach supporting the work must be sensitive to this. Team engagement adds value to the entire process by allowing access to team members' cumulative experience. There is no realistic prospect of constructing a perfect process at the first attempt. Testing out new processes over time using Plan-Do-Study-Act cycle allows incremental improvement. This helps staff to see active use of quality improvement principles at all stages of the work.

Tools for 5S

There are various tools that can be used for implementing a 5S programme (Graban, 2009; Stark & Hookway, 2019).

5S Tags

5S Tags, also known as 'Red Tags', are commonly used during the Sort phase of 5S. These tags are attached to items that are not often used and therefore no longer add value to the work facility. A Red Tag is a piece of paper or card that includes the details of the item, the reason it is being removed, and what is to be done with the item (dispose of, recycle, etc.). A Red Tag is easy to see and makes the process of sorting through different bits of equipment and supplies simple and

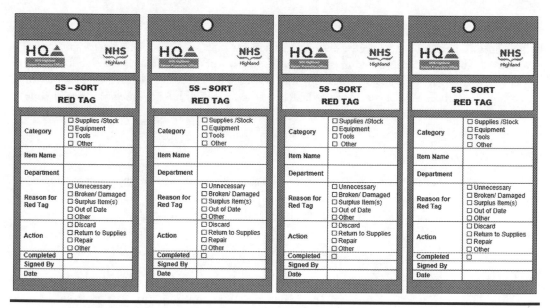

Figure 2.1   NHS Highland Red Tag template.

straightforward. Items that are being considered for removal can be placed in a designated area for review. By looking at the tags, employees can easily determine what is going to stay and what is going to go. It is useful to use a Red Tag when there is doubt over something's necessity to the area. Attaching a tag and reviewing it in an agreed time can help give evidence of whether something is needed or not (Figure 2.1). As with all activities in 5S, it is a team effort.

Floor Markings

Floor markings are common within a workplace. They can be used for a variety of different purposes from identifying where a piece of equipment should live, to warning people of a hazard. They can help patients navigate the often-labyrinthine corridors of Outpatient Departments. Floor markings using coloured tape can be amazingly effective with little cost. Agreement with infection control colleagues over acceptable materials is essential.

Shadow Boards

Shadow boards can be a helpful tool when implementing and sustaining the processes of 5S. Shadow boards feature an outline of where pieces of equipment belong and allow employees to quickly identify which tools are missing.

Signs

The use of signs in an efficiently run work environment is essential. Not only does signage help increase safety, but it also creates a visual environment for employees to follow. Safety signs can be found in a variety of colours, shapes, and sizes with many different text combinations. They can also be customised to meet any unique marking needs. Signage may be available as floor, wall, or standing signs.

Labelling

Labelling is a big component of efficient organisation for a 5S system. For instance, some things that can be labelled include shelving, storage units, bins, workspaces, etc. When labels are used strategically, employees understand where things belong and can easily identify when something is missing. A small tape label printer costs little, but the impact of having labels can be valuable.

Each Step of 5S

5S is a powerful tool in the workplace and can be adapted to fit into an appropriate time scale (daily, weekly, monthly, yearly). It supports and requires ongoing engagement with the process. Each step of 5S has an associated goal. The goals, and tips that can be of value at each step, are described below to help guide efforts.

Sort

'Sort' is the first step in any 5S process. The goal is to remove anything unnecessary from the area being organised. It also provides a clearer picture on what to build in the four other steps.

Beginning the process of Sort starts out with most things removed from the target area. Taking items from one space and placing them in another provides the opportunity to decide what needs to stay and what needs to go. Actions can then be taken for items that are no longer used or needed.

Sort Tips

- Different spaces require different sorting frequencies. For example, a clinic room should be sorted to ensure tidiness every day it will be used. On the other hand, a storage or filing cabinet may only need to undergo the initial steps of 5S monthly, quarterly, or even annually.
- It is important to audit the sorting process of any space where 5S has taken place. This is to ensure accuracy and maintain the discipline. Sometimes, an emphasis on organisation can overshadow other key areas. It is equally important to check equipment calibration dates, supplies' expiration dates, and any potential safety hazards.

Set in Order

The second step of 5S is 'Set in Order'. Its goal is to minimise the need for employees to repeatedly leave the clinical area or patient to get something required. This focuses on placing essential items (as identified in the Sort phase) back into the work area in a well-organised manner. This step is about finding the most sensible location for the equipment and items within a specific work area.

Every time employees must search around for something to complete their task, time is wasted, and this reduces the value of the service being provided to patients. Setting items in order in an intentional and planned way is essential to minimising 'waste' such as time. Imagine a clinic area where a nurse is seeing numerous patients a day. They may need to leave the clinical area many times during a shift to find items frequently used in the initial examination of the patient. Staff need to have their most frequently used pieces of equipment accessible to save time and to help them manage the patient more efficiently. In some settings, logical organisation paired with knowledge of where equipment and supplies are could make the difference between life and death.

While the stakes may not always be as high every day, every loss of efficiency is waste in the process. When implemented in an acute ward area in NHS Highland, this process produced a 38% reduction in the time it took to carry out an initial assessment.

An effective way to begin this step is to map out the area where equipment and supplies will be stored. During this stage, it is crucial to think carefully about the tasks most frequently performed in or around each area of the ward/clinic. This knowledge should be used to map out the most convenient and comfortable areas for staff to go to or reach. The most frequently used items should be stored in easy-to-access areas with the least barriers and movement to get to them. Less frequently used items can be placed farther away from the immediate vicinity of the patient. Some items are seldom used but must be immediately accessible when required, such as resuscitation equipment, and are an exception to the routine of placing less used items farther away.

Set in Order Tips

- Shadow boards show outlines of equipment wherever they are stored and are an excellent way for setting up a workspace in an efficient and easy-to-maintain way. By doing this, it is easy to see when a piece of equipment is missing and it ensures things are stored in the correct place.
- One of the best questions to ask staff is 'why' – why is something stored where it is? Is it convenient? Could it be stored in a more efficient space? Often staff find that there is no specific reason an item is where it is located – it has 'just always been there' as far as they know. When people have the chance to consider what works for them and are freed of precedent, this can increase their willingness to engage in the process. Staff need to know they have control of the process and that it is not tidiness for its own sake.
- Staff are individuals and what may work for one may not work for everyone. Therefore, involving the whole team will make this step of the process more successful.

Sweep

Following on from Sorting and Setting in Order, the 'Sweep' phase is the discipline of regular cleaning, checking, and tidying of the workspace.

In every case, a clean work area is also safer. For instance, keeping floors clear of debris helps to reduce the risk of trips, slips, and falls, which are extremely common causes of workplace injuries and accidents.

Cleaning can be used as an inspection tool and help prevent tool and machinery degradation. Not only does this improve safety, it can also ensure items last longer, making it less costly for replacement and maintenance in the future. This can be considered a component of Total Productive Maintenance, an approach that aims to reduce or eliminate breakdowns and to always keep equipment in effective working order and so available to staff (Díaz-Reza et al., 2019).

Tips for the Sweep Stage

- The sweep stage should be conducted according to a schedule and not done when an inspection or audit is coming up. It is not a strategy for clearing up the present mess; it is an orderly method for preventing clutter in the first place.
- Allocate a certain member of staff each day to ensure the standard of cleanliness and tidiness is being followed by all members of the team. It is not advisable to make this a

person-dependent role, but one person each shift for example. If many staff participate in the sweep stage, then it keeps the team involved and saves the leader from having to do the cleaning tasks all the time. Active staff involvement promotes engagement and helps to embed preventative and maintenance practices within the wider staff team.

■ Posting imagery nearby that shows the fully cleaned and swept state of a workspace can be a helpful way to keep this communication alive. An information board can be used to show step-by-step instructions for how certain areas or tools are expected to be cleaned at the beginning and/or the end of a shift.

■ Acknowledging the effort the team makes to maintain their workplace cannot be stressed enough. Recognition for achievement is a wonderful way to ensure continued engagement.

Standardise

The 'Standardise' stage builds on the idea of auditing and checking in on 5S efforts regularly. This step is the bridge between the Sweep and the Sustain stages. By standardising the approach to 5S, it can ensure efforts are sustained.

Begin to standardise 5S operations by making the process more than a word-of-mouth agreement. This is the time to implement a clear, universally understood system so that employees are certain about what they are expected to do.

A checklist that asks specific questions about the work area can help to ensure that processes are conducted as intended. Failing to standardise procedures can lead to work becoming sloppy over time and a loss of efficiency.

Standardise Tips

■ Do not make it person dependent. Assign the daily or weekly checking to an identified person but not one person. This can be a named rota or allocation to people working on a particular role on that shift/day.

■ Start to think about the required Standard Work/Standard Operating Procedures. Involve members of the team to reach agreement on what is being asked of them, and why.

Sustain

The last step is 'Sustain', and this focuses on taking the previous steps and transforming them into ongoing habits to ensure continuous improvement. The overall goal is to increase efficiency and reduce waste. Random observation of the 5S process is crucial to ensure all steps are being followed. Formal audits should be conducted by a Quality Improvement expert who is able to observe the process in an unbiased way and reflect on those observations back to the team. More regularly, staff can swap areas and conduct an audit of a neighbouring ward or team area. It is often easier to see issues in an area in which the person does not work, and this can then help them to see waste in their own work area.

Tips for Sustaining 5S

■ Standards are maintained through training, empowerment, and discipline to the method.

■ When a new employee joins a team that uses 5S, one of the best things to do is ask a current staff member to train the new member. Teaching someone else how to do 5S requires the staff to know the process correctly. This also reinforces the team approach to an organised workplace, especially if there are some members of the team not as fully engaged as others.

- Sustaining an organised workplace is all about continuous improvement and progress. To facilitate this, it is important to measure the time saved and increased efficiency.
- Use data to inform your next steps and do not ignore warning signs that suggest the standard is not as you would have hoped for. It is an opportunity to improve on the current state.
- Sustaining 5S is about doing each of the steps over and over until it becomes normal practice for all members of staff.
- Communicate with the team regularly about progress or challenges to ensure there is constructive discussion but without blame.

Safety

Rather than a separate stage, safety should be a consideration throughout the process. It is useful to pause from time to time and think through any steps needed to increase safety or apply error proofing to the project. This should include thinking about any unintended impacts on other services or neighbouring processes. Changes that are entirely internal to the service do not require external discussion. From time to time, however, a change in one team's practice can impact a different team, usually one working on a neighbouring upstream or downstream process or a supporting process such as radiology or supplies. Checking for any adverse impact and discussing it with the other team affected can save time and effort and avoid misinterpretation and confusion.

Common Misconceptions about 5S

As with other Lean strategies, the practice and implementation of 5S also feature some common misconceptions which if not addressed can have a negative impact on 5S efforts and results (Table 2.2).

Kanban

I used to squirrel away supplies 'just in case' stocks ran low, and we needed them at short notice. This was due to a lack of trust in the ordering system within (my organisation).

Kanban are a type of 'visual signal' or 'card' that are commonly used in 5S. Kanban are part of a pull system that controls the timing of production and/or delivery of items, to reduce delays and contribute to continuous flow (Papalexi et al., 2016). There are several types of Kanban including types of production Kanban and supply Kanban (Stark & Hookway, 2019, pp. 158–159). This section discusses supply Kanban, which are used to help visualise stock and can be used as a way of monitoring ordering and providing greater control over stock and supplies. For instance, it can be used to pull supplies from a central store or trigger re-ordering in a timely way to ensure areas do not run out of stock. Using a Kanban method for supplies prevents an accumulation of stock and excess inventory. The template in NHS Highland use for Kanban is shown in Figure 2.2.

Table 2.2   Common Misconceptions on the Application of 5S in Healthcare

Misconception	Issue
5S means throwing away expensive things for no good reason	When it comes to 5S, there is often a big understanding gap of what is worth keeping. Staff can be reluctant to dispose of items they perceive as having monetary value. Items and equipment should not be kept simply because they add value to the outside world. Things should only be kept if they are of value to the organisation and support the process delivered by the team. Some items prove to be out of date or broken and can be disposed of or recycled where possible. Other items are useful but not required for the process and can be redeployed to another service. NHS Highland has an intranet webpage where surplus material can be advertised for other services to request. Many services now have similar arrangements which support sustainability and reduce waste including offering surplus equipment in good condition to partner organisations or voluntary groups.
5S is just a tool	5S is a tool, but it is not 'just a tool'. It is a comprehensive framework that emphasises the use of a specific mindset and tools to create efficiency and value. Everything from being organised to cleanliness is considered. Part of the discipline of 5S is being proactive versus reactive. It forms a fundamental introduction to the practice of Lean and helps to introduce a focus on value.
Label everything and keep things clean and tidy and you are doing 5S	A superficially tidy area does not mean that 5S has been done or is not required. 5S is so much more than adding some labels to shelves and keeping a tidy work environment. Does the team have what it needs? Is something missing? Is time wasted looking for items? Cleaning is a small but necessary component of 5S. 5S is order for a purpose: to support the process for staff, improve processes for patients, and reduce the burden of work. Applying 5S with rigour will make the workplace safer and more efficient.
5S is easy	To introduce and embed 5S, staff need to engage with the process and be willing to learn and participate as well. It is multifaceted and interweaves a mindset with a practical process to assist in creating both culture and discipline. This is not easy, especially when starting off and ensuring it is sustained over time. 5S needs deliberative practice. It is never finished.

Kanban are attached to either an item or a quantity of items, for example in a supply bin. Bulky items are likely to have an individual Kanban, while smaller items will usually have a Kanban associated with several items. In the twin bin system described in the Case Study for an Obstetrics and Gynaecology Ward, the items used are matched against the re-order period. For example, if ten of an item are used a day on average and the re-order period is seven days, then at least $7 \times 10 = 70$ items need to be in stock in the ward/area at the time the re-order is made. In this case there would be two supply bins, each capable of holding 70 items. When one supply bin is emptied, the Kanban from that bin is used to re-order the items, the second supply bin is used

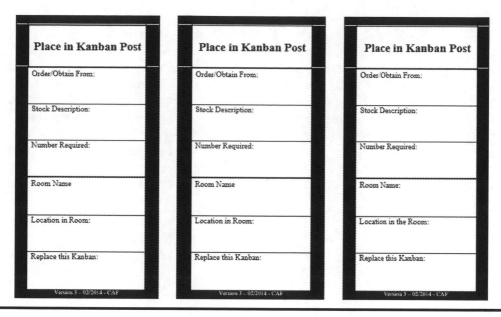

Figure 2.2 NHS Highland Kanban template.

until the first is re-filled, and so on. In practice some leeway may be needed to allow for fluctuating clinical demand and staff will often want several days of additional supply until they become confident in the system.

It can be difficult to convince staff in hospital settings that using a Kanban system is a reliable method for ensuring they have the right supplies in the right amount at the right time. Fear of running out of something important often leads to overstocking of items with an unintended consequence of items becoming expired and wasted. It also means additional space is required for storage and the volume of supplies makes it more difficult to locate the desired item. However, the Kanban system is tried and tested and can ease staff fears about running out of supplies. The case study illustrates the application of a Kanban system in a hospital ward, which also accommodated patients arriving for urgent assessments in an ambulatory care setting.

CASE STUDY: OBSTETRICS AND GYNAECOLOGY WARD

The first step with the ward team in establishing a Kanban system for supplies and stock was to audit what was used within the area over a month. From this, the team established what items were used and re-ordered in the ward. The team identified how many of each item were used monthly and then calculated weekly and daily requirements while considering that demand for some items was more uneven than for others. This was then cross-checked against the time it took to re-order each item if it was coming from a central distribution point within the hospital or from an outside supplier. Some items had longer re-order times than others, and this contributed to decisions about the quantity to be ordered, and how many items should be in stock at the time of re-order.

Laminated cards were created which showed the details of what the item was, where it was stored, where it was to be ordered from, the code for re-ordering, and how many were to be re-ordered at a time. A Kanban post system was used. Once an item was used that had the

Kanban on it, it was a signal to re-order. It was placed in a coloured Kanban box where they were gathered, and items were re-ordered as and when they were required. Once the item was re-ordered, the Kanban was placed in a different coloured box so staff would know it had been ordered and was waiting on delivery. Once the supplies were delivered, the Kanban was placed on the item that would then trigger the next re-order.

For smaller items, the twin bin system where items could be stored in identical tubs. Once the items in the first tub were used, the Kanban at the bottom of the tub would signal a re-order and the second tub would be used while waiting to replenish the first tub. The first tub was restocked and became the second tub and so on. This method also ensured that stock does not expire as it is rotated and used according to when it was delivered.

Standardised work was created to make it easy for the staff to follow the Kanban process, and all staff had to be trained in the use of the Kanban system and what their role was in maintaining it.

Conclusion

It is important not to use Lean tools in isolation from their purpose. The use of 5S is a way of creating a culture that will reduce or prevent waste and increase value to the patients. It can be used within healthcare settings as part of a wider Lean system for improvement and is also an effective way of introducing staff to Lean principles and letting them experience successes.

5S is an ongoing process that supports the processes delivered by healthcare teams. It is a core part of the management system that will help continuous improvement to be embedded as part of daily work. Employee engagement is vital, and empowering the staff to take ownership for improving the area they work in helps to sustain an improvement mindset. 5S contributes to a safer and more efficient working environment and allows time and other resources to add value to patient care.

Learning Points

- The approach in 5S fits well within healthcare settings and is acceptable to most staff.
- Team involvement is essential if 5S is to be owned by the staff team. Active engagement also helps to sustain the improvements.
- 5S requires a focus on the processes it is to support. It is important to set it in an improvement context for staff to avoid it being seen as tidiness alone.
- Work on 5S is an effective way of introducing Lean principles at a manageable scale.
- Encouraging staff to identify problems and seek further improvements helps to build a culture of continuous improvement and can fit well with the introduction of Daily Management.

Bibliography

Ching, I. C., Hui-Chu, H., Huang, I. H., & Yi-Chun, L. (2020). 5S Reduces environmental microorganism colonies in the hemodialysis room. *Tzu Chi Nursing Journal*, 19(5), 84–96.

Díaz-Reza, J. R., García-Alcaraz, J. L., & Martínez-Loya, V. (2019). *Impact Analysis of Total Productive Maintenance. Critical Success Factors and Benefits*. Springer Nature

Graban, M. (2009). *Lean Hospitals*. Productivity Press.

Hadfield, D. (2006). *Lean Healthcare Implementing 5S in Lean or Six Sigma Projects*. MCS Media, Inc.

Hirano, H. (1996). *5S for Operators: 5 Pillars of the Visual Workplace*. Productivity Press.

Hirano, H. (2009). *JIT Implementation Manual the Complete Guide to Just-in-time Manufacturing: Volume 2 Waste and the 5S's*. CRC Press.

Ikuma, L. H., & Nahmens, I. (2014). Making safety an integral part of 5S in healthcare. *Work*, *47*(2), 243–251. https://doi.org/10.3233/WOR-121576

Ishijima, H., Eliakimu, E., & Mshana, J. M. (2016). The "5S" approach to improve a working environment can reduce waiting time: Findings from hospitals in Northern Tanzania. *TQM Journal*, *28*(4), 664–680. https://doi.org/10.1108/TQM-11-2014-0099

Jaca, C., Viles, E., Paipa-Galeano, L., Santos, J., & Mateo, R. (2014). Learning 5S principles from Japanese best practitioners: case studies of five manufacturing companies. *International Journal of Production Research*, *52*(15), 4574–4586. https://doi.org/10.1080/00207543.2013.878481

Jiménez, M., Romero, L., Domínguez, M., & Espinosa, M. d. M. (2015). 5S methodology implementation in the laboratories of an industrial engineering university school. *Safety Science*, *78*, 163–172. https://doi.org/10.1016/j.ssci.2015.04.022

Kanamori, S., Castro, M. C., Sow, S., Matsuno, R., Cissokho, A., & Jimba, M. (2016). Impact of the Japanese 5S management method on patients' and caretakers' satisfaction: a quasi-experimental study in Senegal. *Global Health Action*, *9*(1), 32852. Retrieved 2016/12/01, from https://doi.org/10.3402/gha.v9.32852

Kanamori, S., Shibanuma, A., & Jimba, M. (2016). Applicability of the 5S management method for quality improvement in health-care facilities: a review. *Tropical Medicine and Health*, *44*, 21.

Kenney, C. (2011). *Transforming Health Care: Virginia Mason Medical Centre's Pursuit of the Perfect Patient Experience*. Productivity Press.

Kurmangulov, A. A, Reshetnikova, Y. S., Frolova, O. I., Brynza, N. A. (2019). Introduction of the 5S lean manufacturing methodology in the healthcare system of the Russian Federation. *КУБАНСКИЙ НАУЧНЫЙ МЕДИЦИНСКИЙ ВЕСТНИК*, *26*(2), 140–149. https://doi.org/10.25207/1608-6228-2019-26-2-140-149

Mead, E., Stark, C., & Thompson, M. (2017). Creating and leading a quality improvement culture at scale. *Management in Healthcare*, *2*(2), 115–124.

O'Mahony, L., McCarthy, K., O'Donoghue, J., Teeling, S. P., Ward, M., & McNamara, M. (2021). Using lean six sigma to redesign the supply chain to the operating room department of a private hospital to reduce associated costs and release nursing time to care. *International Journal of Environmental Research and Public Health*, *18*(21), 11011. https://www.mdpi.com/1660-4601/18/21/11011

Papalexi, M., Bamford, D., & Dehe, B. (2016). A case study of Kanban implementation within the pharmaceutical supply chain. *International Journal of Logistics: Research and Applications*, *19*(4), 239–255. https://doi.org/10.1080/13675567.2015.1075478

Rutledge, J., Xu, M., & Simpson, J. (2010). Application of the Toyota production system improves core laboratory operations. *American Journal of Clinical Pathology*, *133*, 24–31. https://doi.org/10.1309/AJCPD1MSTIVZI0PZ

Stark, C., & Hookway, G. (2019). *Applying Lean in Health and Social Care Services*. Routledge.

Take, N., Byakika, S., Tasei, H., & Yoshikawa, T. (2015). The effect of 5S-continuous quality improvement-total quality management approach on staff motivation, patients' waiting time and patient satisfaction with services at hospitals in Uganda. *Journal of Public Health in Africa*, *6*(1), 29–34. https://doi.org/10.4081/jphia.2015.486

Toussaint, J., & Adams, E. (2015). *Management on the Mend*. ThedaCare Center for Healthcare Value.

Vedovatto Klein Kerschner, T., Bohrer da Silva, C., Fioravante dos Santos, V. C., & Ferreira, G. E. (2020). Propositions of coordinating nurses for the implementation of the 5S program in the primary health care. *Revista Eletrônica de Enfermagem*, *22*, 1–8.

Waldhausen, J. H., Avansino, J. R., Libby, A., & Sawin, R. S. (2010). Application of lean methods improves surgical clinic experience. *Journal of Pediatric Surgery*, *45*, 1420–1425. https://doi.org/10.1016/j.jpedsurg.2009.10.049

Murdina Campbell was a senior quality improvement lead in the Programme Management Office at NHS Highland. Murdina trained as a midwife and was a ward sister at Raigmore Hospital in Inverness leading a combined day-patient and in-patient unit. She trained in Lean with NHS Highland's Kaizen Promotion Office (KPO). Murdina later became deputy head of the KPO, where she taught Lean methods and coached staff training to lead Rapid Process Improvement Workshops. Murdina also led work on rapid adaptions to NHS Highland services during the COVID-19 pandemic and supported an organisational improvement programme on out-patient service delivery in NHS Highland's Programme Management Office.

Chapter 3

The Design and Use of Good Data in Clinical Processes

Todd L. Allen

Contents

DOI: 10.4324/9780429346958-3

Aims

- Understand the purposes and links between outcomes tracking systems and "DataMarts" that are used in Lean improvement methods.
- Understand and apply the idea of an outcomes (or causal) chain in the good design and use of clinical data systems.
- Understand the basic steps that are required to build effective clinical and operational data systems in healthcare.
- Describe how data systems fit into the overarching mission of clinical quality improvement.
- Describe central themes which will hopefully help others lead their own quality improvement work.

Introduction

Intermountain Healthcare is a not-for-profit integrated healthcare system in the western United States. It is known for its decades-long commitment to the principles of clinical quality improvement and the successes that have emanated from that steady commitment (James & Savitz, 2011). However, like every other healthcare organization in the world, Intermountain was not born with these capabilities. In fact, it was about in 1995 when we discovered that we were lacking several critical components (gaps) that are required to truly function as a Lean learning healthcare system. One of these gaps was that we did not have a robust, integrated, and accurate clinical data system to match our operations (budget) data. And so, we embarked on a multi-year effort to close this and other critical gaps in the late 1990s. Our world-recognized enterprise data warehouse (EDW) and its attendant clinical DataMarts resulted from this work.

This chapter describes the core theoretic concepts that we used to build our clinical data systems and the concepts that informed that work. Throughout we will use a case study around patients who are hospitalized with the diagnosis of sepsis to illustrate key points.

Using Data for Improvement

Effective data design requires a conceptual model of the problem at hand. These models can come in the form of process maps, fishbone diagrams, driver diagrams, and a myriad of other tools.

Outcomes Tracking Systems

Healthcare produces more data than it consumes. Imagine the dashboard of a jet airplane with knobs, dials, gauges, and readouts everywhere you look. There is more information on display in that cockpit than you could understand on a flight from New York to Miami. And yet, if an airplane dashboard is designed well, it will always have the essential data displayed clearly and prominently featured in the middle of the pilot's field of vision. Good data design in healthcare should be similar. Compared to the potential chaos of all the data we could display, picking outcome measures that are most important to the clinical or operational process of interest requires strategy and discipline. We will call these outcomes tracking systems.

An outcomes tracking system monitors and reports a limited set of data, of intermediate and final outcomes, balanced across outcomes classes (medical, service, and cost), at regular intervals, longitudinally over time (often years) for specific purposes of critical navigation (Nelson et al., 1998).

In clinical medicine, these purposes most often include but are not limited to:

- Inform leadership and operational decision-making (organizational and professional transparency) and focus attention (you manage what you measure) on the things that matter.
- Show you the current position relative to market standards or within a local competitive marketplace (accountability).
- Help you monitor trends so that you know when to react (the voice of the data).
- Help identify improvement opportunities (voice of the customer and voice of the process).
- Track the success of improvement projects (how do you know if it is an improvement?). against a validated baseline.
- Help hold the gains you have earned through demanding work and planning.

CASE STUDY ONE: SEPSIS DASHBOARD ELEMENTS

Intermountain Healthcare has long had an outcomes tracking system related to sepsis. Since 2002, we have reported on: inpatient mortality, Intensive Care Unit and hospital length of stay, overall sepsis-bundle compliance, and total and variable cost for patients with sepsis. These measures have served as our limited and long-term dashboard elements.

All successful organizations have effective outcomes tracking systems that monitor and report on the data elements that are key to their business. We should re-emphasize that successful organizations use these systems to report on a *limited* data set, *balanced* across outcome classes, over an *extended* time. Finally, it is critical to note that while an outcomes tracking system is required for improvement, it does not cause improvement. The work of improvement requires a diverse set of capabilities and behaviors.

Outcomes (or Causal) Chains

Outcomes tracking systems (dashboards) mostly collect high-level data. Therefore, they do not often contain the data necessary to design and manage improvement at the clinical front-line. If you want to drive improvement, you must have both the philosophy and the capability to "drill down" to more granular and workflow-centered data elements.

Both outcomes and processes are hierarchical. They can be reduced to more granular levels until you reach what is called the "decision layer" which often corresponds with where the work happens. The steps between an outcomes tracking system and the decision layer are called the outcomes (causal) chain.

Outcomes chains track the hierarchical elements of a process or outcomes structure, from a "final outcome," through to a series of intermediate outcomes, also known as process steps, down to the level of actual decisions or behavior that represents the place where changes can be designed, implemented, and measured. This is the same as the "Five Whys" in Lean and it is the same as the drill down methodology. Outcomes chains are the only way to properly decide on the data elements that will be necessary to run improvement cycles using Lean methods.

The strength of the links in the chain, the evidence, is important. If you have strong evidentiary or causal links between the outcomes of interest and the process-level measures, you can be more confident that a change in the process measure will affect the outcome measures. Weaker links make those assumptions more tenuous. However, in medicine, we are often challenged by weaker links in the outcomes chain. There are perfectly effective ways to strengthen those links by using good team methods and semi-formal group techniques.

Using the outcomes chain approach will lead you to a series of intermediate process-level measures. These are the data elements that will be used to design and implement improvement cycles. We will call these data elements "drill down" or process measures (Provost & Murray, 2011). Once you settle on the right process measures, they will often be organized in a longitudinal DataMart along with the outcome measures.

CASE STUDY TWO: SEPSIS – CAUSAL CHAIN

There is good evidence from randomized controlled trials that show that mortality due to complications of sepsis can be lessened by limiting acute lung failure and distributive shock. Lung failure can be limited by using a strategy of low-tidal volume ventilation (LTVV) (Brower et al., 2000). Distributive shock can be improved through a good approach to infection control, however, due to many variables the perfect time to administer antibiotics to an individual patient is unclear (Peltan et al., 2017). Therefore, two process (drill down) measures for sepsis might be whether LTVV was used and if antibiotics were given within three hours of presentation. These two process measures are an example of an outcomes (or causal) chain and have different strengths of evidence associated with them and the outcome of interest which is mortality.

Data for "drill down" and improvement work will investigate an extended set of data, which included detailed process and outcome data, over a limited period of time (sometimes a "one shot"), to test whether improvement ideas will work. This is the very idea of an improvement project. While the concept of data for drill down is simple, common barriers might emerge at this point. These barriers can include challenges related to data systems' design, study design, data collection, data management, and analysis.

Remember that data for drill down (or process measures) are fundamentally different from outcome measures that may be featured on a dashboard. For example, the altimeter is a central feature of an airplane dashboard. The weight of material in the cargo hold and tailwind might represent process measures relevant to altitude. Once you settle on the right process measures, you will want to collect and use them for a longer period, and they will often then be organized in a longitudinal DataMart along with the outcome measures. Importantly, what you learn from the process measures will most certainly modify the outcomes tracker.

We must use drill down measures in our work to effectively understand and change the process and the outcomes of interest that follow from the process. Process-level measures massively shorten the cycle time for change and discovery and massively increase the effective sample size for analysis. Both features are critical to Lean improvement cycles. Imagine designing and implementing a change in the process of diagnosing and treating patients with potential sepsis in the emergency department (ED) and then waiting a year to see if mortality was affected. If you want to drive improvement, you *must* have both the philosophy and the capability to "drill down" to more granular and timelier workflow-centered data elements. The key then becomes the strength of the links in that outcomes chain.

Challenges in Finding the Decision Layer

Since outcomes tracking systems mostly collect and report high-level summary data, these systems and data elements often do not reach the "decision layer." Finding the right process-level measures that are linked to the outcomes of interest and can drive change most often requires a bit of work. This relies on a culture of teamwork and learning, a quality improvement methodology (like Lean), and leadership. It also requires good analytic support, literature reviews, and an effective means of collecting and displaying data. A robust clinical information system with the necessary resources to build and maintain an enterprise data warehouse and clinical DataMarts is also critical. Using the tools described in this book will provide the knowledge to design useful and relevant data systems.

General Principles for Data Design

Health systems and caregivers are increasingly asked to report data to national or regulatory agencies in the name of quality. Often, those outcome and accountability measures do not hit the decision layer and do not come with the process measures that are necessary to understand and improve that outcome. Regulatory accountability measures are a fact of modern healthcare and while this can sometimes seem frustrating, the application of good data design principles to this challenge will make success toward any regulatory measures more likely.

For example, imagine if the legislature of Avalon designed a national accountability measure that required you to report the all-cause 30-day readmission rates in patients hospitalized with sepsis. One could make a good case as to why this outcome measure is important to patients, and one might even choose to set a goal for this measure. The measure itself, however, tells you nothing about how your local organization might work to improve. This means that you and your teams will have to do the arduous work of building an outcomes chain, using drill down techniques, from this readmission measure down to the decision layer where you can measure and manage change that will affect the readmission rate. We call this bottom-up data design. It means that you need to organize around core work processes to collect and report data and that your data structures and collection must follow the core work processes themselves. Design your systems (either electronic or manual) to collect the process-level data once, at the front-line (patient level), and then use that data to manage the process all the way up the chain to the outcome level. Notably, in doing this you cannot impede clinical productivity and so make every attempt to integrate data capture into the flow of clinical work.

Intelligently designed, the data should help individual clinicians understand and improve the work that affects readmissions and then report that up to the level of the unit or clinic, the hospital or divisions, the health system, states and regions, and finally national reporting.

While accountability measures are likely to be necessary in modern healthcare, they tend to assume that clinicians and systems can respond to these measures with quality improvement capability and commitment, that ranking systems are accurate, and that consumers will respond to these rankings in a meaningful way. Parts of each of these assumptions are tenuous. Intelligently designed, these data systems and efforts can help with accountability measures bringing learning and improvement. Accurate national reporting and accountability, and the capacity to improve, will only happen when data are generated and used for internal management using the principles described here (Berwick et al., 2003).

Quality Data Needs to Be Complete, Timely, Accurate, and Transparent

Delivering on these general principles is fundamental to delivering quality data:

- Complete means that all necessary elements are captured without "null" fields.
- Timely means that you capture the data elements right within the flow of clinical work such that they could be used to monitor the clinical work in real time if necessary.
- Accurate means that the data is right the first time and that no auditing or validation should be required. Collect the right data once, at its point of origin, and then use it for all necessary applications. More to the point, blend your data collection right into the routine flow of your work.
- The final general principle is data transparency. As a quality leader, you are the guardian of the culture of the data you collect and report. This means that you need to be transparent with what data you are measuring and why, and to deliver your reporting in a climate of trust and learning.

True transparency will be achieved when we have an environment in which those involved in healthcare choices (patients, family, payers, providers) have sufficiently accurate, complete, and understandable information about expected clinical results such that they can make wise choices regarding the care they give or receive. Such choices involve not just the selection of a health plan, a hospital, or a physician, but also the series of testing and treatment decisions that patients routinely face as they work their way through diagnosis and treatment. Most clinicians do not know (do not measure or have easy access to) their own short- and long-term clinical outcomes, and as a result, they cannot accurately advise patients regarding the treatment choices that are so important to them.

Practical Steps for Good Data Design and Good Data Systems

Our experience in building effective data systems that link process and outcome measures was derived from standard clinical trial design (Pocock, 1984). With a little practice and discipline, the method described here can end up providing intermediate and final measures related to clinical, cost, and satisfaction outcomes. These are optimized for process management and improvement and are more extensive and clinically focused than accountability measures. The method also generates a parsimonious set of measures that avoids the bias of availability.

As noted earlier, start with a good conceptual model of clearly defining the problem. This foundation will help you and your teams better find the data elements that represent the voice of the process and link to the outcome measures of interest.

Using the conceptual model (or process map), generate a simple list of the desired reports that will be needed to understand and improve the process. This is a simple list of reports that you and your team think you might need to manage the process. Write out these reports in plain language. Make a simple drawing of the annotated run chart or statistical process control chart that represents that named report. Take that paper with the name of the report and the drawing and test it with your teams and the front-line. Do this for each one of the reports that you think you might need.

CASE STUDY THREE: SEPSIS – METRICS

You and your team have decided to use Lean methods to improve the door-to-antibiotic time in patients with suspected sepsis in the ED. After agreeing on a process map of the steps required to prepare and administer the antibiotic once the decision to treat has been made, you decide you will need the following reports. You write these down on a piece of paper:

1. Proportion of weekly ED sepsis patients who received antibiotics in less than three hours from arrival and registration.
2. Elapsed time from order of antibiotic to pharmacy preparation of the order.
3. Elapsed time from the preparation of the antibiotic to the administration of the antibiotic.

For each of these reports, you would then prepare a drawing of that named report and test this at the front-line. For #1, the drawing might look like as shown in Figure 3.1.

These reports should very carefully match up with the conceptual model. Next generate a list of the data elements that will be required to operate the reports that you have decided you will need. Think in terms of numerators and denominators or the real data elements that are required. You are sequentially building a data specification (coding) manual. Use what you have generated, and underneath the drawing of the chart, write out the specific numerator and denominator required for that chart (Box 3.2). This step assures that your data elements match up with the information that you are trying to generate. Once again test this drawing and the now identified data elements with your teams and the front-line. Ask them, "if we gave you this data and this report, would you use it, and would it make a difference in the work that you do?"

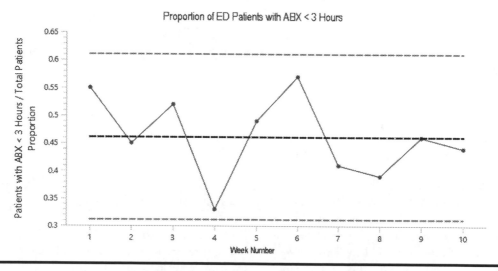

Figure 3.1 Proportion of emergency department patients receiving antibiotics in less than three hours of arrival and registration.

CASE STUDY FOUR: SEPSIS – MEASUREMENT METADATA

Numerator: ED patients with sepsis who received antibiotics in less than three hours totaled by week

Denominator: All ED patients with sepsis totaled by week

Data Elements Needed: Date and time of arrival, date and time of antibiotic order, date and time of completed preparation of antibiotic, date and time of antibiotic administration, medical record number (patients with sepsis), ED patients with diagnosis code = sepsis

Once you have agreed on your reports and the data elements needed for those reports, only now should you go to your data specialists (members of the information system team) to begin discussions about how to capture the data and where or whether the data already exists. At this step, you are negotiating what you need with what you have. Waiting until this point to have these discussions helps you to avoid the "availability bias" that so often can limit learning. Here you will identify and write down the data sources for each element that you need while considering the value of the final reports versus the costs of getting that necessary data.

Now, and again in concert with your data specialist, you can begin to design the EDW and DataMart structure. Once this is done, you can begin to program the analytic routines and the display subsystems. Finally, you will need to rigorously test the reporting system to ensure accuracy and usability.

The reports should also include the final outcomes and be balanced across outcomes classes including medical outcomes, service outcomes, and cost outcomes.

Remember, data costs money and typically this is more than you might expect. Therefore, it is important to explicitly define all the data elements that you will need including where they will be found and how they will be coded. You also must give explicit instructions for unknown data and what to do in the case of blank or null data. You should make every effort to link every data element that you collect to a report. Do not collect data that you will not use. Taken together these general rules help you generate your data specification (coding) manual which can then be implemented either electronically via the electronic health record or through self-coding data forms.

There are several sources of clinical data. Work carefully with your clinical and information system teams to identify those sources and use them for opportunities for improvement and learning.

Learning Activities

To apply these ideas in your own practice:

■ Consider a clinical problem you are working on and write down three outcome measures relevant to that problem. One should come from each of the standard categories of medical outcomes, service outcomes, and cost outcomes.

■ Using an outcomes chain, track back one of the outcome measures to a process measure that is relevant to the problem. This may require two or three steps. At each step, make a notation as to whether the link between the measures is strong, weak, or moderate.

■ Using the process measure you selected, write out the name of a report that would represent that process measure over time and then create a simple drawing of the graph that would illustrate that named report.

Where Does Data Design and Use Fit in an Overall Lean Improvement Effort?

Good data design and use is an important part of Lean theory and its application in healthcare. At Intermountain Healthcare, we have had a standard high-level model that we follow when attempting to apply Lean methods across a broad swath of our clinical work. That method is:

■ Select a *high-priority* clinical or operational process.
■ Generate an evidence-based "best practice" *guideline* that provides detail on the best way to conduct that clinical or operational process.
■ Blend the guideline into the flow of clinical work. Adjust and design training, staffing, supplies, physical layout, educational materials, measurement, and information flow.
■ Build and embed data systems to (1) track protocol variations and (2) short- and long-term patient results.
■ Use the guideline as a shared baseline and *demand* that clinicians vary from that guideline when required based on individual patient needs.
■ Measure, learn from, and over time eliminate variations arising from professionals, but retain variations arising from patients. This is the principle of mass customization.
■ Feed that data back into a Lean Learning Loop to update the guideline, provide transparency to front-line clinicians, and generate formal knowledge that can be shared transparently.

Conclusion

Lean improvement theory unequivocally teaches us that lessening unnecessary variation will improve outcomes. With the health and wellness of our patients in our hands, this work is the moral imperative of our time. Real improvement requires good data and data that ties directly to the front-line where the excellent work happens. Gathering good data is not simply mining any available data to see what might work. There is a methodology toward designing and implementing good data systems. With good data in hand, your clinical teams can really begin to understand the fundamental processes of healthcare and discover how to improve them. At that point, the totality of Lean theory can be brought to bear to make a remarkable difference in the lives of your colleagues, your patients, and your community.

Tips

■ Be patient. Finding and using good clinical data is not always as easy as it might seem.
■ Invite someone with good data experience onto your improvement teams and include them in your discussions and learn from their experience.

- Write down and keep track of your decisions with respect to data. Your data specification manual does not need to be complicated. Make it simple.
- Test your data structures and reports with the front-line workers. If they do not understand it or will not use it, go back to the drawing board and try again.

Learning Points

- Outcomes tracking systems are critical in healthcare and represent a limited set of data critical clinical and operational data reported over time and at regular intervals.
- Outcomes tracking systems do not lead to improvement by themselves without the application of additional capabilities that can be found in Lean theory.
- Process measures represent short-term outcomes that are relevant to improvement strategy and learning.
- Outcome measures link up with process measures through an outcomes (causal) chain.
- The causal chain plus a conceptual model of the problem will reveal the data elements that are necessary to understand, manage, and improve that process.
- Data must be complete, timely, and accurate to be useful at the front-line.
- Data collection must be integrated into the natural flow of clinical work, and data must be transparent to be maximally effective.
- There is a methodology that enables the good design of clinical and operational data systems.

Acknowledgments

I would like to thank and honor my family, my colleagues at Intermountain Healthcare and the Healthcare Delivery Institute (@ATP_QI), and my friend and mentor Dr. Brent C. James. Many of the ideas represented in this chapter arose from his teachings and leadership.

Bibliography

Berwick, D. M., James, B., & Coye, M. J. (2003). Connections between quality measurement and improvement. *Med Care, 41*(1 Suppl), I30–38. https://doi.org/10.1097/00005650-200301001-00004

Brower, R. G., Matthay, M. A., Morris, A., Schoenfeld, D., Thompson, B. T., & Wheeler, A. (2000). Ventilation with lower tidal volumes as compared with traditional tidal volumes for acute lung injury and the acute respiratory distress syndrome. *New England J Med, 342*, 1301–1308. https://doi.org/10.1056/NEJM200005043421801

James, B. C., & Savitz, L. A. (2011). How Intermountain trimmed health care costs through robust quality improvement efforts. *Health Affairs, 30*, 1185–1191. https://doi.org/10.1377/hlthaff.2011.0358

Nelson, E. C., Splaine, M. E., Batalden, P. B., & Plume, S. K. (1998). Building measurement and data collection into medical practice. *Ann Intern Med, 128*(6), 460–466. https://doi.org/10.7326/0003-4819-128-6-199803150-00007

Peltan, I. D., Mitchell, K. H., Rudd, K. E., Mann, B. A., Carlbom, D. J., Hough, C. L., Rea, T. D., & Brown, S. M. (2017). Physician variation in time to antimicrobial treatment for septic patients presenting to the emergency department. *Crit Care Med, 45*(6), 1011–1018. https://doi.org/10.1097/CCM.0000000000002436

Pocock, S. J. (1984). *Clinical Trials: A Practical Approach.* John Wiley & Sons.

Provost, L. P., & Murray, S. K. (2011). *The Health Care Data Guide: Learning from Data for Improvement* (1st ed.). John Wiley & Sons.

Todd L. Allen, FACEP, serves as the senior vice-president and chief quality officer at the Queen's Health System based in Honolulu, Hawaii. He has overall responsibility for regulatory reporting and certifications, quality, safety, infection prevention and control, and the function of performance improvement. He previously served at Intermountain Healthcare in Salt Lake City, UT, as the assistant chief quality officer and as the senior executive medical director for the Healthcare Delivery Institute. His research has been supported by the National Heart, Lung and Blood Institute (NHLBI), and he has authored or co-authored over 45 peer-reviewed publications. Todd also serves as an invited lecturer on quality, Lean methods, and improvement in healthcare for systems throughout the United States and Europe.

Chapter 4

Hospital Flow

Marc Rouppe van der Voort, Anna Roos Vijverberg,
and Frits van Merode

Contents

Aims

This chapter reviews patient flow with the following aims:

- To describe the impact of flow problems on patients and staff.
- To provide examples of in-patient and outpatient flow problems and the response to them.
- To examine the differences between open-loop and closed-loop systems.
- To emphasise the role of executive leadership in embedding and maintaining improvement in health care organisations.

DOI: 10.4324/9780429346958-4

Introduction

Why Improve Patient Flow?

When following a patient's journey, a lot of waiting can be observed. It can feel uncertain what or when the next step will be. There is often rework, rescheduling and small mistakes. The process is often stop-and-go, and for the patient, it is rarely a smooth experience of continuous flow. Yet patients are usually satisfied, even though processes are essentially broken.

High patient satisfaction levels even in the context of service problems probably occur because care is delivered by providers who are skilled professionals and are very committed to the well-being of patients. This creates a high level of trust and gratitude, but in a relationship that is characterised by dependency and vulnerability. The way care is organised adds anxiety and uncertainty to the lives of patients in the most vulnerable moments of their lives. Patients are not satisfied because of high process quality but despite poor process quality.

Perhaps as important, the highly motivated care professionals also experience their daily work routines as stop-and-go. Their working lives are often filled with frustration because they need to spend a relatively large percentage of their time dealing with the broken processes. Fixing means creating workarounds to ensure that their patient receives the right care. Often, they feel powerless to fix root causes in the processes. They know that the problem they are fixing today is likely to return tomorrow and there is not much they can do about it. The statistics on the loss of motivation and people leaving the health sector are alarming, especially since many professions are experiencing a shortage of people.

Summed up, improving flow is important to further enhance the patient experience and reduce unnecessary anxiety. It is also important to reduce the stress and frustration of care professionals. Finally, improving flow reduces wasteful activities.

Improving Flow

Improving flow means reducing 'undesired' waiting in the patient care processes. It addresses 'undesired' waiting because waiting can be functional or desired in some circumstances, such as patients who are considering their options and want time to decide.

One way to define optimal flow is when a patient experiences a smooth, continuous and connected care process (Benjamin & Jacelon, 2021). Putting this more formally: 'Patient flow may be described in terms of the progressive movement of patients through care processes from arrival until they physically leave the hospital, with movement referring to the conversion of an input into an output' (De Freitas et al., 2018, p. 626). In a recent literature review, Benjamin and Jacelon note that 'patient flow' and 'patient flow management' are often not well differentiated. They offer the following definition: 'Patient flow management is defined as the application of holistic perspectives, dynamic data, and complex considerations of multiple priorities to enable timely, efficient, and high-quality patient care' (Benjamin & Jacelon, 2021, pp. 4–5).

Work on improvements in flow can be targeted on a complete patient journey, or on processes that impact several flows within a hospital such as work in the emergency department, radiology department or outpatient clinic. Understanding the flow of groups of patients between departments is important, such as the planning of an operating theatre schedule in relation to the outflow to the intensive care unit and the general wards.

Improving a patient's journey often requires redesigning work processes, for example by introducing one-stop-shop outpatient visits. It involves capacity management and planning methods. Due to its many pathways and shared resources, a hospital can be considered a network through

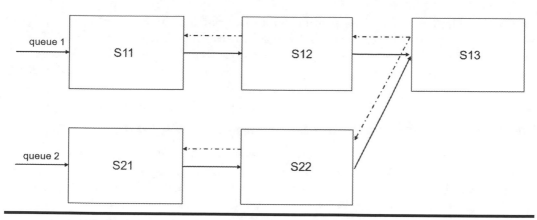

Figure 4.1   Workstations in a hospital. Solid arrows indicate patient flows, and dotted arrows indicate information flows, e.g. blocking of the downstream workstation. Systemic failures appear as a local blockage results in a sequence of local blockages. Through the blocking of shared resources, an increase in the volume of a certain patient stream may lead to blockages in another patient chain which seems at first sight totally unconnected from the first patient stream (source: [3]).

which the patients move (van Merode & Groothuis, 2003). Improving flow is to a great extent about increasing the capacity to absorb fluctuations of patient groups that flow through the network via many routes (Figure 4.1).

In the example in Figure 4.1, two patient flows – termed queue 1 and queue 2 in the figure – pass through a common process labelled S13. An increase in flow in either of the patient streams can overwhelm the shared process and result in delays in the other queue. Through the blocking of shared resources, an increase in the volume of one patient stream may lead to blockages in another patient stream which seems at first sight unconnected (van Merode & Groothuis, 2003).

How Can a Hospital Work on Flow Improvement?

It is important to work on long-term solutions. To obtain lasting improvements, the team must not only solve current problems but also address the deeper root causes. This often requires work on hospital capacity. From this perspective, the following distinction between three levels of flow improvement work is useful:

1. Improvement work that is part of the daily routine of individuals and care teams.
2. Work that is carried out by temporary improvement teams, usually multi-disciplinary. This work can be conducted within a single department or can be cross-departmental that tackle more complex problems.
3. Hospital system-level improvement work that addresses the root causes of flow problems. This is usually the responsibility of senior management and executive-level staff.

Case Examples

Two real-life cases of poor hospital flow and solutions that have proven to be effective are described. The first case is an example of patient flow between departments. The second case is about improving flow within a department. Both cases describe improvement work conducted by temporary improvement teams (Level Two in the three levels listed above). Generic lessons on what and how to improve hospital flow are considered. The chapter concludes with a general reflection on the lessons learned. The root causes of poor hospital flow, and the associated implications for improvement work in the hospital, are discussed.

Context: The Dutch Healthcare System and Hospital Characteristics

If a Dutch citizen becomes ill, they first visit a general practitioner (GP). The GP acts as a gate-keeper and delivers general health care. If planned specialised care is required, the GP can refer the patient to specialist hospital-based care. The patient is referred to one specialty. If other specialised care is necessary, a new referral is needed from the GP (Delnoij et al., 2000; Sripa et al., 2019).

All Dutch citizens are required to have healthcare insurance with a private insurance company. If a patient receives care in the hospital, the hospital passes on the diagnosis code to the health insurer. The hospital is paid a pre-agreed amount based on the condition. The cost reimbursed does not change if more or less care is provided (for example additional outpatient visits).

Case Study 1: Clinical Hospital Flow

This case study demonstrates the use of levelling, and matching capacity and demand.

The chief executive of the hospital received a letter from a group of neurologists. They were frustrated and complained about how their patients were often scattered across various wards in the hospital. This resulted in a lower quality of care, more work for the doctors and less joy in the work of the nurses. Their assumption was that there were not enough beds to accommodate busier periods. The chief executive asked the management team to analyse the problem and work on a solution (Figure 4.2).

Initial analysis of the data showed:

■ Neurology patients as well as patients from several other specialisms were scattered across wards.

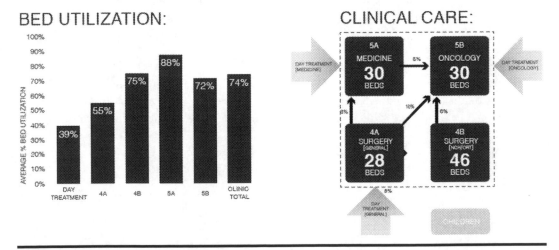

Figure 4.2 On the left is a bar chart of the average bed utilisation of the different wards. On the right the flow of patients between the different wards.

- The average length of stay of patients admitted to a ward of a different specialty was almost a full day longer than for patients with the same condition admitted to a ward of the correct specialty.
- Those mostly urgently admitted were scattered across a range of wards.
- Patients who had same-day surgery (and went home after a few hours of recovery) often did not recover in the same-day ward.
- Patients who had surgery and stayed one or more nights rarely were admitted to other wards.
- There were not enough beds to accommodate the increasing number of patients having same-day surgery.

Further analysis revealed a more nuanced picture:

- Bed utilisation was lower than expected on several wards, including the same-day ward.
- There was a high variability in the number of same-day surgeries per day. On busy days, the overflow of same-day patients were admitted to general wards. To ensure availability, the required beds had to be reserved the day before and remained empty for the remainder of the day and night. This partially explained the low bed utilisation while at the same time wards were often 'full' and could not admit urgent patients from the emergency department.
- The ward for neurology was mixed with orthopaedics. Patients from orthopaedics were almost never admitted to another ward because they were planned admissions with beds reserved the day before. Neurology patients were more likely to arrive as emergency admissions with no bed booked.

A graph was created that showed the average number of admissions and discharges on the neurology and orthopaedics ward per hour of the day (Figure 4.3).

When a nurse saw that the peak in admissions was between 7 and 10 am and the peak of discharges was between 10 and 12 am, she queried, 'why do we admit patients before surgery?'

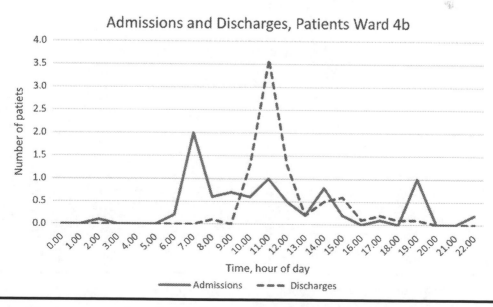

Figure 4.3 Average number of admissions and discharges per hour of the day.

Everyone was baffled. No one could explain why patients were asked to arrive at the ward as early as 7 am and then waited on their beds before being transported to the operating theatre. If no one can explain why we do it, we can stop it.

A test of change began with one day, one specialty and four patients. The patients went directly to a room next to the operating theatre and went through the hospital admission procedures while seated. In the beginning it took a lot of improvisation. For example, the IT system would not allow the provision of medication for surgery if a bed was not assigned to the patient. The staff had to create virtual (fake) beds to fool the system. Later, an admission lounge was created next to the operating theatre. Two years later all patients were admitted via the admission lounge. They then went from the operating theatre to the ward, into a bed previously used by a patient who had been discharged earlier that morning.

The second solution came from a student interacting with the surgery planning department and the capacity manager. There were four teams of planners that planned almost all surgeries per group of specialisms. This meant that each group planned several same-day surgeries every day and no group could know how many same-day surgeries were planned per day in total. So, the planners used a large chart on the wall to keep track. Vertical squares depicted the number of available same-day surgery beds. Each time they scheduled a same-day surgery patient, they coloured an empty square with a particular colour per specialty (Figure 4.4).

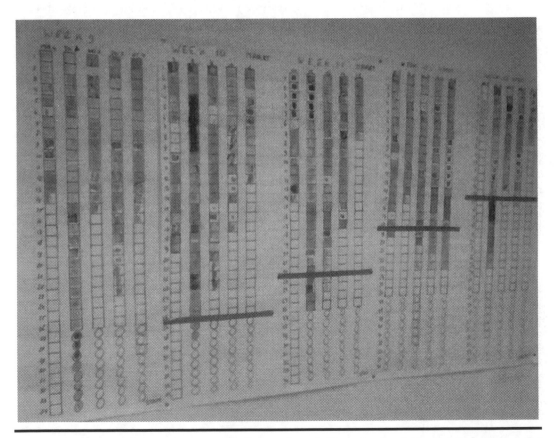

Figure 4.4 Photo of the paper on which the planners kept track of the number of planned same-day surgeries. Photo provided by authors.

When all beds were filled, they coloured a circle, indicating a patient who needed to be admitted to a regular clinical ward. This meant that a bed had to be reserved and was shown as 'occupied' from the day before the planned admission, making that bed unavailable for other patients, even though it was not physically occupied. As can be seen in Figure 4.4, the system was complicated.

After a few weeks, the team looked at the coloured squares and learned several points:

- The overflows from the same-day ward happened most often on Tuesdays.
- Over a week, there were more than enough beds: the number of empty squares per week was substantially higher than the number of coloured circles.

For a few weeks, the supporting quality improvement team hoped that the planners would spontaneously change the planning to prevent the overflow. Unfortunately, this proved unrealistic. The quality improvement experts wanted the solution to come from the planners themselves because the planners and other staff knew best how the complexity and fine-tuning of the planning process worked and what changes could be sustainable. The supporting team challenged and motivated the planning group to try a solution. They started using moving horizontal red lines as a visual indicator of the maximum number of same-day surgeries to be planned per day for a certain period ahead. Unfortunately, this only further increased their frustration of not being able to improve the situation.

In the meantime, a student had calculated the ideal mix of surgeries per day to create a levelled presence of orthopaedic patients in the regular ward. This was first calculated with complex simulation software and then translated into simple planning rules:

- Plan surgeries on Monday and Friday if a patient needs to stay two nights or longer.
- Plan surgeries on Tuesday and Wednesday if a patient needs to stay one night.
- Use Thursday as the overflow day where all lengths of stay can be planned.
- Spread the same-day surgeries evenly over the days of the week.

Applying these rules produced a small improvement with slight lower peaks of planned patients in the ward on a single day but fell far short of the expected improvement. The manager asked the planners to make a note each time they had to break the planning rules. The cause turned out to be simple: the surgeon who operated on a particular day was often specialised in a type of surgery that required a different length of stay. Particularly, on Tuesday two surgeons often performed a high number of same-day surgeries. This explained the regular overflow from the same-day ward on Tuesdays.

The planners and the manager explained the situation to the surgeons, and they agreed to switch operating days. This enabled the planners to follow the simple rules more closely, resulting in a levelled presence of planned patients in the wards. This in turn reduced the peak bed occupation and the number of urgently admitted patients on the wrong wards.

This gave the idea for the last solution: the planners identified the days when the specific surgeons operated that resulted in more same-day admissions than usual. On these marked days, they planned surgeries with at least one night's stay to prevent the same-day ward from overflowing. This almost completely solved this overflow problem.

Together, these interventions had an enormous impact on hospital flow: fewer patients were admitted to 'wrong' wards. The work pressure on the doctors and nurses improved. The system became more productive because substantially more patients could be admitted using the same number of beds. Furthermore, the emergency department was less crowded and frustrated. In addition, the nurses loved the new 'admission without a bed' process. They were so enthusiastic that there was an increase in applications from nurses who liked the idea of working in a ward where leadership listens to their ideas and gives freedom and guidance to make improvements.

Lessons from This Case Study about Flow

There is an enormous impact on patients, staff and productivity when there is no or poor flow in the system:

- Many parts of the hospital continuously change and interact with each other. This means the whole system needs to be studied.
- The importance of integrated planning is paramount. The impact on the wards from different expected lengths of stay needs to be considered when deciding which operations will be performed on which days.
- The power of a good analysis based on data, from a system perspective (vs individual departments or specialties) and discussing it with the involved professionals.

Most variation is a consequence of individual clinician choices, such as the design of surgery schedules and patient planning methods, and it is important to reduce this variation.

Lessons on How to Improve Flow

- The strong ideas that produce improvement are often surprisingly simple once the root causes are clear. However, it can take many months to figure these out and even more time to implement them. This is because they require a new way of thinking, which means that the implementation must deal with the old way of thinking pushing back against the solution.
- There is power in sharing data without judgment with the professionals to encourage free thinking and experimentation, and coaching this process.
- Flow and capacity management requires a mix of skills: analytical, change management, process improvement and ideally coaching. Coaching helps to make it sustainable and increase the capabilities that will allow the team to be able to better deal with similar challenges in the future.

Case Study 2: Outpatient Specialist Care Flow

This case study demonstrates that services often change in response to service pressures. When the root cause of the problem is not apparent, changes made with the best of intentions can cause further problems. The case study also describes changes made in isolation, which when combined with other changes being made by other people, can add to confusion and delays.

The situation was that three medical specialists started a new outpatient specialist clinic. They agreed that they would each perform four outpatient sessions (half days) per week. In the early months after the clinic opened, there were not enough patients to fill all the available slots. The doctors dealt with the empty slots in their sessions differently. The first doctor regularly cancelled half-full sessions on short notice. This generated extra work for the administrative staff, but they did not complain. The second doctor did not cancel sessions but used the free time to perform paperwork. The third doctor enjoyed improving processes in the clinic and instructed the administrative staff to schedule patients in her sessions consecutively; she finished her clinics earlier than her colleagues did because of the lack of gaps in her clinic schedule.

After a while, the third doctor became popular, and more patients were specifically referred to her. Her sessions were now full and her access time, the number of days between the day a patient's appointment was requested and the day the appointment could be offered, rose steadily to four weeks. The popular doctor now saw 25% more patients compared to her colleagues, but the doctors divided their income equally. This became a cause of irritation for the third doctor. She instructed the administrators to have four fixed slots each week in the clinic schedule of all three doctors where only new patients could be booked. This makes sense because the doctors were paid a fixed amount per new patient per year, regardless of how many follow-up visits are performed. With the creation of the new patient slots, the doctor sought to ensure that everybody brought in the same amount of income for the group. A direct consequence was that her access time for new patients rose from four to eight weeks because she now sees fewer new patients per week. However, her follow-up visits could be planned on short notice because she now had more clinic space available.

Meanwhile, another difference between the three doctors took effect. The first doctor saw follow-up patients more frequently than his colleagues. In combination with the extra new patients and his routine practice of regularly cancelling sessions because of other activities, he did not have enough slots for all the patients. His access time began to rise and fluctuated between two and six weeks, depending mostly on how many sessions he cancelled.

Sometimes the medical condition of patients requires them to see the doctor within a few days. The first and the third doctor do not have enough available space for these patients. Therefore, the third doctor decided to reserve a slot in every session for urgent appointments. After a while, the first doctor notices that these urgent slots are often not used. He instructed the administrators to use these slots for new patients if they were unfilled until 24 hours before the clinic. His own access time now fluctuates between one day and four weeks.

Because the third doctor checked the sessions of all three doctors, she noticed that the first doctor still saw fewer new patients. This meant that the measure to fix four slots per session was ineffective. The second and third doctors performed more sessions and thus saw more new patients than the first doctor. Therefore, the third doctor instructed the clinic planners to schedule routinely a fifth new patient at the cost of follow-up slots at the sessions of the first doctor.

As the first doctor now saw more follow-up patients, performed fewer sessions and sometimes had a fifth new patient in a session, he did not have enough space for all his follow-up appointments. Access time for follow-up patients rose to greater than three months. He instructed the clinic planners that if a patient needed to be seen sooner, then the administrative staff could double book the first two appointments. It may seem illogical to start with more patients, but he considered that sometimes appointments can be short. So, if he added additional patients, he would have a healthy pressure to keep appointments short and try to finish on time. This did not work often, but he felt that he was doing the best he could.

Demand for the clinic grew steadily. The second doctor also found that he did not have enough follow-up appointments. He heard from the clinic planners about the double-booking rule of his colleague, but he considered it patient unfriendly that all patients need to wait longer. He instructed the planners that they could book a maximum of three extra follow-up appointments at the end of each session and he and the other staff would just work a little longer. The third doctor wanted extra patients only planned during the morning sessions but did not mind which slots. She sought to finish the afternoon on time, because of other obligations.

Because the first doctor still did not have enough space for his follow-up appointments, he sometimes performed an extra session on Friday afternoon. It took some effort to convince the administrative staff to work additional time on a Friday afternoon, which they did not like. He instructed them to plan only follow-up appointments in these sessions.

The third doctor had a sub-specialty interest and dedicated one session a week to this group of patients. In the beginning, these sessions were half-empty. She instructed clinic planners to also schedule follow-up appointments from the regular sessions in these sub-specialty clinics. Later, when the specialised session became full, she forbade further regular appointments from being scheduled in these sessions. When the access time for the specialised session became longer than two weeks, she asked for the specialised appointments to be booked in the regular sessions.

Because of the continuous changes in the planning rules, the work became very complex. The experienced clinic planners understood the rules, but new assistants struggled and made many mistakes. The planners became very irritated with all the changing rules per doctor and their apparent lack of understanding of how difficult it was for the administrative staff to avoid errors. They felt unable to provide a good service to patients in this increasing complexity. The waiting room was often very full and discussions on the phone with patients increased.

The doctors, clinic assistants and planners were all frustrated with their work. The doctors had a meeting to discuss the problems. They agree that it has become very hard to schedule clinics and they were frustrated with the whole situation. Something must change.

What are the general patterns in this case?

- Several solutions isolate capacity by producing dedicated slots for new patients, urgent patients, specialised sessions etc. This makes the system more vulnerable to fluctuations in supply (the number of sessions performed per week) and demand (the number of requests for an appointment per week).
- Fluctuations in supply (sessions) are causing more flow problems than fluctuations in demand (Figures 4.5 and 4.6).
- Even though there are long access times, there is also a waste of unused slots, due to the increased complexity of the planning system. One speciality in our experience used more than 50 types of slots with dozens of planning rules.

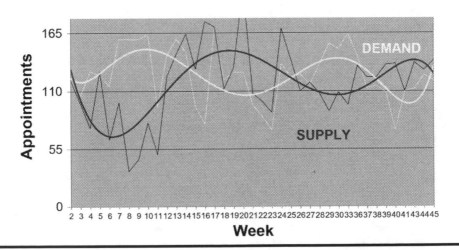

Figure 4.5 Demand and supply of outpatient clinic slots for new patients per week.

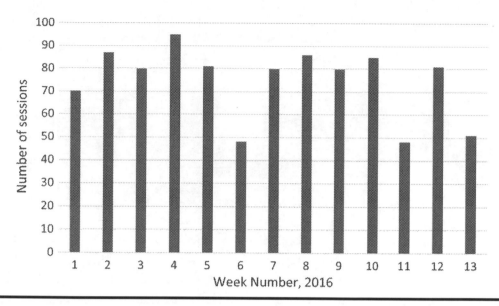

Figure 4.6 Number of sessions per week.

■ Long waiting times decrease efficiency. Many people believe that waiting times are required to work efficiently by preventing empty slots, but the opposite has proven to be the case with long waiting times increasing waste.

More important are observations about how the clinic 'learned' to improve and the impact of behaviours.

Incremental Improvements without Root Cause Analysis: Many small problems emerged over time and many small changes were made to address these problems. Each solution was unproblematic in isolation but together created a more complex system. This complexity led to less flow, more waste and frustration. While there was a constant impulse to change, there was no culture of continuous improvement with explicit measurement.

Figure 4.7 shows an example of the unintended consequences of a higher follow-up rate resulting in a higher demand for follow-up slots. A new planning rule is created to give more priority to urgent patients by assigning dedicated slots to them. This results in more capacity for urgent patients and thus lower access time. The GPs refer more patients to the outpatient clinic because of low access time resulting in more demand. At the same time, the planning rule creates less capacity for follow-up patients. The access time for follow-up patients keeps rising and a new planning rule is created to gain more capacity (at the beginning of a session two patients may be booked extra). The double-booking results in sessions running late and unsatisfied patients which eventually leads to a lower demand.

Uncoordinated Improvements: The three doctors did not act together for the overall benefit of the system. By not involving her colleagues in her improvement efforts, the third doctor also did not improve the 'system'.

The doctors changed schedules often, but they did not reflect on the impact of the changes. Consequently, there was no systematic learning and double-loop thinking is totally absent (Figure 4.8). With adaptive or single-loop learning, an event like rising demand is solved by a planning rule that reacts to the event. Generative or double-loop learning looks at the system and

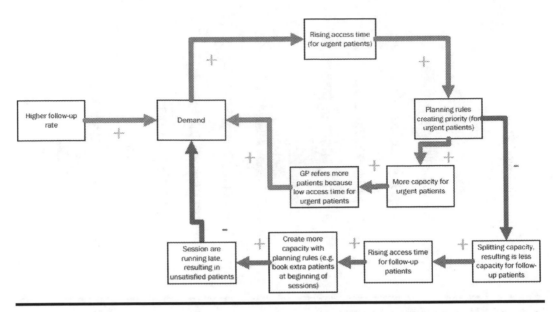

Figure 4.7 Impact of increased frequency of return appointments.Example of a system dynamic loop diagram to depict the impact of a local solution on the system. This example shows that a higher follow-up rate results in a higher demand for follow-up slots and a higher access. A new planning rule is created to give more priority to the urgent patients by assigning dedicated slots to them. This results in more capacity for the urgent patients.

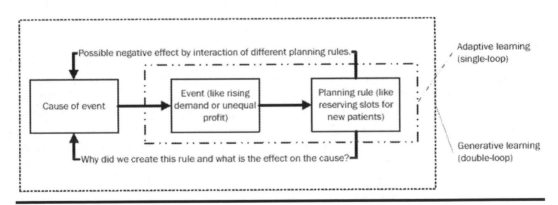

Figure 4.8 Single-loop and double-loop systems. With adaptive or single-loop learning, an event like rising demand is solved by a planning rule that reacts to the event. Generative or double-loop learning looks at the system and the impact of the solution on the system. Why was this solution created and what is the effect of the solution on the cause? There is a possibility of interaction between solutions resulting in a reserved effect on the system.

the impact of the solution on the system. This allows explicit consideration of why the change was introduced, and measurement of the effect of the change. This also allows for identification of unanticipated interactions that may have an unwanted effect on the system.

Working with Multiple Teams

Applying these lessons at scale, we worked with more than 50 outpatient specialist clinics in collaborative breakthrough projects organised by CBO, the former Dutch Institute for Healthcare

Improvement. We studied the interventions and results of the first participating 21 clinics (Van der Voort et al., 2010). Many outpatient specialist clinics were able to reduce access times from four to eight weeks or above, to three to ten days for each involved specialist without adding capacity. Further research five years later showed that the improvements had been maintained. Services were able to keep access times short, with better patient experience and work satisfaction with less waste (van der Voort et al., 2014).

Each clinic formed a multi-disciplinary team with a doctor in the lead. They measured and analysed their delays, efficiency and planning methods. The team was taught relevant planning principles and Lean methods and examples of possible changes were shared. In combination with the results from their own analysis, they decided which changes to implement. They measured the effects and learned from the changes. They also shared learning amongst the wider group of participating teams. Then they decided on more or different changes and continued to learn. Most achieved excellent flow, and increased work satisfaction in staff within 6–12 months. The implemented changes differed per clinic with anything from 3 to 13 changes being applied. Two general flow principles proved successful to increase their responsiveness to better match supply and demand.

First, they applied levelling by reducing fluctuations in the number of clinic sessions per week. One popular intervention to improve this was the introduction of a 'holy horizon': within, for example, six weeks it is agreed not to cancel sessions. Another intervention was to add or change the type of sessions for some doctors in periods where their colleagues could perform fewer sessions to make use of the unused clinic capacity.

Second, they became much more flexible to allow them to absorb fluctuations in demand. All clinics markedly reduced the number of types of appointments and increased the flexibility on how many appointments of a certain type, such as new or return, could be booked per clinic session, within the overall clinic capacity.

Importantly, not only did they change the way they worked, they learned how to keep improving and how to avoid counterproductive changes. They learned how to analyse their clinic from a system perspective and to continue monitoring, learning and adapting. In the research five years later, their clinics had on average applied three new interventions to their planning method after the project ended which the teams explained they had done to keep access short. Most organised regular meetings with a doctor, planner and management to reflect on changes in supply and demand. They also used these meetings to discuss changes in the supply of sessions for the next period and to evaluate and discuss interventions in their clinic planning methods when necessary.

In interviews, participants stressed the importance of clinical leadership and a shared belief that they could and should keep access times short together as a team. Some described this as the most important different way of thinking. They did not associate long waiting times as a sign of a good doctor anymore, but instead they started to view long waiting times as a sign of a poorly organised doctor.

Conclusions

General Reflection

Why do almost all hospitals deliver care characterised by poor flow? The root cause has to do with the way hospitals tend to be characterised as push systems, or 'open-loop' systems.

Push refers to the dynamic that the next step in the process is determined after a step is finished. The patient is then 'pushed' to the colleague or department. Care professionals and departments can feel overwhelmed by the patients being 'pushed' towards them. The root cause of much waiting time however is that capacity is often decided well before demand is known. This refers for example to:

- The number of outpatient clinical sessions per week or month and the number of each type of appointment within those sessions.
- The number of operating theatre sessions per (sub)specialism per week or month.
- The number of beds per specialism (or group of specialisms) in a specific department.

The chosen supply per week or month often has little or no relation to predictions of demand. There are few closed-loops systems used to determine the best planning choices and to create pull systems. Loops between departments as well as loops that make use of learning from previous periods allow better choices on how to match supply and demand in the next period.

Waiting lists are often used as buffers to protect services from too much pressure and at the same time ensure a well-filled clinic or theatre schedule. Staff can also be buffers, often over- and underutilising their time. When analysing care pathways, both patient and staff buffers should be considered.

At the same time, a lot of healthcare professionals are very good at locally organising their practices. However, this is not enough to create high-quality care chains. It may contribute to an 'open-loop', with no synchronisation between the activities of the departments and care institutions involved. So, the challenge is how to create a system that uses the power of healthcare professionals with a system approach realising closed-loop healthcare. 'Closed-loop' means that the healthcare chain is regulated by feedback without delay from downstream to upstream.

Focus of Improvement Work

The logical focus is to create a flow experience for patients and reduce waiting times. However, the improvement of patient pathways is required to achieve this. This is not only intended to reduce waiting times between steps but also to connect the steps across disciplines and departments to allow continuous flow from a patient's perspective.

The systemic root causes need to be addressed at the senior management and executive levels because the improvement work can go against the dynamics that characterise most hospitals. The improvement work will become more difficult, and progress will be hard to sustain if the hospital remains oriented on managing departments rather than looking at pathways and patient flow. Some may argue that this is where improvement work needs to start because it is the root cause. But we think it is very difficult to start here. First, the managers, professionals and executives must learn together the impact of poor flow and what is required to improve it. Otherwise, we deem it unlikely that there will be enough willpower and knowledge to invest in addressing the root causes.

Executive-level and senior management improvement work should be at the system level. Change the system from a predominantly push system to a more pull-characterised system (it will always be a mix). Create more closed-loop processes instead of the typical open-loop processes with insufficient feedback to make the right decisions across departments.

Executive leadership can work on changing hospital governance systems from a vertical silo orientation towards a model that is also oriented towards pathway management. For example, they can ensure that departmental year plans have goals and Key Performance Indicators on patient flow and that management reports pay attention to patient pathways and measures of flow results as well as departmental results. One example of how this can be delivered is by implementing a care chain structure around one disease with a doctor, nurse and manager forming the daily management of the care chain. The focus of this daily management team is to create a structure and a culture to continuously improve with a multi-disciplinary team, connecting all the silos.

Executive level and senior management increase the ability of care teams to look at their processes from the perspective of flow and enable them to work on daily improvement work to address problems in their direct influence. One way of stating it is that fewer project improvement teams are required if problems are addressed within the influence of the directly involved professionals. But they need freedom and support to make the required changes, and they sometimes need advice from logistical or process improvement experts to maximise results.

Focusing on deeper systemic root causes and transitioning from open loop to closed loop requires a double-loop learning culture in the hospital. A hospital functioning as a closed-loop will develop as a system. This is only possible when the members know how the hospital as a system functions. This is one of the anchors of the Shingo operational excellence model where core values and guiding principles determine the individual focus (Edgeman, 2018). A typical example is 'waste' which is a non-value-added activity. In focused Lean projects waste is identified and put on the agenda to be removed. But consideration of waste must take account of 'redundancy'. Both are visible in hospitals as waiting times, resources that are idle, and doctors waiting for patients. However, where 'waste' is always 'redundancy', but 'redundancy' is not always 'waste'. The perfect organisation with an exact match for capacity and demand does not exist and there is always a need for available capacity to keep the system moving. This is also true for hospitals and is one of the lessons of the view of organisations as information processing systems as developed by Galbraith (1971). No hospital can operate at 100% capacity and some redundant capacity is required.

Organisations often fail to see their redundancies and their dependency on them. Redundancy can include underutilisation of staff, equipment etc., but also waiting times of patients. Two mistakes can be made here. First, all redundancy is considered waste. This might lead to over-anxious organisations (van Witteloostuijn, 1999) harming themselves by reducing their ability to flex to meet fluctuations in demand. Second, redundancy can be accepted where it is waste. Both mistakes should be avoided as redundancy is needed, but it should be an element of a conscious system of organising.

Earlier we described that in a push system, a step is finished, and the responsibility is transferred to the next station. It is essential to realise that organisations that work in this way are not managed as a system. It does not learn how to identify problems in the system. In the first case study, we saw how important it is that the planners figure out the root causes and learn to discover new ways of thinking about problems. It shows how a coaching style of management is important to learn (see Chapters 12 and 13 for further discussion of management approaches to a Lean system). In the sessions when the planners come back to discuss their findings, they discuss improvement actions. Coaching and double-loop learning are important and a prerequisite to developing an organisation into a pull system. Understanding feedback loops, which can be reinforcing (positive) or balancing (negative) (Senge, 2006), is essential.

In the second case study, no effort was made to analyse the feedback loops. It was more like a trial-and-error process. It was driven by educated guesses, but there was still no double-loop learning. In a pull system operations and processes are regulated by feedback and so produce a closed-loop system. Organisations that only operate push systems do not sufficiently use feedback and thus are open loop. Their ability to design and function as a system fails. Hospital flow management should design and develop a system view of the organisation. Munavalli et al. recommend using the terms 'open-loop systems' and 'closed-loop systems' instead of 'push systems' and 'pull systems'.

In an open-loop system there is a delay in utilising the feedback and taking action to improve the workflow (Munavalli et al., 2021, p. 59). To design and keep improving the hospital as a system, double-loop learning is necessary. When changes are implemented as a reaction to problems or because opportunities to improve are identified, the before and after situation should be measured. The changes should be deliberate. This allows systematic learning from these changes – this is single-loop learning. To create operational excellence, how a hospital system learns from change is of paramount importance.

Learning Points

- Problems with patient flow are usually visible as waiting time problems. Flow problems inconvenience, distress patients and cause stress for staff.
- When staff identify problems in patient flow, they do their best to find solutions.
- However, problems can arise when root causes are not identified, the impact of changes is not monitored and evaluated and team members do not coordinate improvement actions.
- Many patient flow problems result from mismatches between capacity and demand and systems that are not designed to flex to meet changes in demand.
- Hospital systems often focus on departmental silos rather than on patient value streams. Governance arrangements can reinforce this focus.
- Building multi-disciplinary improvement teams, providing coaching and supporting learning can produce dramatic improvements in apparently intractable problems.
- Levelling and reducing complexity are important considerations in improving flow.
- Hospitals cannot operate at 100% capacity. Distinguishing between waste and necessary redundant capacity is important. Waste can be eliminated, but some flexible capacity is required to allow response to varying demand.
- Executive teams play an essential role in helping to promote and embed an improvement culture over time.

Bibliography

Benjamin, E., & Jacelon, C. (2021). An analysis of the concept of patient flow management. *Nursing Forum*, *57*(3), 429–436. https://doi.org/10.1111/nuf.12681

De Freitas, L., Goodacre, S., O'Hara, R., Thokala, P., & Hariharan, S. (2018). Interventions to improve patient flow in emergency departments: an umbrella review. *Emergency Medicine Journal*, *35*(10), 626–637. https://doi.org/10.1136/emermed-2017-207263

Delnoij, D., Van Merode, G., Paulus, A., & Groenewegen, P. (2000). Does general practitioner gatekeeping curb health care expenditure? *Journal of Health Services Research & Policy*, *5*(1), 22–26. https://doi.org/10.1177/135581960000500107

Edgeman, R. (2018). Excellence models as complex management systems. *Business Process Management Journal*, *24*(6), 1321–1338. https://doi.org/10.1108/BPMJ-02-2018-0049

Galbraith, J. R. (1971). Matrix organization designs how to combine functional and project forms. *Business Horizons*, *14*(1), 29–40. https://doi.org/10.1016/0007-6813(71)90037-1

Munavalli J.R., Boersma H.J., Rao S.V., & van Merode G.G. (2021). Real-time capacity management and patient flow optimization in hospitals using AI methods. In Masmoudi M., Jarboui B., & Siarry P. (Eds.), *Artificial intelligence and data mining in healthcare*. Springer. https://doi.org/10.1007/978-3-030-45240-7_3

Senge, P. M. (2006). *The fifth discipline: The art and practice of the learning organization* (2nd ed.). Random House Business.

Sripa, P., Hayhoe, B., Garg, P., Majeed, A., & Greenfield, G. (2019). Impact of GP gatekeeping on quality of care, and health outcomes, use, and expenditure: a systematic review. *British Journal of General Practice, 69*(682), e294–e303. https://doi.org/10.3399/bjgp19X702209

van der Voort, M. R., van Merode, F., & Berden, B. (2010). Making sense of delays in outpatient specialty care: A system perspective. *Health Policy, 97*(1), 44–52. https://doi.org/10.1016/j.healthpol.2010.02.013

van der Voort, M. R., van Wijngaarden, J., Janssen, S., Berden, B., & van Merode, F. (2014). Sustainability of improvements in access to outpatient specialist care in the Netherlands. *Journal of Health Services Research & Policy, 19*(2), 94–101. https://doi.org/10.1177/1355819613509083

van Merode, G. G., & Groothuis, S. (2003). *Hospitals as complexes of queuing systems.* Health Sciences Simulation.

van Witteloostuijn, A. (1999). *De anorexiastrategie: over de gevolgen van saneren.* De Arbeiderspers.

Marc Rouppe van der Voort, MSc, studied Business Administration at Erasmus University Rotterdam and performed his PhD research at Maastricht University. He currently leads a transformation process in St Antonius Hospital to free up capacity by improving the way care is delivered and developing digitally supported healthcare. He has also led nationwide hospital programs on improving flow and reducing waiting and has worked in several management consulting roles. He has published three books on the application of Lean thinking in Dutch Healthcare. Van der Voort has led the Dutch Network for Lean in Healthcare (Lidz) for eight years and is currently on the advisory board of Lidz.

Anna Roos Vijverberg, MSc, studied medicine at Leiden University. Since 2018, she has been a PhD student at the Care and Public Health Research Institute (CAPHRI) of Maastricht University and the Department of Lean and Health Logistics at the St Antonius Hospital. Her research focuses on the Lean philosophy and the concept of value-based healthcare. More specifically, she investigates whether changes in the process design of the colorectal cancer care chain can lead to an improvement in quality of care, clinical outcomes, and flow.

Frits van Merode, MSc, MA, BSc, BA, PhD, studied economics and philosophy at Erasmus University in Rotterdam and technical mathematics at the Eindhoven University of Technology. Since 2001, he has been a full professor of Logistics and Operations Management in Healthcare at the Care and Public Health Research Institute (CAPHRI) of Maastricht University and Maastricht University Medical Centre+. Van Merode was dean of the Faculty of Health Sciences (2004–2006), dean of the Faculty of Sciences (2011–2015), and a member of the Executive Board (2008–2018) of the Maastricht University Medical Centre+. His main research projects are directed to the design of the layout of hospital buildings, intelligent operations management systems for healthcare, and real-time scheduling systems both for patients and for staff.

Chapter 5

Value Management

Kay Cordiner, Poonam Gupta, Salah Arafa, and Cameron Stark

Contents

DOI: 10.4324/9780429346958-5

Aims

The aims of this chapter are to:

- Describe the importance of Value Streams in delivering patient outcomes.
- Note the risks of silo working, and silo accounting, adversely affecting patient experience.
- Explain how a focus on value can deliver improvement activities aligned to patients' needs and organisational aims.
- Demonstrate core principles of Value Management including Visual Management, Value Stream Management and continuous improvement.
- Illustrate the role of the Box Score.

Introduction

In Lean, for something to be of value it must meet the needs of a patient or service user, be done correctly the first time and change the product or service in some way (Stark & Hookway, 2019, pp. 16–17). Waste is any activity that does not produce value for the patient. There are many sources of waste, and some arise from processes used in the organisation. Waiting is a common type of waste and one which often distresses patients. Other wastes can be less visible but can cause problems for the delivery of care.

Traditional accounting reports expenses and budgets within departments, rather than across the functions required to deliver a product, or as in health and social care, the steps required to deliver care for a particular condition (Rao & Bargerstock, 2013). Looking only at departmental and directorate budgets can result in a focus on internal processes, at the expense of patient flow which often cuts across departmental boundaries. For instance, imaging, laboratory and medical physiology components are often treated as different services rather than as a core part of the clinical process experienced on a patient's journey. This means that the costs of a service are easier to measure than the added value provided to patients. Cost savings or efficiencies in one department (or cost centre) may be made at the expense of the overall process producing the service experienced by the user (Kroll, 2004).

Lean Accounting, developed by Brian Maskell, aligns accounting to Value Streams, the processes used to produce value in a Lean organisation (Maskell et al., 2011). Value Streams are the sequence of steps that together produce a patient's journey. The boundaries of a Value Stream can be wide. For example, a patient may see a generalist, such as a general practitioner, and be referred to a specialist out-patient clinic. The specialist at the clinic may arrange tests that result in a decision for in-patient hospital treatment, such as an operation. The operation will involve a booking process, an admission procedure, the operation itself and the aftercare. There may be out-patient follow-up and then a referral back to the original referring generalist for any ongoing care. While the whole process affects the patient, any individual service involved is unlikely to be aware of the entire sequence. Awareness of this overall Value Stream, and the contribution of individual services to the patient experience, can help to avoid decisions based only on their impact on individual departments. Lean accounting enables organisations to focus "on their internal processes so that the process also meets the value definition of the customer" (Arora & Soral, 2017, p. 54).

Examples of problems that can arise when organisations lose sight of the entire Value Stream include introducing apparent improvements in one service that worsen flow elsewhere; creating push processes that result in queues; administrative and clinical processes that do not mesh and result in repeated questions, investigations and paperwork that do not add value, and cost-shifting that improves the bottom line in one service but worsens care overall.

In Value Management the accounting process becomes an integral part of the Lean processes used in the organisation (Kennedy & Widener, 2008). This requires a much faster turnaround of cost information, allowing it to be used in tandem with up-to-date information on process and quality. Rather than retrospective monthly financial reconciliation, financial data is needed week to week, for the previous week. This enables the organisation to link process and cost measures and so allows a visible focus on service quality. Staff do not have to cast their minds back to a previous quarter. Accountancy teams and finance departments need to be tightly integrated with the process and to be seen as key members of the delivery team. There are challenges for accountancy processes in moving to these more process-aligned methods, and considerable support for finance departments may be required (Fontenelle & Sagawa, 2021).

The key components of Lean accounting are Visual Management, Value Stream Management and continuous improvement (Maskell & Kennedy, 2007). This chapter discusses how these principles can be applied in health and social care and gives examples of their application in hospitals in Scotland and Oman.

Development of Value Management

Value Management is a response to the pressures in health and social care systems. Health systems survive on thin operating margins, with pressure to both reduce costs and improve care. This is a very challenging working environment and delivering these apparently opposed imperatives can seem like an impossible task.

Within healthcare systems, variation in practice remains a driver of poor quality and variable cost. Several chapters in this book document situations where different teams, services or hospitals work in different ways and where the lack of Standard Work affects the value for patients. Marc Rouppe van der Voort and colleagues discuss in Chapter 4 the need to look at flow across teams, and between hospitals and the community. Maintaining improvement work in diverse settings such as these while also maintaining a focus on strategic priorities is difficult. In Chapter 6 Fiona Keogan and Anne-Marie Keown describe challenges in standardising Value Streams within a large organisation including across different models of provision.

Cost and quality data are plentiful in many healthcare systems but do not always deliver the benefits that should be associated with them. Financial and quality data can be delayed, aggregated and hard to find. This data is not always visible to clinical teams, and when it is, its context and meaning may be difficult to understand. Linking information to events is very difficult, and the delay between actions and identified costs makes interpretation very challenging.

Approaches to this are often top-down. Services often try to squeeze costs on non-clinical activities and seek to reduce supply costs, for example by identifying preferred suppliers. Labour costs can also be a focus of attention. Where standardisation is introduced, it can be imposed rather than agreed upon, resulting in clinicians feeling that things are being done to them, rather than that they are co-producing improvement. This can result in resistance and bad feeling, and a reduction in morale with unhappy clinical staff, and equally unhappy managers.

An alternative approach is to link data on cost and quality and use performance improvement methods to drive change. For this to be effective at scale, there needs to be a link to a management system. It is this tension of linking improvement to identified problems, embedding it in a management system and putting clinical teams at the centre of the work that Value Management seeks to address.

Context

The work described here happened at Raigmore Hospital in Inverness, Scotland, and at Heart Hospital in Doha, Qatar. Raigmore Hospital and the Scottish health system are described in more detail in Chapter 2. Raigmore Hospital was an international pilot site for Value Management, while Heart Hospital was a very early adopter of the method and worked with Institute for Healthcare Improvement (IHI) colleagues to develop the method further.

Healthcare in Doha is publicly funded, although private healthcare is also available. Heart Hospital is a specialist hospital in Qatar for cardiology and cardiothoracic surgery patients. It is made up of a state-of-the-art 20-bed coronary care unit, a 12-bed cardiothoracic intensive care unit (ICU), a 24-bed surgical high-dependency unit (HDU) and a 60-bed ward. To provide the safest and most effective care, and to respect patient privacy, every bed in the hospital is in a single room and the 60-ward beds are individually monitored through an electronic system called telemetry.

Value Management

The components of Value Management are:

- The use of a Box Score.
- Pareto analysis.
- Plan-Do-Study-Act (PDSA) cycles.
- Visual Management Board.
- Daily Management.
- A weekly huddle with representatives from multiple teams.

This section uses examples from NHS Highland in Scotland, and Hamad Medical Corporation in Qatar. Examples from NHS Highland are from a Respiratory ward in Raigmore Hospital in Inverness, a 450-bed District General Hospital. Examples from Hamad Medical Corporation are from Hamad Heart Hospital in Doha.

Preparing the Service

To introduce Value Management into a system, consider the following steps.

Identify the Existing Quality Improvement Capacity of the Organisation

Be honest. Is Quality Improvement embedded in the organisation, or are examples isolated and unconnected to one another? Consider what Quality Improvement expertise exists in the organisation, as this will affect the introduction and later rollout plan.

The range of expertise can vary from enthusiastic staff members with limited training on Quality Improvement, through to a small number of trained people in different parts of the organisation, to a specialist team or even a specialist team that work with people with different levels of Quality Improvement training across the organisation, and with the experience and capacity to train others. Precisely where the organisation is on this continuum will affect how Value Management is introduced, supported and spread.

Understand Finance Team Capacity

Value Management requires a shift in the way financial information is produced and shared. Rather than producing retrospective statements a month or more after the event, Value Management strives to link financial data to clinical data so that teams can see, assess and respond to the information in close to real time. This requires a willingness to move to a new system, but also the capacity to continue to run the old accounting system, which is likely to be required for wider organisational reporting, at the same time. Much of this relates to the degree of management support and a willingness to re-direct finance team capacity.

Assess Management Interest

Teams do not need extensive management support to begin to do PDSA cycles in their own area. Value Management, however, needs to link to a discipline of Daily Management and, ideally, organisational alignment. As noted above, integrating finance into a rapid reporting cycle is necessary, and this needs management will.

Review Strategic Alignment

Teams can and do create their own targets, but to have a greater impact, alignment with organisational aims is essential. This requires organisations to know and communicate their priorities, and to understand the relative value they place on competing priorities. This helps the clinical teams undertaking Value Management to select at least some work that fits with the organisational priorities and makes reporting across the organisation much more straightforward if everyone understands the areas of organisational focus.

Look for the Right Fit for a First Adopter

Deciding where to start is a big decision. There may be a clear preference, for a service with a team who have experience in Quality Improvement; a team manager who is interested, engaged and preferably trained in Quality Improvement methods; an accountant who is interested in the idea; and a service manager who wants to provide a link to the organisation's senior management and strategic direction.

In most cases, some of these things can be obtained but not all. This needs the organisation to weigh up the pros and cons of different locations. It is important that the first implementation is given the very best opportunity to succeed so this decision should make deliberatively.

> **PRACTICE TIP: STRONG CHARACTERISTICS
> FOR A PILOT CLINICAL TEAM**
>
> Team includes a charge nurse or equivalent role; junior nurses who can support the work; an interested accountant; an engaged physician lead; and a supportive senior sponsor.

The Team Lead has analytical skills and basic knowledge of Quality Improvement methods.

Positive team attributes:

■ Existing regular connection between team lead and finance department.
■ Good links between the team lead and their next-level leader, which go beyond day-to-day operational discussions and firefighting.
■ Existence of a junior "bench" of talent that the team lead is eager to develop.

Team attributes that are worth further review:

■ Frequent turnover in the team.
■ Chaotic feel to the service – go to the gemba – go and see the team and spend some time there.

Preparing a Team

The IHI has developed a standard method for supporting new services, and new teams, to begin Value Management. This is based on experience gained in Doha and Inverness, and now in other services across the world.

IHI can support services who wish for their support. The general stages are applicable in any setting and include:

Training – in the first implementation, if not partnering with IHI, relevant training modules will need to be developed. The necessary components will include the purpose and use of a Box Score; an introduction to Quality Improvement if the team do not already have those skills; information on how and why to use financial data; and the use of Visual Management and huddles.

Pre-Work – this will include agreements on the roles, such as finance lead, medical lead, executive sponsor, team lead and Quality Improvement coach. The team will also want to look in detail at their capacity, staff satisfaction and their main processes and begin to think about possible performance measures for their service.

As part of the preparation, the team will need to identify the key activities in their work, usually by process mapping where the steps of the clinical process are laid out. In some systems a flow chart may work better for the service, but agreeing the main activities helps to focus the work (see also Pareto diagrams, discussed further below). A Process Diagram laid out in blocks is shown in a diagram from Heart Hospital (Figure 5.1).

Understanding how local work links to overall organisational strategy can also be done at this stage by mapping linkages. An example from Heart Hospital in Doha is shown in Figure 5.2, with linkages across from their system strategy to the hospital-specific strategy, leading across to measurements including in their Value Management process.

This can then be simplified to make the linkage between the measures more visible (Figure 5.3).

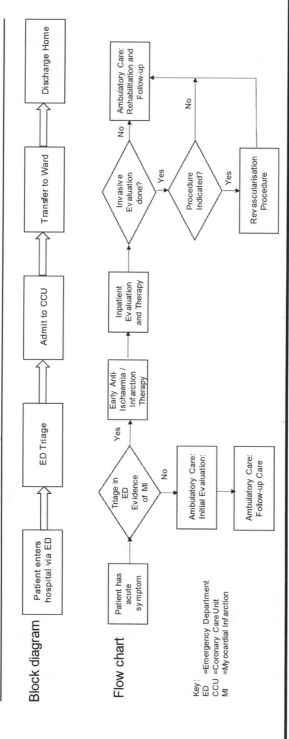
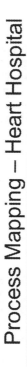

Figure 5.1 Heart Hospital process map.

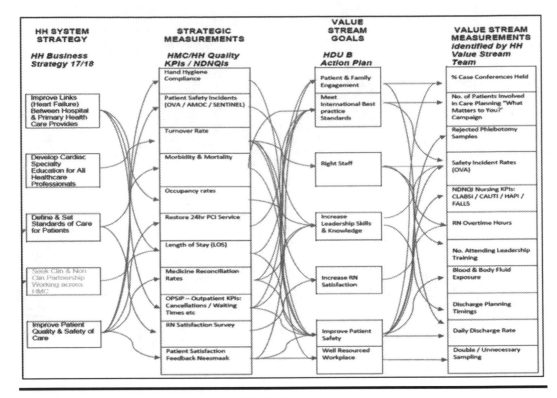

Figure 5.2   Heart Hospital linkage chart in Doha.

Heart Hospital Pilot: HDU-B

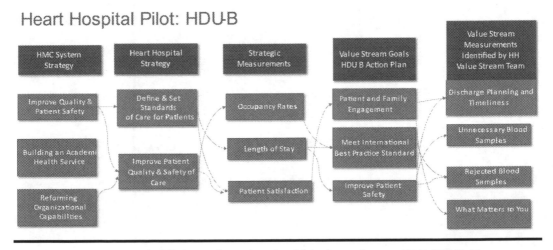

Figure 5.3   Heart Hospital linkage chart showing high-dependency unit B (HDU_B).

Looking at the elements of Value Management, the team will work on each of these in turn, and they are described in more detail below.

Detailed Components of Value Management

Box Score

The Box Score contains three items – a financial statement; performance metrics such as quality, follow and service user satisfaction and capacity – which are the measures of the use of team resources. Capacity includes consideration of how resources are used, such as the proportion of time spent on direct and indirect patient care. Box Scores can be aligned with organisational Balanced Score Cards (Kaldirim, 2021).

Balancing measures are important in Quality Improvement. Improving things in one area but inadvertently worsening things in a different area is a significant risk. If something goes wrong without being noticed, it can discredit the whole process. Two key areas are patient safety and staff satisfaction. These are topics where any compromise will rightly lead staff to question the purpose of the work. Any Box Score must include a balancing safety measure and staff satisfaction. If improvements in throughput, for example, result in increased stress to staff or more adverse events for patients, the whole enterprise has failed. Acknowledging this upfront and including explicit measurements in the weekly plan can go a long way to reassuring staff that the intention is not quality reduction at any cost.

Deciding on the metrics for a Box Score needs collaborative work across the team, and the wider organisation. It is essential to engage the relevant stakeholders in measurement selection, including doctors, service managers, nurse managers and the wider staff group. Performance Measures should, as described above, be directly linked to the strategic aims of the organisation. Frontline multi-disciplinary teams prioritise and select the measures based on the linkage chart exercise. They use process mapping to identify the dominant processes in the unit and potential gaps in those processes. The team then prioritises in the region of five to seven measures to avoid overload. The metrics selected should be measurements that can be easily gathered and reported and should include information on quality, flow and efficiency.

When choosing measurements, it is important to choose measures with enough variation to merit weekly measurement. If the team already has a good idea of what a high-performing service will look like, this will help with measurement selection. Criteria to consider include:

- Links to a strategic goal.
- Evidence of variation in performance.
- The measure is easy for staff and patients to understand.
- The team is accountable for performance and improvement of the factor being measured.
- The sample size will be large enough to allow collection of meaningful weekly data (a measure that is either zero or one, for example, is unlikely to be appropriate).
- The data is readily accessible.

An example of a Box Score from Raigmore Hospital is shown in Figure 5.4 and an example from the Heart Hospital in Figure 5.5. The similarities demonstrate that the same format can be used in different settings.

Ward 7a Value Stream Box Score	06/06/2018	13/08/2018	20/08/2018	27/08/2018	03/09/2018	10/09/2018	17/09/2018	24/09/2018	01/10/2018	08/10/2018	15/10/2018	22/10/2018
Number of Discharges	35	36	30	55	40	26	36	27	32	35	32	42
Median length of stay	4.6	2.7	3.5	5.6	4.1	4.7	5.2	5.8	6.6	3.0	2.9	3.7
Median time of discharge	10:45	11:51	11:30	12:00	12:15	11:22	11:20	10:30	12:00	10:45	10:00	11:00
Joy At Work Green/Black as %	100/0	95/5	100/0	95/5	90/10	100/0	90/10	95/5	100/0	100/0	100/0	100/0
Days between Falls	14	21	28	4	2	9	7	5	11	18	25	33
% Non respiratory patients	52%	55%	38%	35%	35%	41%	17%	20%	31%	34%	41%	41%
% Non-acute patients	21%	21%	10%	14%	10%	17%	10%	17%	24%	13%	10%	7%
% Readmissions rate to any NHSH hospital	14%	14%	18%	16%	18%	18%	13%	10%				
Direct care Day				53%					50%			
Indirect Day				35%					30%			
Available Time %				12%					20%			
Direct Care Night				40%					40%			
Indirect Care Night				45%					40%			
Available Time %				15%					20%			
Nursing Pay Costs (Excluding Bank)	£20,051	£20,472	£20,283	£20,074	£20,362	£20,661	£20,406	£20,648	£20,670	£20,625	£21,998	£22,029
Nursing Pay Bank Costs	£1,560	£1,735	£0	£1,775	£1,825	£1,825	£2,950	£2,670	£2,180	£1,790	£895	£1,350
Other Pay Costs	£0	£0	£0	£0	£0	£0	£0	£0	£0	£0	£0	£0
Drug Costs	£5,082	£5,082	£5,082	£5,082	£5,082	£7,156	£7,156	£7,156	£7,156	£3,690	£3,690	£3,690
Direct Clinical Care Supplies Costs	£2,159	£2,159	£2,159	£2,159	£2,159	£3,919	£3,919	£3,919	£3,919	£2,498	£2,498	£2,498
Other Non Pay Costs	£385	£385	£385	£385	£385	£361	£361	£361	£361	£859	£859	£859
Income	-£575	-£375	-£575	-£375	-£575	-£562	-£562	-£562	-£562	-£770	-£770	-£770
Total Costs	£41,480	£42,076	£40,152	£41,718	£42,055	£44,368	£45,238	£45,201	£44,733	£41,877	£41,755	£42,841
Costs Per Patient	£593	£647	£618	£564	£561	£704	£611	£646	£573	£544	£588	£542
Total # pts seen	70	65	65	74	75	63	74	70	78	77	71	79
Total costs excluding medical staffing	£28,263	£28,858	£26,935	£28,501	£28,839	£31,297	£32,167	£32,129	£31,662	£28,747	£28,625	£29,711

Figure 5.4 Raigmore Hospital respiratory high-dependency unit B (HDU_B) ward Box Score.

HBL/HDU-B Value Stream Box Score	Jan 2018	Feb 2018	Mar 2018	Apr 2018	May 2018	Jun 2018	Jul 2018	Aug 2018	Sep 2018	Sep 2018
Discharge timing to improve the patient access to bed	9%	36%	25%	44%	91%	67%	72%	80%	71%	85%
Patient Days Since admission mean			220	212	276	195	191	198	204	208
Patient Days Since admission median			22	13	19	7	6	5	4	9
Patient experience -What matters to you WMTY-Patient awareness on treatment plan and EDD		97%	80%	91%	100%	100%	100%			
VTE Risk assessment	5%	10%	30%	25%	25%	26%	39%	83%	79%	94%
Prevalence study of HDU -B Skin Issues	2	0	4	0	0	1	0	0	2	0
Rejected samples	4	6	4	0	1	1	0	0	1	1
Total number of Blood samples	163	190	213	158	118	154	149	194	159	187
RN Overtime hours	160	160	120	72	48	72	144	64	40	88
Direct Nursing care hours/Day Shift	57%	57%	61%	63%	63%	70%	74%	75%	75%	75%
Indirect Nursing care hours/Day Shift	42%	42%	37%	25%	25%	18%	14%	13%	13%	13%
Available Nursing hours /Day Shift	1%	1%	2%	12%	12%	12%	12%	12%	12%	12%
Direct Nursing care hours /Evening shift	55%	55%	60%	62%	62%	65%	66%	68%	68%	68%
Indirect Nursing care hours/Evening Shift	30%	30%	25%	22%	22%	19%	18%	16%	16%	16%
Available Nursing hours /Evening Shift	15%	15%	15%	16%	16%	16%	16%	16%	16%	16%
Direct Nursing care hours/Night Shift	40%	40%	40%	40%	40%	43%	44%	44%	44%	44%
Indirect Nursing care hours/Night Shift	25%	25%	35%	37%	37%	35%	35%	35%	35%	35%
Available Nursing hours /Night Shift	35%	35%	25%	23%	23%	22%	21%	21%	21%	21%
Pharmaceutical costs	6465	7535	23362	7533	6320	9372	7706	7128	13609	8086
Consumables costs	18,541	15,871	9,416	15,680	10,990	16,110	14,091	14,386	18,210	11,753
Laboratory costs	11,750	11,790	16,080	12,590	6,640	6,550	9,810	10,450	8,920	13,260
Total cost per patient days			1384	1410	1305	1360	1348	1361	1482	1442

Figure 5.5 Heart Hospital Box Score.

If performance measures are chosen poorly, it can lead to lack of engagement by staff who see it as irrelevant to themselves. This is often an issue with doctors. If measures are chosen which are not within the team's control, then rapid disillusionment and boredom are likely. If a measure is chosen for a process that is already going well and has little variation, then few improvement opportunities are likely to be identified. Avoiding these hazards is likely to lead to more rapid staff engagement and greater likelihood of ongoing engagement.

Pareto Analysis

A Pareto analysis is a way of identifying high volume, high cost or large time commitment activities. It assists prioritisation decisions. Teams may have strong views on what takes up their time, and often they will be correct. Some issues can stick in people's minds, however, and they can over-estimate the number of times something occurs or the amount of time it takes up, in line with the availability heuristic and related cognitive biases (Valdez et al., 2018). This can happen particularly if an issue is contentious or requires a lot of attention when it happens.

A way of displaying the proportion of activities, costs of, for example, cause of admission is to plot them on a graph. In a Pareto chart the categories are put in numerical order from left to right. A second axis is used to show the cumulative percentage of the total that is contributed by the categories. Pareto charts are often associated with the "80/20" rule, the idea that often 20% of things take up 80% of the time or contribute 80% of the total volume (Grosfeld-Nir et al., 2007).

There is no hard and fast rule about this, but the general principle – that a small number of categories may make up a high proportion of the total activity – is a common finding. For example, in the NHS Highland respiratory ward example, admissions of people with Chronic Obstructive Pulmonary Disease proved to be a high proportion of the total admissions.

An analysis of this type supports teams to make decisions about where they want to focus their efforts. This is not to suggest that people with less common conditions should be disregarded. Making a difference to high-volume activities can often improve processes across a whole team, and free up time that can then be allocated to higher value-added activities, including time for less common conditions.

PDSA Cycles

Plan-Do-Study-Act cycles are the engine which drives change. Identifying opportunities and monitoring performance have no value if they are not tied to change. PDSA cycles, and the discipline of completing the whole process, are essential steps in moving from aspiration to completed action (Stark & Hookway, 2019). They also have the value of being self-correcting. Rather than launching a whole project and continuing it regardless of impact, PDSA cycles allow for rapid feedback on success and then give the opportunity to make changes, with fast re-assessment of impact in the following improvement cycles. PDSA cycles and their use are covered extensively in Quality Improvement literature, websites and training materials, so the method is not discussed in detail here.

Examples of the use of PDSA cycles in Value Management in the Raigmore Hospital example include:

Capacity – Moving indirect care (e.g., completing documentation on care bundles) from day shift to night shift when there was more staff capacity, and so increasing the available time during waking hours for patient education.

Safety – Consistent management of falls, and the introduction of a new falls prevention bundle.

Cost – Reducing duplicate drug orders and bank nursing hours and substituting lower-cost drugs of equivalent efficacy.

Experience – Testing of new measures for patients and staff intended to increase understanding of areas which can be improved.

Quality – Determining common causes of readmission and improving links with community colleagues.

Visual Management Board

The purpose of Visual Management is to:

■ Share information with the wider team in a more accessible way than circulating spreadsheets.
■ Display time series data graphically.
■ Give a way of rapidly recognising defects, successes and further opportunities for improvement.
■ Connect the whole system, from strategic management to the front line.

The NHS Highland example shows these elements in use (Figure 5.6).

The Visual Management Board includes the Box Score, Run Charts, Pareto analyses and Improvement ideas, divided into the categories of Capacity, Safety, Cost, Experience and Quality. Each has its place, and none is concealed. A drop in quality or safety because of cost savings would be readily visible to everyone and would prompt review at the weekly huddle.

A team is likely to work on five or six PDSAs at any given time. The board brings together all the team's ongoing improvement work and addresses the fragmentation that is often seen in improvement activities. The board functions as an "at-a-glance" view of the team's entire performance and

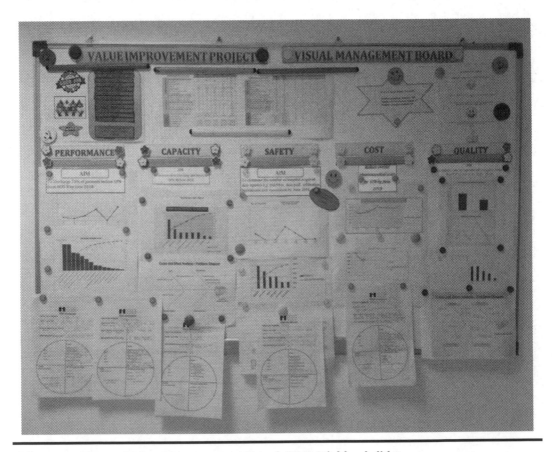

Figure 5.6 Photo of Visual Management Board (NHS Highland slide).

should be helpful to all levels of management, particularly when they become used to the layout and process.

BOX 5.2 PRACTICE TIPS FOR THE VISUAL MANAGEMENT BOARD

■ Delegate. Distribute pieces of the Visual Management Board's responsibility across your team.
■ Train and empower your staff to lead huddles.
■ Apportion the same time every week to make your Visual Management Board updates.
■ Work with a coach. Don't try to do it all yourself!
■ Reach out to other teams: some of your most powerful improvement work will involve the relationship between your team and other teams.
■ Report upward: remember that some problems will require action by higher-level leaders; give them the data to demonstrate the nature of the problem.

Weekly Huddle

The huddle happens with the interdisciplinary team every week standing in front of the Visual Management Board, including finance and pharmacy representatives, physicians and the team staff (Figure 5.7).

The huddle is more a report-out than a time for in-depth discussion. The biggest indicator of progress is having a handful of strong, targeted pieces of improvement work at any given time.

The huddle should last no more than 15 minutes and cover the agenda items:

■ Review of the Box Score: are there any items above or below control limits? Is there any evidence of special cause variation?
■ Review of all key quality measures.
■ Review the improvement work: what did the team do last week? What will the team work on this week? (See Table 5.1.)

Daily Management

Daily Management embeds Quality Improvement into everyday work. There are efforts to review performance on the previous day/shift; identify any problems that arose and consider how to resolve them; share any new learning or changes to Standard Work since the previous day; and review the work of the day including agreement of any changes required, for example because of staff absence (Stark & Hookway, 2019, p. 208). Daily Management is a core part of many healthcare systems' approach to Lean (Marsilio et al., 2022).

This is usually done via daily huddles lasting no more than 10–15 minutes and with related Standard Work. Senior leaders play an important role in Daily Management by demonstrating its use and by engaging with and supporting staff to apply their own Daily Management practice. To transmit information up the organisation, there will often be a hierarchy of huddles, beginning at the team/ward level, then with team leaders going to a huddle focused on the whole department, or the relevant Value Stream. This results in all services being aware of current pressures and sighted on solutions being applied. When applied consistently across an organisation, the method can produce excellent staff engagement (Maurer et al., 2018).

Figure 5.7   Photo of weekly huddle at high-dependency unit B (HDU_B).

Table 5.1   Common Challenges and Responses in Huddles

Challenge	Responses
Team does not huddle every week	Be present as the coach Remind the team that the huddle should help them solve problems every week Engage the Executive Sponsor
Same person leads huddle every week	Remind the team lead to delegate Frame as a professional development opportunity for staff
Huddles are running over time – more than 15 minutes	Time the huddles every week and let the team know if they went over time Give a five-minute warning, Interrupt and close the huddle if timing is a chronic issue – reinforces the timing discipline
Team members are not speaking up	Create norms via coaching: "there is no wrong answer, and no stupid comments" Assertively and repeatedly encourage feedback Talk to the lead; sometimes, they are setting subtle norms
Declining attendance	Clarify with the lead who should be there: at least a couple of frontline staff, at least one physician, the coach, a senior sponsor and the accountant Figure out what the problem is; may need to rotate attendance in some staff groups if some need to be on the floor

Leaders should incorporate Lean tools into their Daily Management practice, including daily huddles, "gemba" walks, Visual Management, analysis tools such as scatter plots, A3 thinking, teaching Lean methods/tools, Standard Work, Value Stream mapping and Plan-Do-Study-Act (PDSA) cycles (Marsilio et al., 2022). Organisational leaders can use their own Leader's Standard Work which specifies actions for that day ensuring that they are present on the gemba, the place that work is done and that over the course of a week or month they observe all aspects of the work of the organisation. In a Value Management introduction leaders will often begin their day by attending the huddles of pilot units to show their engagement and to share in the learning. Leaders must also provide the support to engage the involvement of the wider team required to allow Value Management to have an impact, including the clinical teams, finance, IT and pharmacy.

Daily Management ties together the weekly huddles used in Value Management with day-to-day management. The information collected at the huddles also informs future improvement efforts. Daily Management is also discussed in Chapters 8 and 12.

The approach to the implementation of Value Management is important and must be done with deliberation and consistency over time.

PRACTICE TIPS: KEY ELEMENTS FOR SUCCESS IN VALUE MANAGEMENT

- Clinical leadership and engagement.
- Fundamental understanding of improvement methodology.
- Senior-level sponsorship and permission.
- Creation of wider team – finance data support.
- Knowledge transfer through skilled coaching.
- Visual display of weekly data.
- A weekly report-out and holding to account.
- Nurture creativity.

Conclusions

Value Management links cost and quality and uses performance information to drive Quality Improvement. By aligning financial accounting to Value Streams and providing much more rapid financial information than the norm, it allows clinical teams to take control of their work and understand how quality, finance and performance are linked.

Putting staff at the heart of the development of the Box Score and basing changes on evidence promotes a scientific approach to improvement and shifts control to the clinical team. This helps to demonstrate the value and trust the organisation places on staff and their expertise. Alignment of team objectives with organisational priorities leverages team-based improvement work into improvements along Value Streams and ultimately across the organisation. The link to Daily Management brings the improvement activity together with day-to-day performance in a way that is meaningful for both the team and the wider organisation. The health systems described here have produced evidence of gain in very different contexts, demonstrating the broad applicability of the approach.

Learning Points

- Value Management links cost, quality and performance along Value Streams rather than in organisational silos.

■ The approach is built around individual teams and places their expertise in their service at the heart of Quality Improvement activity.

■ Accounting systems report financial data very quickly allowing teams to consider activity, performance and finance at the same time.

■ The key components of Value Management are the development of a Box Score showing dimensions of quality; Pareto Analysis; Visual Management Boards; the use of PDSA cycles; and weekly improvement huddles.

■ When developing Value Management in an organisation, the selection of the early adopter teams required careful consideration to maximise the likelihood of success.

■ Introducing Daily Management helps to maintain and widen the improvement activity and link it to daily performance.

■ Organisational leaders play a vital role in the adoption, maintenance and spread of Value Management.

Acknowledgements

We acknowledge Heart Hospital and Hamad Healthcare Quality Institute leadership, including Dr Nidal Asaad (Medical Director), Dr Awad Al Qahtani (Chairman Cardiology), Mr Ian McDonald (Executive Director Nursing) and Mr Nasser Al Naimi (Deputy Chief Quality) for their continuous support to this program.

We are grateful to Kadar Mate (President and Chief Executive Officer), Dr Azhar Ali (Executive Director), Ms Maryanne Gilles (Director), Lisa Mackenzie (Director), Tricia Bolendar (Improvement Coach), Kevin Little (IHI Faculty) and Jeff Rakover (Senior Research Fellow) at the Institute for Healthcare Improvement for their valuable support.

We thank Brian Maskill (BMA Inc) and Jess Rickards for their accountancy expertise.

In NHS Highland, we thank David Park (Deputy Chief Executive), Evelyn Gray (Associate Nurse Director, Acute Services), ex-Finance Director Nick Kenton, Amy Noble (Senior Charge Nurse) and Susan Clifton (Finance Lead for Value Management).

Bibliography

Arora, V., & Soral, G. (2017). Conceptual issues in lean accounting: a review. *IUP Journal of Accounting Research & Audit*, *16*(3), 54–63.

Fontenelle, A. O., & Sagawa, J. K. (2021). The alignment between management accounting and lean manufacturing: rhetoric and reality. *Journal of Business & Industrial Marketing*. https://doi-org.uhi.idm.oclc.org/10.1108/JBIM-04-2020-0216

Grosfeld-Nir, A., Ronen, B., & Kozlovsky, N. (2007). The Pareto managerial principle: when does it apply? *International Journal of Production Research*, *45*(10), 2317–2325.

Kaldirim, Y. (2021). Performance measurement and reporting in lean manufacturing environment: integration of balanced scorecard and lean accounting box score. *İşletme Araştırmaları Dergisi*, *12*(2). https://doi.org/10.20491/isarder.2020.898

Kennedy, F. A., & Widener, S. K. (2008). A control framework: insights from evidence on lean accounting. *Management Accounting Research*, *19*(4), 301–323.

Kroll, K. M. (2004). The lowdown on lean accounting: a new way of looking at the numbers. *Journal of Accountancy*, *198*(1), 69.

Marsilio, M., Pisarra, M., Rubio, K., & Shortell, S. (2022). Lean adoption, implementation, and outcomes in public hospitals: benchmarking the US and Italy health systems. *BMC Health Services Research*, *22*(1), 1–10. https://doi.org/10.1186/s12913-022-07473-w

Maskell, B., Baggaley, B., & Grasso, L. (2011). *Practical Lean Accounting* (2nd ed.). CRC Press.
Maskell, B. H., & Kennedy, F. A. (2007). Why do we need lean accounting and how does it work. *Journal of Corporate Accounting & Finance*, *18*(3), 59–73.
Maurer, M., Browall, P., Phelan, C., Sanchez, S., Sulmonte, K., Wandel, J., & Wang, A. (2018). Continuous improvement and employee engagement, part 2: design, implementation, and outcomes of a daily management system. *JONA: The Journal of Nursing Administration*, *48*(4), 209–215. https://doi.org/10.1097/NNA.0000000000000601
Rao, M. H. S., & Bargerstock, A. S. (2013). Do lean implementation initiatives have adequate accounting support? the debate of duality. *Management Accounting Quarterly*, *14*(4).
Stark, C., & Hookway, G. (2019). *Applying Lean in Health and Social Care Services*. Routledge.
Valdez, A. C., Ziefle, M., & Sedlmair, M. (2018). Studying biases in visualization research: framework and methods. In G. Ellis (Ed.), *Cognitive Biases in Visualizations* (pp. 13–27). Springer Nature. https://doi.org/10.1007/978-3-319-95831-6_2

Kay Cordiner joined the Institute for Healthcare Improvement in 2018 as Faculty. She supports the spread of the methodology across other health systems including Hamad Medical Corporation in Doha, Northwell Hospital in New York and Western Health and Social Care Trust in Northern Ireland as well as in Scotland. She is also faculty for the Royal College of Physicians on Quality Improvement and has published on Value Management in the *Harvard Business Review* and *British Medical Journal*.

Poonam Gupta, MBBS, MScPH, CPHQ, CMQ/OE, is a physician and currently head of quality improvement at the Heart Hospital of Hamad Medical Corporation, Doha, Qatar. Gupta is trained as an improvement advisor and patient safety executive with the Institute for Healthcare Improvement, Boston, and trained in Lean for healthcare at the University of Tennessee Knoxville, Haslam College of Business. As program director for value improvement in Heart Hospital, her work has been highly successful and has gained local and international attention. She is a faculty and improvement advisor for Institute for Healthcare Improvement, Boston. Gupta is the author of many published papers and abstracts in international peer-reviewed journals and teaching resources. She has earned more than 15 awards for several Quality Improvement and Patient Safety (QIPS) initiatives and has been a local and international speaker at various patient safety forums. Additionally, she collaborates with the Ministry of Public Health, Qatar, as healthcare facilities licensing inspector.

Salah Arafa is an interventional cardiologist at the Heart Hospital of Hamad Medical Corporation, Doha. He graduated from Tripoli University Libya and completed his post-graduation in the UK. He has more than 30 years of clinical experience. In addition, he is the director of performance improvement and has experience in quality improvement and risk management leading many initiatives at the facility level. He is a key member of many patient safety committees at the facility and corporate levels. Salah has many research, posters, and presentations under his name.

Cameron Stark, MB ChB, MPH, MSc (Dist), MRCPsych, FFPH, is an Honorary Reader and Part-time Lecturer at the University of the Highlands and Islands (UHI) Outer Hebrides. Stark leads the UHI postgraduate module on the application of Lean in healthcare. After graduating from the University of Glasgow, he trained in psychiatry and public health and worked as an NHS Public Health Doctor for over 30 years. Stark was the quality improvement science lead for NHS Highland and trained as a Lean leader with Tees, Esk and Wear Valley NHS Foundation Trust. He has published over 60 papers in peer-reviewed journals and has written or edited 5 previous textbooks.

Chapter 6

Building a Model Value Stream for Older People Living with Frailty in Ireland

Fiona Keogan and Anne-Marie Keown

Contents

DOI: 10.4324/9780429346958-6

Aims

This chapter aims to:

- Outline work on a clinical pathway to ensure that older people living with frailty admitted to an emergency department are identified and offered appropriate support, and treatment.
- Describe how to build capability and capacity to support sustainable change at a system level using Lean.
- Share how Irish hospitals and care systems changed to deliver a service focusing on the needs of older people that is less hospital based.
- Explain the importance of taking a partnership approach for the delivery of services across emergency care pathways for frail older people.

Introduction

> Lean is not a programme; it is not a set of quality improvement tools; it is not a quick fix; it is not a responsibility that can be delegated. Lean is a cultural transformation that changes how an organisation works.
>
> **(Toussaint & Berry, 2013, p. 74)**

Hospitals cannot deliver transformation alone, and the chapter includes a case example describing work on a Frailty pathway that crosses hospital and community service boundaries. The improvement work sought to offer a seamless service to prevent, identify, and manage frailty to improve outcomes for service users.

The context of the work is a complex public/private system, the Ireland East Hospital Group (IEHG). IEHG was established in 2015 and is the largest in Ireland, providing public and private care for approximately one million people. It has an annual budget of over €1 billion. The group comprises 11 hospitals (six voluntary and five statutory) with University College Dublin (UCD) as its academic partner. Hospitals are categorised as: Model 4 (Tertiary Referral), Model 3 (Regional Hospital), or Model 2 (Community Hospital) (Figure 6.1).

The group spans eight Counties of Ireland and works with four Community Healthcare Organisation (CHO) partners. The Model 3 sites, Regional Hospital Longford and Mullingar, St Luke's Hospital Kilkenny and Carlow, Wexford General Hospital, and Our Lady's Hospital Navan were the focus of the Lean improvement work.

The Irish health system is not integrated, and hospitals and social services have separate budgets and staff. Thirteen per cent of the population are 65 years of age and older and this is expected to double by 2040. There are often few alternatives to emergency admissions for frail older people.

In 2016, the IEHG commenced a transformation improvement journey. The chief executive had previously learned about the positive impact that adopting Lean from the Toyota Production System could have on improving patient care and introduced it to the group (Figure 6.2).

True North and Adopting Lean for Healthcare Transformation

True North reflects the vision, strategy, and agreed outcomes developed and adopted by IEHG and is underpinned by a series of objectives and metrics (Figure 6.3).

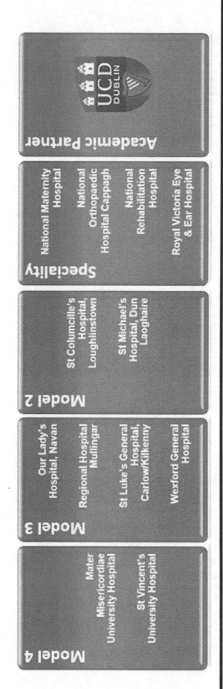

Figure 6.1   Overview of Ireland East Hospital Group.

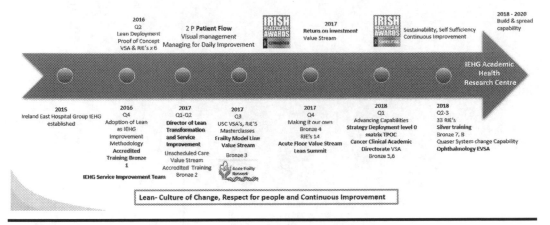

Figure 6.2   Ireland East Hospital Group improvement journey 2016–2020.

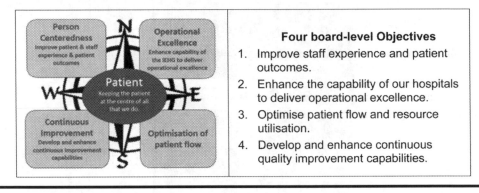

Figure 6.3   True North for Ireland East Hospital Group transformation programme board level.

Setting four board-level objectives helped to ensure strategic alignment and the prioritisation that would be necessary to achieve transformational change. This disciplined approach adopted from the Toyota Production System allowed for decision-making by consensus and enabled rapid testing and implementation through Plan-Do-Study-Act cycles.

Lean is built on two pillars: (i) respect for people and (ii) continuous improvement (Koenigsaecker, 2012). While it is a credible scientific approach to delivering sustainable transformation, it is not a silver bullet. Working to achieve breakthrough results for every patient every time requires disciplined leadership, with a clarity of purpose and focused delivery. Kim Barnas expands on True North and the importance of leadership in Chapter 12 of this volume, 'Executive Leadership in Sustaining Lean Transformation'.

The transformation model for IEHG is set out in our Deployment Triangle which was developed in partnership with our Technical Partner – IBM Watson Health Simpler (Figure 6.4) – and adheres to the key principles of Lean (Figure 6.5).

From Getting Started to System-Wide Implementation: Frailty Case Example

In 2016, the IEHG undertook several engagement events across the Hospital Group as an introduction to Lean.

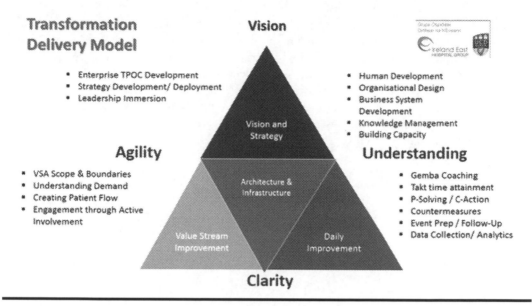

Figure 6.4   Ireland East Hospital Group strategic deployment triangle: transformation delivery model.

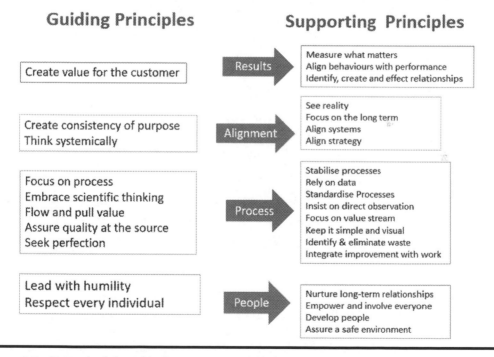

Figure 6.5   Key principles of Lean.

This included A3 thinking – so-called after the size of the paper on which it is presented – and problem-solving training. IEHG also employed a nine-box version which encourages a systematic and standardised approach to problem-solving, education, Lean training, Value Stream Analysis (VSA) and Rapid Improvement Events (RIE). The initial work consolidated the application of Lean starting to build a new learning culture including growing the capacity and capability to deliver change at pace.

As a result of this first tranche of work, the Hospital Group decided to focus on frailty. Older people living with frailty experienced the longest waits in emergency departments across Model 3 hospitals. People who are frail tend to have higher rates of hospital admission, increased length of stay, and increased risk of death, but there is evidence that improvements in care can benefit these patients. Older people are more likely to be alive and in their own homes at follow-up if they receive a comprehensive geriatric assessment on admission to hospital (Ellis et al., 2017). The following year work got underway to design a new model of care for older people living with frailty across the group to improve their care experience and outcomes.

ABOUT FRAILTY

Findings in The Irish Longitudinal Study on Ageing (TILDA) reported 31% of the Irish older population aged 65 and over were robust, 41% were pre-frail and 22% were frail (O'Halloran et al., 2020).

Frailty relates to the physiological decline that takes place in late life, making people particularly vulnerable. It limits a patient's capacity to recover and is a consequence of the cumulative decline in many physiological systems over a lifetime. Even small challenges such as a minor infection or a change in medication can have a disproportionate, sometimes catastrophic, impact on a frail person (Clegg et al., 2013). Frail people tend to be older, have worse health, and have lower levels of education. They also experience more falls, have more disabilities, and use more medications and healthcare services. The following statistics set out some of the challenges facing both the individuals and the service:

■ Almost half (48%) of the people over the age of 85 die within one year of hospital admission (Clark et al., 2014).
■ Crowded emergency departments are correlated with increased length of stay (McKenna et al., 2019).
■ Patients who experience admission delay in the ED have a 12% increase in their length of hospital stay (Huang et al., 2010).

In Ireland in 2018, there were 43,665 emergency presentations of those aged 75 years or older with 23,907 admissions. On average 820 beds per day are occupied by this group of people. Around half of the patients seen in the emergency department showed signs of frailty. These worrying statistics, however, are not an inevitability.

Best practice indicates that older people admitted to the hospital should have their care needs met as soon as possible, with follow-up happening as close to home as possible. Providing older people access to a specialist and coordinated geriatric assessment service on admission to the hospital increases the chance that they will be alive in their own homes at follow-up assessment (Ellis et al., 2017). Before 2017, this was not a standard practice in IEHG. Historically health systems have evolved around the needs of the service and service providers and not the needs of the patients.

A visual was prepared for presentations for staff to set out the building blocks of a system-wide process (Figure 6.6). In practice, this is not a linear process, but the diagram helps to convey key components of the approach.

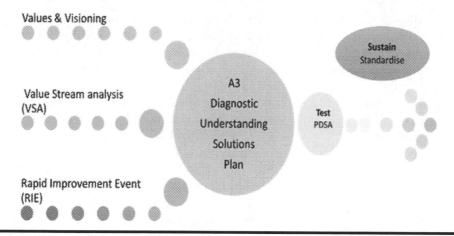

Figure 6.6 Creating a system-wide approach to transform frailty pathway using Lean. Artwork provided by authors.

Core parts of the work in the hospital group are:

- *Values and Visioning* workshops with all stakeholders working on the frailty pathway were held across the hospitals and community partners. While there is a national context and direction of travel, each hospital site had its own unique set of issues and cultural identity. The purpose was to set a vision and agree on the culture (values and behaviours) believed necessary to make improvements. These events created a constancy of purpose for all staff involved in delivering care to older people living with frailty while acknowledging any specific local context. Akin to the analogy of playing for the Barbarians rugby team while we would all wear the 'Frailty team jersey', we kept our club socks.

- *Reflecting the Voice of the Patient.* It was important that the various organisations involved maintained their cultural identity while delivering the change and agreeing to new standard ways to work and behave. The voice of our patients told us they wanted to 'stay in my own home'. However, the predominant model of care in Ireland and in our hospitals was failing to meet this need. The drive to keep older people in their homes became the dominant mantra for the IEHG.

- *Partnership and Knowledge Management.* Throughout our IEHG's Lean improvement journey, we have been supported by the Acute Frailty Network (AFN) in the UK. This facilitated opportunities to share expertise and experiences. This collaboration offers the staff access to international communities of practice, research opportunities, and to join with 150 other hospital sites in developing a community of practice and a shared learning network for frailty.

- *Value Stream Analysis* is a process review across a patient pathway from referral (or entry to the service) through to discharge. This is usually a high-level view of the pathway, supported by data which informs where there are bottlenecks and constraints to flow. The analysis highlighted that care was variable in quality and delivery, both across and within hospitals, and was often unresponsive to individual needs. Considerable rework and waste were evident in the process. Notably, older people experienced the longest waits in emergency departments and had multiple and often inappropriate bed moves, with a corresponding lack of coordination of their care. This was inevitably delivering poor outcomes causing significant stress to patients, carers, families, and staff. The need to redesign existing pathways of care was apparent to both improve patient outcomes and meet increasing demand. Following on from the outcomes of the Value Stream Analysis a series of Rapid Improvement events were planned.

■ *Rapid Improvement Events (RIE)* (sometimes referred to as Rapid Process Improvement Workshops, RPIW) are delivered over four intensive days with a report out by the team on the fifth morning. Each day usually takes place from 8 am to 4 pm.

The work to implement the Frailty Model Line started in St Luke's General Hospital. This is a large acute hospital in Kilkenny City that provides acute healthcare services to the people of Carlow and Kilkenny. The hospital began working on improvements to its Unscheduled Care Service in October 2017. A key element was to design, develop, and implement a Geriatric Emergency Medicine Service (GEMS) for older people living with frailty. This work began to change the culture around the provision of care to older and more vulnerable patients in a way that put the 'patient first' the focus of all service improvements. The scope of the improvement work was from presentation to the emergency department to the point of discharge and was structured around the A3 thinking and problem-solving format (Figure 6.7). This is an A3-sized piece of paper, with nine boxes used to apply discipline to the work of problem solving. The Current or Initial State is shown in detail in Figure 6.8.

Some of the early works identified the following issues:

1. Older people can be afraid to attend the emergency department. Some people leave it until they are unwell and in crisis.
2. Lack of preventative services results in greater problems at the time of presentation, such as immobility, pain, malnourishment, undiagnosed cognitive impairment.
3. Carers are stressed and overburdened and can only get support in a crisis.
4. The only way to access services is through the emergency care pathway.
5. Lack of same-day responsive services with rapid intensive support for the short duration needed.
6. Lack of options for an alternative to conveyance by emergency service.
7. Once an elderly, frail person presents at the ED, it is easier to admit than discharge.

Based on the Initial State, the need for Rapid Improvement Events were identified in four areas of the frailty pathway:

1. *First 72 Hours* – frailty identification and response mechanism.
2. *Admitted Care* – patient cohorts, interdisciplinary working utilising navigational hubs and ward boards.
3. *Onward Care* – rehabilitation, transitional care, long-term care, end of life, etc.
4. *Integrated Care* – working with primary and community partners, social care, voluntary sector, local authorities.

While it is not possible to describe all the work undertaken in detail, hopefully using one example helps convey our approach and some of the key activities and results.

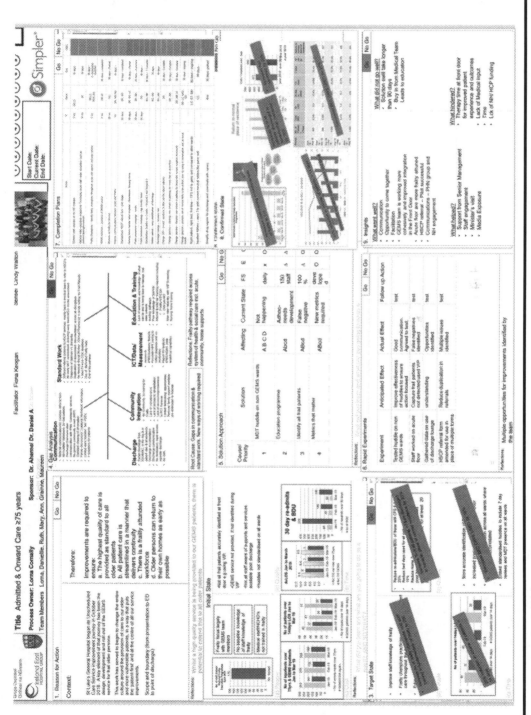

Figure 6.7 Photo of an example of A3 tool developed for the work in St Luke's General Hospital. Photo provided by authors.

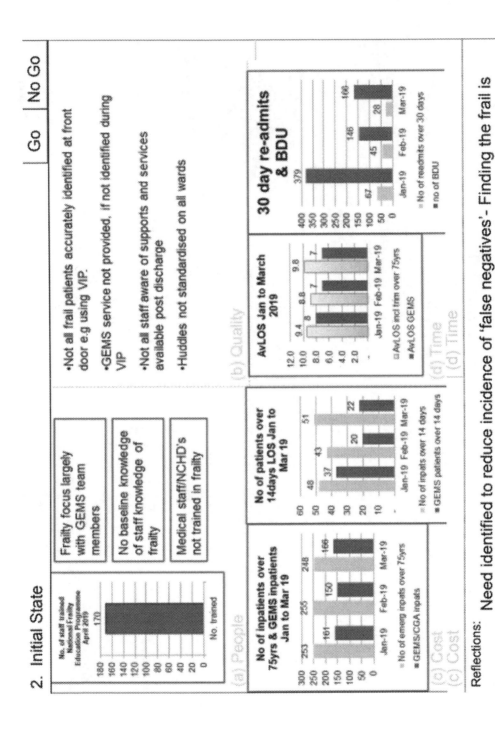

Figure 6.8 Photo of initial state of frailty pathway at St Luke's General Hospital. Photo provided by authors.

Example of a Rapid Improvement Event at St Luke's: 'First 72 Hours – Frailty Identification'

Preparation

When holding Rapid Improvement Events, significant time and attention must be afforded to the preparation phase. The team must be selected and coached in advance and supported to complete their initial A3 (Boxes 1–3), along with identification of the A3 sponsor, owner, and team.

The team must be guided to participate in six to eight weeks of preparation in advance of the event. During this period, participants are encouraged to hold a healthy respect for the work underway and commit to the time required. This includes committing to being present and engaged over the five days of the event. This is all part of the standard work to prepare for an RIE. Activities included preparing process maps, collecting and analysing data, carrying out waste walks, and understanding the voice of the customer. This stage is integral to ensuring a viable event and gaining an understanding of the current state, prior to the start of the event.

If the event is being held in person, the room(s) to host the event is also important. The team must be able to use the walls to display process maps and display the data. Walking the walls is key to engagement opportunities and storytelling. Space to break out into workgroups is desirable.

The value of the preparatory work, in our experience, determines the quality of the event outputs and progress within the week.

Days One to Five

Day one began with an overview of the fundamentals of Lean and work to further understand the current state.

This is validated with the application of tools such as high-level process mapping (Figure 6.9) and identifying waste. Day one aims to test the understanding of the team of their current state, aiming for clarity of purpose and intent. It also entails direct observation of the process of care and identification of non-value-added activities and any barriers to flow. Often workarounds have developed and rework is necessary because of flawed processes.

Figure 6.9 demonstrates that high-tech solutions are not necessary: flip chart paper and sticky notes can work well. Working with a team to capture their experience and ideas is a powerful

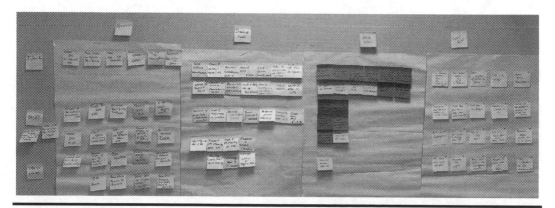

Figure 6.9   High-level process map of frailty pathway. Photo provided by authors.

process, and much of the value comes from listening and sharing experience and expertise across the group.

The day includes exploration of both Value and Waste. Lean commonly considers seven wastes (Stark & Hookway, 2019). IEHG includes an eighth waste, that of unused human potential. Waste hides in plain sight. Once teams begin to look, it is common for them to identify a great deal of waste. This is not a fault of the clinical team, and it is important to avoid a blame culture. Processes evolve organically often around the immediate needs of teams and the organisation, and multiple small defects build up in any system over time.

Day two focused on defining the target state, value from the patient's perspective, and designing and testing the new process. Work took place to identify the gaps between the initial and target state. The team undertook rapid experiments, defined, and measured Key Performance Indicators, and finalised a proposed new process. Rapid experiments included:

- Testing huddles on non-care of the elderly wards.
- Developing a system for identifying older people with frailty.
- Developing an out-of-hospital care system.
- Developing a visual management hub to support patient flow.
- Data gathering on the use of the discharge lounge.
- Single referral form designed to replace multiple forms.
- Developing an education and training programme to deliver a frailty attuned workforce.
- Building system capability and capacity for change.

Day three activities focused on developing standard work to implement the new solutions The team generated 63 improvement ideas in seven broad categories (Figure 6.10).

On day four participants reviewed and refined the standard work developed. Boxes 7–9 on the A3 are also completed at this stage. New processes were adjusted and training on agreed standard work undertaken. A storyboard outlining the week's journey was prepared ready for presentation on the final day, known as the report out.

Day 5 – The report out is an opportunity to highlight the results achieved during the week including the new frailty pathway. The report out usually takes 10–15 minutes following the A3 format. Other team members, executive sponsors, executive directors, senior managers, and leaders attended. Many participants had never spoken publicly before taking part in an RIE and it was an opportunity to celebrate collective efforts to improve patient care as well as for personal development.

Sustain and Standardise

The week of the RIE was followed up with ongoing support from the service improvement team at weekly huddles either face to face or virtually with the A3 team. The standard work from the event was displayed using visual management and the A3 shown on a process board. The A3 was updated as the solutions are tested, and the countermeasures developed.

To further support sustaining the changes tested or proposed, there are follow-up sessions with 30-, 60-, and 90-day report outs. The work leading up to these report outs focused on the implementation of the solutions and the ability to demonstrate the metrics. Dashboards were developed to make data visible and accessible and enable the team to know how they were doing at a glance (Figure 6.11). The findings from 90-day report out as presented are highlighted (Figure 6.12).

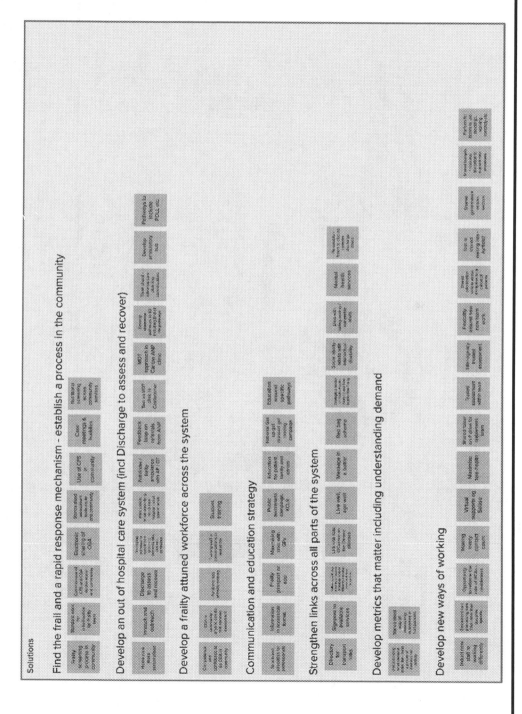

Figure 6.10 Proposed solutions and activities.

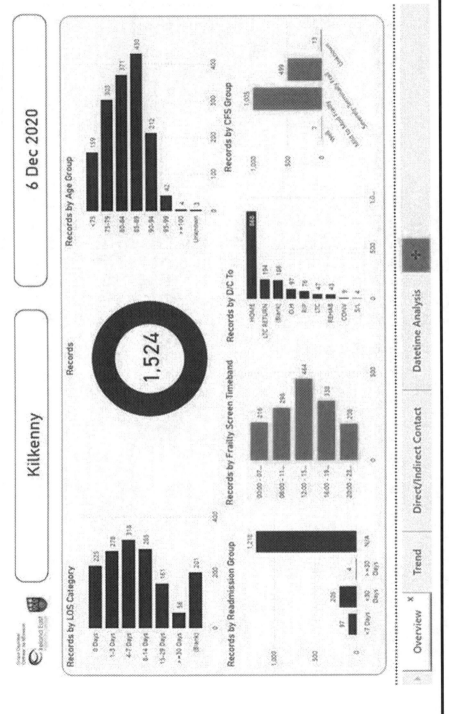

Figure 6.11   Example of a dashboard developed for St Luke's Hospital, Kilkenny.

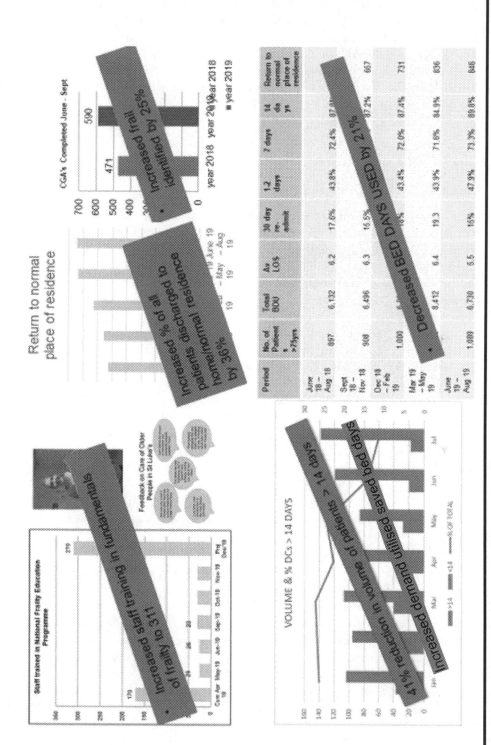

Figure 6.12 Photo of findings from report out at 90 days. Photo provided by authors.

In addition to the work described above, staff developed an '#End PJ Paralysis' campaign including using social media. This was based on the work of Professor Brian Dolan to encourage patients to get up and get dressed each day (Arora, 2018). Research has shown that most people feel better in their clothes and have shorter average lengths of stay in hospital when they get up, get dressed, and get moving as soon as possible (Arora,2018). The Geriatric Emergency Medicine team in St Luke's Kilkenny delivered a reduction of 29% on inpatient falls and a 64% reduction in hospital-acquired pressure ulcers.

Learning and Reflections

The Role of Leadership in Transformation

Leadership for transformation must operate at all levels of the organisation or system; however, it must begin with the chief executive and the executive team. They must take ownership and accountability for the organisation's Lean principles. They must be authentic in their engagement and commitment to the transformation journey. Crucially they need to be grounded in a belief in Lean philosophy and principles, not merely the deployment of a toolset. This leadership must be visible where the work is being done. In Lean this is termed 'going to the gemba' and is referred to various chapters in this volume. This can only be achieved through a willingness for deep personal immersion in Lean transformation, at Lean events and undertaking the leader's standard work. Resilience, humility, and a steely determination to succeed are key attributes. Having said all that leadership and buy-in at all levels is critical, but without strong senior executive support there will be no transformation.

When asked about what to do if the chief executive was not interested in Lean, Patti Gabow the much-respected former chief executive of Denver Health said, 'Either forget about implementing Lean or find a new job' (Gabow & Goodman, 2014, p. 143). To expand and embed transformation, the IEHG was supported by a technical partner or sensei, IBM Watson Health. While the IEHG executive and improvement team are the primary agents working with hospital frontline staff, the technical partner brought specialist skills and experience in large-scale transformational change and in coaching those leading the change.

Culture, Context, and Insights

The first Enterprise Value Stream Analysis (EVSA), undertaken was emergency care flow across eight hospitals. On reflection, this was far too ambitious. A change in basic assumptions in thinking, culture, and behaviour was first required. We quickly understood the need to focus and identify key priorities and to deprioritise those improvement activities not directly impacting the agreed objectives. Patient stories were used to understand how patients were experiencing care and share this with staff to validate the need for change. These were very insightful and often difficult for staff to accept. While they were working hard to provide the best care, they were limited in the way things were organised and managed. Not everyone was on board from the outset, and some challenged the rationale for using Lean. For many Lean was a programme running in the background without their personal involvement and this included some members of the executive team with only half embracing Lean thinking, attending events, and participating in training.

The organisation also encountered challenges from some senior middle managers and clinicians concerned about releasing staff to participate in the week-long improvement events.

Notably, however, more traditional management approaches can also be time consuming, often with multiple meetings and minutes yet with no clear outcomes or opportunities to build important relationships. At the week-long events, it was common to hear stories of staff who had worked in the same location for 15 years and never met. From when staff enter the room on day one, hierarchies are flattened, paving the way for solutions to be co-designed and tested. This occurred repeatedly as teams supported each other within and across organisations to make improvements. The experience of those who participated in the events was positive and RIE quickly proved their worth.

IEHG learnt to involve clinicians when and where they could best contribute. The feedback from those who have actively engaged in these RIE was that they gained a renewed understanding of the work of their teams, the system in its entirety, and how patients experience care. The improvement cycles often resonate with the clinical decision-making processes. Nevertheless, at times clinicians challenged the need for standard work stating it was contrary to making autonomous decisions and akin to cookbook medicine. This emphasised the need to explain to senior clinicians the benefits of standard work. It aims to reduce any unwarranted variation in the care that patients experience and to take the opportunity to standardise where possible and desirable.

It can be a challenge to engage staff in a new way of thinking and working when they are often firefighting, albeit the very reason transformation was required. It is essential to listen actively and respect the work they do. Going to see the work being done is an essential component of Lean. Helping staff to remove waste and work to the top of their licence improves patient access, outcomes, and staff experience. From the Value Stream Analysis and Rapid Improvement Events, it had become apparent that up to half of the staff were not being freed to work at as high a level as their skill allowed but rather were being asked to deliver components of care that could be provided by less skilled staff. The work in IEHG indicates that there are many more improvements to be made to allow staff to deliver the care they wish to be able to offer, and to deliver the care patients desire.

A key learning was the variability in access to and quality of the data recorded by the hospital. While sites complied with sending in reports and audits up the line, initially they did not understand how to use data for improvement. Measuring for improvement and measuring for performance management are distinct disciplines. Teams needed to be supported to understand the variability in their systems and measure the impact of changes they make. To this end, the use of Statistical Process Control (SPC) charts was adopted and a group-wide training program for all staff including board and executive teams was implemented. Performance Reports now reflect a new focus on driving systematic improvement (see Chapter 3 for further discussion of the use of data to drive improvement).

For IEHG, it was something of an '*a-ha*' moment for hospital staff to learn just how much community partners knew about patients, and how often they held the solutions to problems. They are an especially important part of the healthcare system, yet often are not communicated with during hospital admissions or discharges. Lean has enabled hospital and community staff who would otherwise work in a non-integrated way to join forces to create better outcomes for patients. Adopting Lean philosophy is helping to compensate for an otherwise siloed system, encouraging both vertical and horizontal integration between the acute and community services. The shift in mindset came from bringing people together – from laboratory staff to nurses, porters to general practitioners and surgeons to social workers. Lean was immensely powerful in this context with staff going back to their workplace to continually think about how they can improve their processes and the requisite skills to do this.

Pace and Scale

A Rapid Improvement Event is a way of enabling social collaboration in order to decrease waste and increase value (Koenigsaecker, 2012; Liker, 2004). Koenigsaecker found that the optimum duration of an RIE was one working week. This seems very brief, but a week of concentrated effort supported by the wider organisation can produce a remarkable incredible momentum for change. Participation in workshops enabled the development of relationships and respect across the system and collectively improved the understanding of issues and barriers to better care.

The events were the engine that drove the Lean transformation process. They need to be strategically planned and deployed at scale and at pace to realise benefits. Across three years, over 20 frailty events took place. More than 500 people participated in masterclasses, improvement events, and workshops. These were critical in making the frailty pathway a sustainable reality. After each event, it was important to continue to provide coaching support to help teams to gain confidence and continue to test changes. It is important to avoid defaulting to a project management mindset. Transformation requires a different skill set, and having better conversations with the right people at the right time adds more value. Sometimes with Lean you need to go slow to go fast.

Global Pandemic

A global Covid-19 pandemic early in 2020, necessitated a rapid pivot to a virtual approach to delivering and supporting the Lean transformation work. The first frailty RIE was successfully delivered in this format in November 2020, using an online system, '*Mural*' as a virtual platform. The ability of teams across the IEHG system to respond and adapt to ensure the work of improvement continued was commendable. Their belief in the priority that this work should hold in the face of unprecedented adversity and challenge to the system is testament to how the philosophy of lean and methodology had been embraced across the group.

Conclusions

Lean challenges most traditional management and administrative schools of thought, empowering all to make the changes required and devolving leadership. Deploying Lean philosophy and tools builds towards continuous improvement. It is a way to drive a new culture leading to better outcomes for patients and was successfully adopted during the unprecedented restrictions faced during the pandemic.

Starting with St Luke's General Hospital helped to create an example of a new care pathway that could evidence sustainable delivery of breakthrough improvements in all the True North domains. This process was adopted, adjusted, and rolled out across four other sites.

On reflection, a key challenge was the failure to immerse senior leadership, particularly middle managers, in the Lean approach from the outset. Some were fundamentally wedded to the status quo and to overcome this required them to be supported and encouraged to adopt new ways of working. This was far from easy. Middle managers can often feel disenfranchised and threatened as they are caught between the executive team from which the strategy has been deployed and the frontline teams who are immersed in the change.

Not surprisingly, therefore, the demands of transformation leadership are not for the fainthearted. Brave leadership from the top is essential and they need to be supported by external experienced technical partners. This can then pave the way to foster leadership and buy-in at all levels.

There are critical steps at the start of the transformation journey that should not be ignored. While much has been achieved, there is much more to be done.

Learning Points

- A change in basic assumptions in thinking, culture, and behaviour was first required before progress could be made.
- Don't be over-ambitious at the start and judge the pace.
- Immerse senior leaders in the Lean improvement work from the outset.
- Lead with humility, visibility, and respect for the agency of every individual.
- Work in an integrated way with other agencies and industries.
- Invest in building lean capability and capacity into your system to deliver a workforce.
- Early on executive leaders did not truly understand the full extent and importance of standard work.
- Involve clinicians when and where they can best contribute.
- Helping clinical staff and managers to see waste is perhaps one of the most valuable lessons they will learn in their Lean personal experience. Leaders at all levels must be trained to see waste.
- There was variability in data (access, quality, and ability to use it).
- Develop the competency to harness the power of data for improvement
- Transformation is vulnerable to a change at the top and if not addressed will undermine the improvement effort and sustainability.

Acknowledgements

The staff and patients of the Ireland East Hospital Group.
Our Partners in Community Health Organisations across Ireland.
Our Technical Partners – IBM Watson Health Simpler.
Professor Simon Conroy and the Acute Frailty Network.
Liz Sargent and Peter Gordon, NHS Emergency Care Improvement Programme.
Professor Brian Dolan, End PJ Paralysis Campaign.

Bibliography

Arora, A. (2018). *#EndPJParalysis: The Revolutionary Movement Helping Frail Older People.* NHS England. Retrieved 04 March 2022 from https://www.england.nhs.uk/2018/06/endpjparalysis-revolutionary-movement-helping-frail-older-people/

Clark, D., Armstrong, M., Allan, A., Graham, F., Carnon, A., & Isles, C. (2014). Imminence of death among hospital inpatients: Prevalent cohort study. *Palliat Med, 28*(6), 474–479. https://doi.org/10.1177/0269216314526443

Clegg, A., Young, J., Iliffe, S., Rikkert, M. O., & Rockwood, K. (2013). Frailty in elderly people. *Lancet, 381*(9868), 752–762. https://doi.org/10.1016/s0140-6736(12)62167-9

Ellis, G., Gardner, M., Tsiachristas, A., Langhorne, P., Burke, O., Harwood, R. H., Conroy, S. P., Kircher, T., Somme, D., Saltvedt, I., Wald, H., O'Neill, D., Robinson, D., & Shepperd, S. (2017). Comprehensive geriatric assessment for older adults admitted to hospital. *Cochrane Database of Systematic Reviews, 9,* CD006211.

Gabow, P. A., & Goodman, P. L. (2014). *The Lean Prescription*. Productivity Press.

Huang, Q., Thind, A., Dreyer, J. F., & Zaric, G. S. (2010). The impact of delays to admission from the emergency department on inpatient outcomes. *BMC Emergency Medicine, 10*, 16. https://doi.org/10.1186/1471-227x-10-16

Koenigsaecker, G. (2012). *Leading the Lean Enterprise Transformation* (2nd ed.). Productivity Press.

Liker, J. (2004). *The Toyota Way: 14 Management Principles from the World's Greatest Manufacturer*. McGraw-Hill.

McKenna, P., Heslin, S. M., Viccellio, P., Mallon, W. K., Hernandez, C., & Morley, E. J. (2019). Emergency department and hospital crowding: causes, consequences, and cures. *Clinical and Experimental Emergency Medicine, 6*(3), 189–195. https://doi.org/10.15441/ceem.18.022

O'Halloran, A., McGarrigle, C., Scarlett, S., Roe, L., O'Shea, M., Romero-Ortuno, R., & Kenny, R. A. (2020). Living with Frailty in Ireland 2018. In R. A. Kenny, S. Scarlett, & P. O'Mahoney (Eds.), *The Older Population of Ireland on the Eve of the COVID-19 Pandemic* (pp. 25–49). The Irish Longitudinal Study on Ageing. https://doi.org/10.38018/TildaRe.2020-10

Stark, C., & Hookway, G. (2019). *Applying Lean in Health and Social Care Services*. Routledge.

Toussaint, J. S., & Berry, L. L. (2013). The promise of lean in health care. *Mayo Clinic Proceedings, 88*(1), 74–82. https://doi.org/10.1016/j.mayocp.2012.07.025

Fiona Keogan, BSc, MSc Physiotherapy, Post Grad Dip Stats, is the director of Lean transformation at St James's Hospital Dublin where she led the Older Person's Value Stream in Ireland East Hospital Group from 2017 to 2021. After graduating from Trinity College Dublin, she trained in musculoskeletal physiotherapy and worked as an advanced practice clinician and manager for almost 20 years. Fiona was hospital lead for the development of frailty intervention services in her role as Clinical Services manager 2015–2017 (the first service of its type in Ireland) and trained in Lean methodology with Cardiff University. She led multiple improvement projects in Ireland East Hospital Group, and her work on frailty won three Irish Healthcare awards and first prize at the Stanford Lean Transformation Conference in 2020.

Anne-Marie Keown, BSc Physiotherapy, MSc, and PhD candidate, University College Dublin Health Systems, is executive lead for Regional Integration and service redesign. Prior to this, she was the director of transformation and chief operating officer in the Ireland East Hospital Group. She has been a Lean practitioner for 18 years and has a proven track record in delivering large-scale improvement and transformation of services. Her work with the National Acute Medicine programme in the implementation of a National Early Warning Score received the Taoiseach's award. Ann-Marie's career spans 30 years, and she has worked in Ireland, the United Kingdom, Canada, and the Middle East.

Chapter 7

Using Lean at Scale in Mental Health Service Provision

Louise Roig and Jens Normand

Contents

DOI: 10.4324/9780429346958-7

Aims

This chapter aims to share the experiences and lessons learned from the implementation of Lean in Region Hovedstadens Psykiatri (RHP) which provides mental health services in the capital of Denmark. It focuses on the following elements:

- Implementation of Lean in RHP.
- Improvement work, described in two specific case studies. This will illustrate the same focus and approach to management that contributed to a reduction in the number of belt restraints and a reduction in outpatient waiting times.
- Common themes that the hospital carries forward in its work to create a management-driven improvement culture.*

Introduction

RHP is the primary provider of psychiatric treatment for citizens in the Capital Region of Denmark. These services form part of the total, public, tax-payer-financed health services. The political leadership is in the hands of a Regional Authority elected by the citizens of the region.

RHP is Denmark's largest mental health hospital, and in 2018 it treated approximately 50,000 patients. It employs approx. 5,200 staff and provides services across nine mental health centres. These offer both general and highly specialised assessments and psychiatric treatment for children, adolescents and adults.

The hospital was established when four psychiatric hospitals were merged in 2007. The hospitals had widely different cultures and approaches to treatment, care and service. Rather than taking an approach from one of the merged organisations, the RHP senior management team decided to seek a common method of operation that could be promoted across the new organisation. The implementation of Lean started in 2010 with several pilot projects, focusing on creating better, more uniform quality and a higher level of efficiency.

---

* The Mental Health Services of the Capital Region of Denmark have published a book on improvement work, intended for managers in the organisation. Follow this link to get to the English version of the book: www. psykiatri-regionh.dk/english/Sider/default.aspx.

Lean in Psychiatry: Is That Possible?

Healthcare organisations often begin their use of Lean in highly structured environments. Tools such as 5S, discussed in Chapter 2, lend themselves to use in environments that require structure and order. Work on flow often begins in areas with relatively steady numbers and is later extended to areas where work on levelling may be required. When RCP explained that it planned to apply Lean to mental health, common questions raised were:

- Is it at all possible to plan something systematic in mental health, given that patients are very different and the way they present can be unpredictable?
- Is it possible to provide value for the patient, given that patients in mental health services may not always want to be there and perhaps do not think that they are ill in the first place?
- Can patients with a psychiatric illness always provide clear feedback on their wishes, and can they assess their own needs?
- Is it difficult to give the patient medication and plan a treatment pathway that mainly consists of individual consultations and group sessions?

Such questions often come from the public, clinical staff, Lean consultants and patients, when you talk about Lean and improvement work including creating value for patients in mental health services. Yet these views paint an outdated and stereotypical picture of the treatment offered by mental health services. They indicate a lack of understanding of what Lean and improvement work is all about.

The most acutely ill, psychiatric patients need to have planned and structured days during their admission to counteract the chaos they often experience because of their illness. Inner chaos should not be met by chaotic treatment. Patients attending mental health outpatient treatment have the same wish for quick access as those attending physical health services. They also need to be able to contact their healthcare professional when necessary. Treatment is most effective if the patient has been involved as much as possible in planning their care package, to ensure that it reflects their wishes and needs. When everyone involved knows the level and standards of service, a larger number of patients can be offered the same level of treatment delivered at the same, high, professional level.

The more calmness, predictability, as well as clear agreements, and easy access there is, the better. More shared standards for good treatment based on the individual patient's wishes and needs are better. The reality of mental health services is often long-term, complex patient pathways and many handovers of responsibility and so the need to understand problems and remove waste in processes is as necessary as in all other types of organisations.

The thinking behind improvement work is like the clinical way of working. Medical and therapeutic treatment and a patient's recovery path consist of small Plan-Do-Study-Act (PDSA) cycles. The important thing is to collaborate to identify wishes and needs, set goals, and test whether they work as intended. This is the same mindset that needs to be applied when improving processes and developing the value streams.

Patients are more than diagnoses; they are individuals with widely different backgrounds and varying degrees of illness. Many will undergo lengthy treatments involving acute and stable phases of their illness. This means that they have time to observe our processes and the way we structure treatment. Patients see things from the inside and the outside. They can be a goldmine of knowledge about waste and improvements – provided we, as an organisation, are curious and ensure we involve the patients.

It is one thing to *talk* about a focus on creating value for patients, it is another to do it. It can challenge the autonomy of the individual staff in their role, as well as the formal and informal hierarchies that typically exist in a hospital setting. It demands new ways of working. Developing a culture in which improvements are made through addressing long-term problems, rather than firefighting and quick-fix solutions, takes time and requires a shared mindset.

Introducing Lean in RCP

At the hospital, the implementation of Lean started with several pilot projects in individual wards, with the assistance of external Lean consultants. This demonstrated three things:

1. Lean is a thoroughly tested, solid and very involving improvement model. Most of the pilot wards expressed satisfaction and were able to see early results.
2. Typically, several wards are involved, so the improvement of patient pathways must work across wards, centres and sectors. That was why managers of all wards had to learn the new way of working at the same time.
3. A recognition that in the future, Lean work would have to be supported by internal experts, to ensure that expertise and knowledge were disseminated to all staff.

The management team, therefore, decided that Lean was to be implemented in all wards, centre by centre, within three years. To this end, a small central team of Lean specialists was established at each centre to support and train managers to deliver improvement work locally.

Value for the Patient

From the very outset, RHP has focused on creating a common understanding throughout the organisation of how to define 'value for the patient'. This is expressed in the 'V' for *value* (Figure 7.1).

Figure 7.1 Value for the patient.

Figure 7.2 RHP's commitment to the patient.

While Lean tools and thinking were essential for reaching a new organisational culture, it is a means, not an end. Creating value is all about meeting the wishes and needs of the individual patient promptly. To achieve this, continuous work must be done to ensure the best possible quality of treatment is delivered as effectively as possible. Staff now talk about the ambitious goal to create a management-driven improvement culture because it helps:

■ The organisation, the individual manager and the staff member to move in the same, shared direction with a joint focus on creating value for the patient – before everything else.

■ To ensure that treatment has high, uniform quality and the best possible effect so that the hospital uses public-financed resources as appropriately as possible.

■ To systematically transform all the valuable, human capital present in the organisation in the form of knowledge, talents and competences – to the benefit of the patient, the individual staff member and the organisation.

■ The organisation to convert, innovate and implement new initiatives in an ever-changing world systematically and swiftly.

Today, the aim of the hospital's work is described as a commitment that reflects a recovery-oriented approach, focusing on the wishes and needs of the patient (Figure 7.2).

Two Ambitious Goals

In addition to the ongoing daily improvement work, two ambitious goals have been the focus in recent years:

■ To reduce the use of belt restraints by half over five years, without any increase in other coercive measures.*

---

* The Danish Mental Health Act permits hospital physicians to prescribe coercive measures in the form of detention, physical restraints, belt restraints, and medication under special and specific circumstances. Isolation (seclusion rooms) is not permitted under Danish legislation.

■ To reduce waiting times from 30 days from referral to treatment for non-acute patients.

Two case studies illustrate the hospital approach and the integration of Lean.

Case Study 1: Reducing the Use of Coercive Measures

The purpose of strapping a person down with belts in mental health services is to constrain a person, who represents an immediate danger to themselves or others. The procedure is usually performed by nursing staff who use leather or fibre belts to secure the patient to a bed (Bak et al., 2015). It has no therapeutic or treatment-related effect. Mechanical restraint is used in many countries (Steinert et al., 2010), including Denmark (Mårtensson et al., 2019) and other Scandinavian countries (Laukkanen et al., 2020). The Danish Mental Health Act permits hospital physicians to prescribe coercive measures in the form of detention, physical restraints, belt restraints and medication under special and specific circumstances (Bak et al., 2014). Isolation (seclusion rooms) is not permitted under Danish legislation. The research found that Denmark had a higher rate of use than, for example, nearby Norway (Bak & Aggernæs, 2012).

International literature reviews show that patients experience a high degree of powerlessness, humiliation, anger, anxiety, guilt and shame when they are exposed to such coercive measures (Cusack et al., 2018; Strout, 2010). In Denmark, the use of coercive measures in psychiatric services increased nationally over a decade from 2000 to 2010, even though several initiatives had been taken to reduce the use of coercion.

Following this in 2011, the hospital started a pilot project at one mental health centre, focusing on coercion where a reduction of 44% was achieved. In 2014, the hospital's executive management agreed with the Danish health authorities that RHP could decrease the number of belt restraints by 50% over five years. The goal of cutting belt restraints by half caused major worries amongst many staff members, clinicians and managers. It was suggested that if belts were not used, the use of medication, incidents of violence against staff and fellow patients and staff absenteeism due to illness would all increase and with a typical response:

> We are not using belts for the fun; we use belt restraints when necessary.

Once a situation has escalated and a patient harms themself (or has a strongly externalising, agitated behaviour), it is difficult to avoid the use of force. Improvement works, therefore, had to focus on establishing a de-escalating approach rather than entering into conflict. Analyses showed a need for:

■ Agreement that belt restraints must always be the last resort and considered an adverse event.
■ Shared professional knowledge about the new approach to ensure that staff did not escalate or provoke a conflict.
■ A higher number of meaningful activities for patients during admission.
■ Staff being more accessible to patients.
■ Strengthened collaboration with patients on individual conflict prevention and management.

Two mental health centres took the lead. Their results showed that it is possible to reduce the use of coercion. When they had paved the way, the other centres were able to learn from them and be inspired.

The situation at RHP today is the result of five years of improvement work, developed locally at the mental health centres and across the organisation. The work demonstrates Lean principles of working to understand the problem, engaging staff and valuing patients. The journey has required multiple PDSA cycles including exploration of times and circumstances that were associated with a higher frequency of conflict. Arrangements that made it difficult for staff to be present encouraged physical restraint as an early option, reduced availability of group activities during the day and leisure activities were all found to be important issues.

Other problems identified were inadequate attention to patients' preferences on the ward of admission and the doctor who looked after them; limited information on what to expect during admissions and a perception that the voice of the user was not adequately heard.

This section describes how these identified problems were addressed systematically to add value to the patient's journey.

Trust, Kind Words and Mutual Expectations

'Steal with pride' is one of the central mantras of Lean thinking: learn from others who have solved the same problem, instead of re-inventing. Consequently, the hospital decided to learn from a British, evidence-based model for psychiatric nursing called Safewards (Bowers, 2014; Bowers et al., 2015).

The goal of the Safewards model is to improve safety and security in intensive psychiatric wards by reducing and preventing conflicts and the use of coercive measures. For this purpose, ten specific, recovery-oriented interventions have been identified which contribute towards increased cooperation between patients and staff (Ward-Stockham et al., 2021).

The work on the ten interventions helped the ward staff see the patients differently. It also helped staff members reflect on their role in the relationship with patients, and the fact that power must be administered with discretion and respect for the wishes and needs of the individual patient.

Competency Development

Several centres established intervention teams of specially trained staff, who can be called upon when there is a risk of belt restraints (or other coercive measures) to avoid such situations. The team is also tasked with sharing its experiences and competences. Staff in psychiatric intensive care wards are also offered a training programme focusing on cognitive methods for conflict prevention and de-escalation. In addition, competences in dialectical behaviour therapy are strengthened.

Patient's Involvement in Improvement Work

In some intensive care wards, patients are involved in improvement meetings. The typical feedback from patients is that they feel they have an influence and that they are being seen and heard. This may contribute towards lowering the level of conflict.

Patients have contributed to the information material given to new patients about what constitutes a good admission and discharge. They have also given input to help staff understand how they better motivate patients to contribute towards shaping their crisis and treatment plans.

Another example is the contents of the rules on the wards. These describe what is expected from patients, and they define the good behaviour required for the ward to function. The wording was developed with patients so that the message is clear and easy to understand for all parties involved.

Trust between patients and staff can be crucial in addressing a potential conflict. Therefore, based on what patients described as being of value to them, the centres endeavour to admit patients to their preferred ward and clinician (based on previous admissions), thereby building on the rapport previously developed.

Changing the Physical Surroundings

The physical environment can promote or inhibit the culture desired. Conflict more often arises in wards if staff members are not present when problems arise for patients and consequently intervene too late. An element in 'nudging' staff behaviour and habits in their daily work, wards in several centres were modified to make the nurses' office smaller and the communal areas bigger. Open offices were established in the communal areas, so staff members can carry out most of their work in the environment where the patients are located. This markedly increases the availability of staff and opportunities to recognise distress, intervene and de-escalate.

Previously, some beds had restraint belts already in place. Both staff and patients felt this gave an implicit message that belt restraint was acceptable. Beds with restraint belts have now been abandoned on all wards. If belts are to be used, they can be obtained from a cabinet. The focus, however, is on developing staff skills with an expectation of a reduction in moving directly to restraint.

Meaningful Activities

During the most acute phase of an admission, the priority is on giving a patient peace and rest to be able to recover. Patient satisfaction surveys and discussions with patients and patient groups found that patients felt bored. Many patients missed having opportunities for meaningful activities. Boredom can also contribute to an increased level of conflict. Addressing these concerns was an important part of showing respect for service users.

To counteract this, the hospital has worked with occupational therapists and physiotherapists to increase access to fitness facilities and physical activities in general. These services are also available in the evenings as observation data showed that evenings were common times for conflict to occur. Some centres have also re-established their art studios, woodwork workshops and needlework groups. These activities provide patients with the opportunity to explore or rediscover their creative sides, which may not have been a focus during their illness.

Providing Sensory Integration

The intensive care wards of the mental health centres have sensory rooms. A sensory room is a treatment room for patients who experience anxiety, anger, unrest, or sadness and need to feel safe and to be calmed through their senses. Stimulation of specific senses activates soothing processes in the body and may remove restlessness and racing thoughts. The tools applied are massage chairs and massage balls, weighted blankets, soothing lights, sound and film. As with all new initiatives, investment in a sensory room was not enough in itself. The nursing staff had to learn how to use the sensory room alongside other professional nursing interventions. Training on the use of the room and the tools was necessary, as well as increased insight into sensory-motor therapy. Implementation required close managerial monitoring and follow-up.

Ongoing Lessons Learned from Coercion Episodes and In-Depth Data Analyses

When the initial improvements had been introduced and the first results had been achieved, goals were adjusted to become even more ambitious. To reach goals, managers and staff now go into more detail with each coercion episode to understand the problems, identify patterns and learn from these episodes at the centres.

There is a systematic review of all incidents of physical restraint, as well as any nearby incidents. This is to facilitate any learning and enhance shared understanding of what the individual patients need in a crisis. This review is made in a 20-minute meeting called 'Second Opinion'. It is multi-disciplinary with the participation of nursing staff, ward management, physicians and other relevant staff members. The aim is to prevent future crisis, explore other options for intervening early and support the message that the organisation wants to avoid the need for belt restraint wherever possible.

Analyses of local data and information regarding each coercion episode are now gathered and used to identify patterns and understand the problem better. This has been of significance locally and has resulted in adjustments in the wards, for example, staffing levels and activities during the evenings.

Results

The aim to reduce belt restraints has been successful (Figure 7.3). The number of annual belt restraint incidents has been reduced by more than half from 1,974 incidents in 2013 to 739 in 2018. Balancing measures are important, and they illustrate the need to maintain efforts over time and work on further improvements.

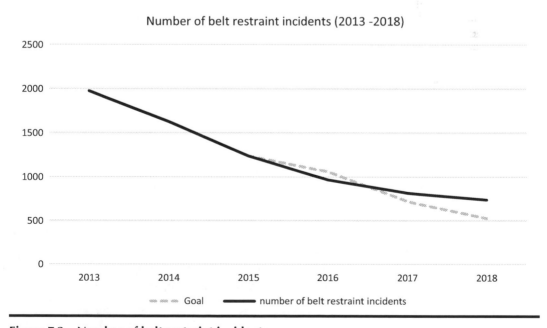

Figure 7.3   Number of belt restraint incidents.

The number of physical restraint incidents and forced administration of medication is unchanged (Figure 7.4). There was an initial increase in other forms of physical restraint as the use of belt restraints began to reduce, but the use of physical restraint is now no higher than it was at the beginning of the programme.

There has been a decline in the number of cases of physical and psychological violence directed against staff since 2014 (Figure 7.5).

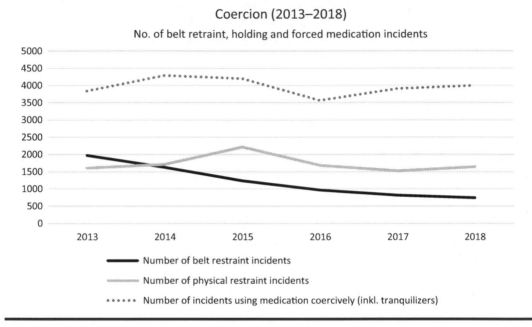

Figure 7.4   Number of belt restraint, holding and forced medications (Coercion 2013–2018).

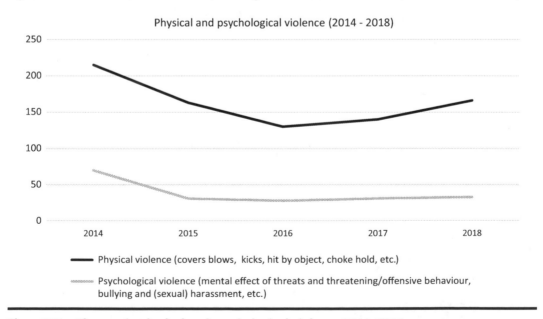

Figure 7.5   Changes in physical and psychological violence 2014–2018.

Conclusions

Recording balancing measures demonstrated that the initial worries of some staff members concerning the consequences of reducing coercion did not happen in practice. As well as far fewer patients being exposed to belt restraints during their admissions, staff also reported an increased pride in the work they do, as well as a calmer and better working environment. In the wards that have made the most progress, there is a feeling that a new culture has emerged.

This work will continue in the coming years with a focus on reducing all types of coercion and on strengthening the recovery approach further in the intensive care wards. To increase the prevention of coercive treatment and interventions, the outpatient clinics will now also be involved; they treat many of the patients in their more stable periods.

Case Study 2: Reducing Waiting Times

In Denmark in 2015 mental health services set a goal to reduce the waiting time from assessment to treatment. This meant all mental health outpatients had to be assessed within one month or have a plan for the ongoing assessment process.

Through two previous Lean pilot projects in outpatient units, the hospital learned how to make more time for direct patient contact and how to shorten waiting time by better planning. However, the hospital was far from the goal of 30-day waiting time for outpatient treatment for most diagnoses. For a few diagnostic groups, the waiting time was more than a year.

Many managers and staff members found the goal of maximum 30-day waiting time impossible to imagine. They were already very busy, and the demand for shorter waiting times was seen as a criticism of their current efforts. They saw only one way that waiting time could be reduced, and that was by employing more staff.

Unlike the work of reducing belt restraints and coercion, work on waiting times was a less familiar area of work for the traditional, professional field of psychiatry. Timely treatment is important when creating value for the patient. When the patient is motivated to seek help, they should not have to wait many months for treatment to start. Reduction in waiting time constitutes an essential part of Lean thinking by reducing the waste of waiting.

An initial analysis of the problem found that:

- Staff and managers were very dedicated to the patients already being treated, but the long waiting times were seen as a condition which new patients had to deal with.
- The number of patients seen per day varied markedly within teams. Many staff members were used to a high degree of autonomy, planning their daily work and their time for treatment based on their views. There was often no systematic, joint coordination of daily tasks amongst the clinicians in a team.
- Managers had been trained or instructed to analyse, plan and manage capacity. Concepts such as Value Streams, takt time and levelling were unknown.
- IT systems were inadequate for planning treatment in the outpatient units.
- Accurate and real-time data were limited.

Examples of Flow Improvements

As the hospital became more familiar with analysing value streams and flow, it became clear that no systematic approach had been taken to the planning and use of resources to ensure a good flow.

A system had to be built to solve this if the goal of reducing waiting times was to be reached. The hospital's executive management was responsible for overseeing and addressing this.

Standard Work for Assessment and Treatment

There was a lack of Standard Work. The triage of referred patients was carried out using locally determined guidelines, descriptions of groups of patients and eligibility criteria created at the individual centres. This meant that the waiting times varied from centre to centre, and the hospital resources were not utilised optimally across the organisation.

The hospital had already developed diagnostic-specific, time-limited outpatient pathways, to ensure a more standard quality of treatment, but these were not used across the treatment centres. The descriptions for these patient pathways became the basis for enabling, systematic joint planning and better capacity utilisation. A central triage unit was created to undertake triage for the whole hospital, to ensure standards and better management of the patient flow across the hospital.

New Management Tasks and Competency Development

Establishing a single point of entry was not enough to reach the goal of reducing waiting times. Daily planning in the outpatient units had to be changed to create more time for direct patient care which data and observations had revealed to be a problem.

There was a need for stronger general management competencies to understand the tools available for managing resources and capacity. This included better work procedures and processes, relevant data and tools to help outpatient managers with their tasks.

The hospital established a new central unit responsible for managing data and patient logistics. The specialists in this new unit help the hospital's executives with the improvement of capacity planning and management. The task of this central unit is to train and develop the management competencies of the outpatient unit managers. To support this, they have collaborated with service managers to develop capacity management tools and a data scorecard. Weekly teleconference meetings are now held to maintain the focus on managing capacity across the organisation. These meetings involve managers of the outpatient and central assessment units.

Managers of the outpatient units have carried out much of this change and have assumed a high level of responsibility. This has required new management skills with a firm understanding of Lean tools. Awareness of their value streams is essential. Managers now ensure that resources and tasks are properly matched and distributed and delegated fairly. They also assume the responsibility for ensuring that staff members deliver evidence-based treatment.

Both individually and as a team, staff members have a joint task in planning the treatment of patients and adapting their daily and weekly plans within a standard framework. Staff members now also take the responsibility for ensuring that patients receive treatment within 30 days of referral.

Data-Driven Management

Concurrently with the introduction of the 30-day assessment and treatment guarantee, the number of patients referred for assessment and treatment has risen steadily. In 2013, 2,995 children and adolescents were assessed for outpatient treatment. Since then, the number has risen year by year. In 2018, the number had gone up to 4,318, an increase of around 30%.

A better understanding of individual value streams; knowledge of the patient groupings and their requirements; identification of takt time to meet the demands; reduction of waste in the system; levelling of the outpatient clinic capacity and demand; and the introduction of Standard Work resulted in considerable improvements in capacity and reduced waits for patients.

Analysis of capacity and demand data and attention to value identified when improvements in flow management alone and could no longer deliver the required waiting times. The organisation decided to add more resources to child and adolescent psychiatry to reach the waiting time target, and the additional finances required for this were identified. This was an easier decision than would otherwise have been the case because there was much better information and the improvements that had already been made were visible to the organisation.

In adult psychiatry, the number of patients requiring assessment and treatment in outpatient services also increased from 7,833 in 2013 to 12,634 in 2018 – an increase of 61%. In this case, the increasing pressure was managed through a minor reallocation of resources from inpatient wards to outpatient services and by improving planning. Most of the improvements in flow were produced by improving planning rather than by increasing capacity.

The difference from the past is that the hospital's executive management can support the management by making decisions on extra resources based on solid knowledge, facts and forward-looking analyses of capacity – not based on retrospective data, gut feelings and assumptions. A firm knowledge of the value streams involved, the capacity available and the daily, weekly and monthly demand allows much better control of the system and helps the organisation to reduce waste by matching demand and capacity.

Results

The average waiting time for children and adolescents has been reduced from 47 days in 2013 to 28 days in 2018 despite the increase in demand. For adult patients, the average waiting time was 53 days in 2013 and 19 days in 2018 (Figure 7.6). In both cases, there was an increase in demand of around 30%

Today in RHP it is rare that patients wait for more than 30 days and the variation in waiting times had reduced substantially. In September 2019, 97% of patients had been assessed or started treatment within the 30-day target.

Conclusions

The organisation is proud that patients rarely have long waits (>30-days) for treatment. While it has been a difficult process, staff report the advantages of greater transparency in what is expected from them. They say that tasks are now more distributed, there is better daily coordination using daily management, and there is more managerial understanding of the time and competencies required for the different tasks linked to the mapping of the value streams.

Shared Features from the Two Case Studies

The two cases address two very different issues at the hospital. The improvement work affected different professional groups and different patients. The problems and the improvements are also widely different in terms of their nature and their content.

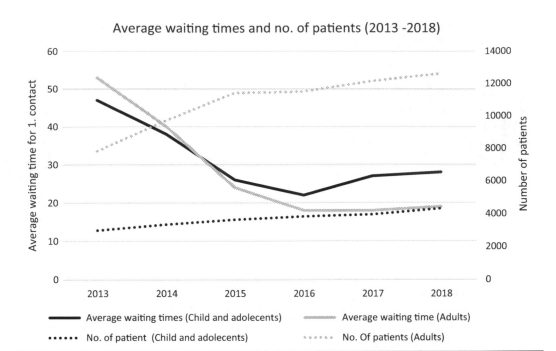

Figure 7.6 Average waiting time and number of patients (child and adolescents and adults, 2013–2018.

In the first case study reducing the use of coercive measures dealt with how the patient is viewed and approached by the professionals, staff commitment and motivation were achieved and increased over time. Many staff members have contributed to the goal of reducing the use of coercive measures. This has been done not only by implementing new processes and new standards, but also by taking a critical look at individual practices and understandings of professional approaches. More and more improvements come directly from staff members, and new initiatives developed elsewhere in the organisation are disseminated across centres on an ongoing basis. This echoes the discussions in this volume on staff engagement (Chapter 2), the importance of working with staff and service users (Chapter 10) and the importance of scientific thinking (Chapter 11).

In the second case study, looking at improving analyses of waiting times showed that there was a basic need for a system for planning patient treatment and for supporting the goal of reducing waiting times. Ensuring that the right processes, tools and competencies are in place is a management task. That is why improvements had to be initiated by management. Chapter 8 from Iceland similarly reflects the importance of training and capacity building on Lean skills, and Chapter 3 provides further information on the leverage that can be gained from good data and analysis.

There are several common traits in how the hospital approached these issues and why the outcomes were a success. Additionally, some of the difficulties and the dilemmas encountered on the way were also of the same nature. These general lessons learned will be taken forward by the hospital in its ongoing improvement work: Common themes included the following.

Meaningful Goals as a True North

In both cases, the goal was to be patient-focused and to create real value for patients. Furthermore, the goals were very ambitious and were initially seen as impossible to reach. When the most obvious improvements had been implemented and the first goals had been reached, new goals were set, pushing the organisation to be even more inventive to reach the goals. This strategic alignment, or Hoshin approach (Stark & Hookway, 2019), was important to our success.

Managerial Focus and Willpower

Ongoing managerial attention and follow-up has been crucial. Every day, week in, week out, year in, year out, all layers of management and all staff members have had to relate to new goals and progress reports and make new plans whenever required. It has been clear for all to see and feel that the hospital's executive management was not going to give up on the goals – not even when there was resistance in the organisation.

Continuous Systematic Improvement Works Locally and across the Organisation

The use of detailed data and Lean tools including A3, Value Stream Analysis, 5 Whys, etc., has allowed RHP to understand and analyse the problems in detail, before solutions were sought. Improvement meetings have been the driver for staff input and have been the way to influence the work on improvement measures and their systematic implementation in the clinic. Chapter 5 on Value Management in this volume gives a further example of the impetus gained from allowing staff to have a regular focus on improvement.

Management Decisions Driven by Data, Facts and Knowledge

The use of data and analyses were significant factors allowing managers at the hospital to understand the problems and help the next level in the organisation to work towards reaching the goals. For example, the work on capacity analyses meant that management was able to make decisions to add resources while at the same time expanding the existing capacity by changing planning procedures.

In both cases, analyses also showed a need to enhance professional and managerial competences if the goals were to be reached. As a result, the hospital's executives decided to invest in relevant competency development to reach the goals that had been defined.

The Importance of Courage and PDSA Thinking

Sometimes, the road was bumpy, with both successes and mistakes on the way. Ongoing analyses, testing of new improvements and lessons to be learned have been needed. It takes managerial courage and trust to work in this way from the very beginning. Furthermore, when the going gets tough resistance is to be expected. Equally, you need to be able to change direction, if it turns out that you were wrong, or the improvement does not work as intended. Therefore, you must learn to live with doubt.

Let Someone Pave the Way: Model Cell Thinking

In both case studies, some centres took the lead in working with the goals, while others waited to learn from their findings. Gradually, as the results emerged, it became clear that the goals were possible to reach. It was at this point colleagues from the leading centres started sharing their knowledge and experience in how to achieve the goals. Colleagues in Iceland, in Chapter 8, also reported on the importance of early successes that can then be shared with the wider organisation.

This approach allows some colleagues to show the way to others who may have doubts. It also makes sense not to have everyone re-inventing the wheel at the same time. It also ensures that major initiatives have been tested and adapted before being adopted across the organisation.

Copy Kaizen and Gemba

A typical dilemma for management is how to disseminate good solutions in a big organisation. As a manager, it is tempting to insist that a solution that works in one location is to be implemented everywhere. However, such a requirement may often create reluctance, no matter how good the solution is. What the hospital has learned is that it is usually better to set goals and a direction. Then to create opportunities and a framework for sharing knowledge to allow room for solutions with a local touch. This is the point of 'copy kaizen' which builds in the importance of local context. Instead of 'one size fits all', units copy the process of continuous improvement and staff engagement and build on the solutions of others, rather than trying to implement every aspect of the improvements identified in a different area.

Knowledge sharing has been more extensive in the two case studies described than in previous development work. Going to the gemba has allowed colleagues to learn from the frontrunners and be inspired to change their practices. Furthermore, sharing has also included problems and improvements via forums, data and improvement meetings.

Creating a Sense of Purpose: Patient Experienced Value and 'What Is in It for Me'

Creating a sense of purpose is a management task, and it is essential to achieve ambitious goals. How an organisation sets direction and creates a sense of purpose needs to be adjusted to each situation and group of employees. If the goals are to create a direct benefit for the patients, then you have made good progress. It is, however, not always sufficient to use the patient's focus as the only argument to engage the employees initially. It can be important to facilitate a dialogue about what the benefit is for those who must change practice. Staff want to do well for their patients and to deliver high-quality services. Lean helps them to do this without increasing the burden of work. It decreases waste and increases the proportion of value-added work that staff can provide. When staff become confident that this will not be at the expense of themselves and the organisation respects their efforts, their confidence in the value of the approach increases.

Some questions to support learning activities have been set out that may prove useful for organisations starting on a Lean journey or towards reviewing their progress.

QUESTIONS TO SUPPORT LEARNING ACTIVITIES

- What do you want to achieve by implementing Lean?
- What creates value for your customers? What do they want from you?
- Has your organisation set sufficiently ambitious goals?
- Do the goals support the direction and behaviour you wish to see?
- Does everyone in the organisation understand why you chose those goals? And how they can contribute?
- How well are your managers prepared for managing improvement work and driving it forward?

Conclusion

A key management requirement is to set the framework for implementation and follow up on it continually, to ensure fidelity to the improvement model as well as to ensure that there is clarity of why the improvement activities are important.

The two case studies show, that with the right management focus, meaningful objectives, good data support and a high level of engagement, ambitious goals can be delivered because of systematic improvement work. However, if solutions are to be disseminated, the opportunity for modifications must be permitted. Otherwise, in our experience, it is likely to be less successful or even fail.

The hospital has learned a great deal from our Lean experience. Region Hovedstadens Psykiatri's goal is to continue to create a management-driven, improvement culture, which is not dependent on the efforts or will of individuals. Rather an integral part of the whole organisation in the way it acts and works. Neither the organisation nor the world is standing still. On the contrary, new patients, new staff members and new managers come all the time. With new problems, challenges and demands, the hospital must and will have to respond. Applying Lean as an integrated management and improvement system allows Region Hovedstadens Psykiatri to do this now and in the future.

Learning Points

- Quality improvement is a journey. There is no perfect service, and it is always possible to identify and deliver further improvements.
- Successful Lean implementation depends on the mindset and behaviour of managers.
- Managers must set the direction towards joint, ambitious goals and create meaning in the work through dialogue and collaboration.
- Ongoing managerial focus on goal achievement is essential for success.
- The manager's role is to help staff create the best possible value for patients and to remove any barrier stopping this from happening.
- Understanding the root causes of problems is important. Staff and patient insight and involvement is essential if sustainable solutions are to be found, and goals achieved.
- Go to the gemba and ensure management decisions are based on knowledge and facts.
- Do not let the wish to achieve the best stand in the way of better; work towards gradual improvements – through PDSA cycles.
- View mistakes and problems as opportunities for learning and improving.
- Work with development and major improvements in model cells.
- Support knowledge sharing and copy kaizen practices.
- Lean tools and methods are essential, but their application is not the goal. The point is to understand what can be achieved by using them.

Additional Resource

The Mental Health Services of the Capital Region of Denmark have published a book on improvement work, intended for managers in the organisation. Follow this link to get to the English version of the book:

www.psykiatri-regionh.dk/english/Sider/default.aspx.

Acknowledgements

A big thank you to all the patients, staff members and managers in the Mental Health Services of the Capital Region of Denmark. They have challenged themselves and each other contributed to improvement work and to the achievement of the great results we have obtained. Without their sterling efforts, there would have been no success.

Also, to the many passionate Lean colleagues and Lean networks in the hospital sector, both locally and globally. Your expertise and support have been invaluable. Their honesty and willingness to share and learn from each other's experiences – good, as well as bad – is crucial if our sector is to continue to improve and create more value for patients.

Bibliography

Bak, J., & Aggernæs, H. (2012). Coercion within Danish psychiatry compared with 10 other European countries. *Nordic Journal of Psychiatry*, 66(5), 297–302. https://doi.org/10.3109/08039488.2011.632645

Bak, J., Zoffmann, V., Sestoft, D. M., Almvik, R., & Brandt-Christensen, M. (2014). Mechanical restraint in psychiatry: Preventive factors in theory and practice. A Danish-Norwegian Association Study. *Perspectives in Psychiatric Care*, 50(3), 155–166. https://doi.org/10.1111/ppc.12036

Bak, J., Zoffmann, V., Sestoft, D. M., Almvik, R., Siersma, V. D., & Brandt-Christensen, M. (2015). Comparing the effect of non-medical mechanical restraint preventive factors between psychiatric units in Denmark and Norway. *Nordic Journal of Psychiatry*, 69(6), 433–443. https://doi.org/10.3109/08039488.2014.996600

Bowers, L. (2014). Safewards: A new model of conflict and containment on psychiatric wards. *Journal of Psychiatric and Mental Health Nursing*, 21, 499–508. https://doi.org/10.1111/jpm.12129

Bowers, L., James, K., Quirk, A., Simpson, A., Stewart, D., & Hodsoll, J. (2015). Reducing conflict and containment rates on acute psychiatric wards: The Safewards cluster randomised controlled trial. *International Journal of Nursing Studies*, 52, 1412–1422. https://doi.org/10.1016/j.ijnurstu.2015.05.001

Cusack, P., Cusack, F. P., McAndrew, S., McKeown, M., & Duxbury, J. (2018). An integrative review exploring the physical and psychological harm inherent in using restraint in mental health inpatient settings. *International Journal of Mental Health Nursing*, 27(3), 1162–1176. https://doi.org/10.1111/inm.12432

Laukkanen, E., Kuosmanen, L., Selander, T., & Vehviläinen-Julkunen, K. (2020). Seclusion, restraint, and involuntary medication in Finnish psychiatric care: a register study with root-level data. *Nordic Journal of Psychiatry*, 74(6), 439–443. https://doi.org/10.1080/08039488.2020.1733658

Mårtensson, S., Johansen, K. S., & Hjorthøj, C. (2019). Dual diagnosis and mechanical restraint – a register-based study of 31,793 patients and 6562 episodes of mechanical restraint in the Capital region of Denmark from 2010–2014. *Nordic Journal of Psychiatry*, 73(3), 169–177. https://doi.org./10.1080/08039488.2019.1582695

Stark, C., & Hookway, G. (2019). *Applying Lean in Health and Social Care Services*. Routledge.

Steinert, T., Lepping, P., Bernhardsgrütter, R., Conca, A., Hatling, T., Janssen, W., Keski-Valkama, A., Mayoral, F., & Whittington, R. (2010). Incidence of seclusion and restraint in psychiatric hospitals: a literature review and survey of international trends. *Social Psychiatry and Psychiatric Epidemiology*, 45(9), 889–897. https://doi.org/10.1007/s00127-009-0132-3

Strout, T. D. (2010). Perspectives on the experience of being physically restrained: An integrative review of the qualitative literature. *International Journal of Mental Health Nursing*, 19(6), 416–427. https://doi.org/10.1111/j.1447-0349.2010.00694.x

Ward-Stockham, K., Kapp, S., Jarden, R., Gerdtz, M., & Daniel, C. (2021). Effect of Safewards on reducing conflict and containment and the experiences of staff and consumers: A mixed-methods systematic review. *International Journal of Mental Health Nursing*, 31, 199–221. https://doi-org.uhi.idm.oclc.org/10.1111/inm.12950

Louise Roig, MA in History and Minority Studies, is a trained Lean facilitator and coach. She has contributed to the Lean journey at the Mental Health Services of Greater Copenhagen for over a decade with her co-author Jens Normand. During the last five years, she has been responsible for leadership training supporting the hospital's senior management team with their strategic work and policy deployment.

Jens Normand has a MA in Economy and Leadership. For over a decade, together with the chief executive, he is responsible for the development of a culture of continuous quality improvement at the Mental Health Services of Greater Copenhagen. Before that, he worked as a senior consultant in other hospitals, helping and coaching leadership in quality improvement work. For six years, Jens was also the chief development leader in Danske Bank. He has published two books about leadership and management in Improvement cultures.

Chapter 8

Organisation-Wide Implementation of Lean in Iceland

Páll Matthíasson, Benedikt Olgeirsson, and
Gudrun Björg Sigurbjörnsdottir

Contents

DOI: 10.4324/9780429346958-8

Aims

- To describe the hospital-wide introduction of Lean in the National University Hospital of Iceland.
- To outline the stages of introduction, including the importance of organisational ownership of the method.
- To demonstrate how approaches such as kaizen, Rapid Process Improvement Workshops, and 3P events can be integrated into one organisation.
- To share the successes of this Lean application.

Introduction

Most health systems have used quality improvement approaches and often find consistency over time and the maintenance of gains challenging. When new systems are being adopted, this is likely to be in the context of previous efforts to embed quality improvement methods. Staff may be dubious about new quality improvement efforts because of their experience of problems in previous introductions. Moving from the use of quality improvement methods to the application of an integrated system is challenging.

This chapter discusses the application of Lean methods in Landspítali Hospital in Iceland. At the time the work began there was staff dissatisfaction with the long-term maintenance of quality improvement efforts in the hospital. There was no lack of engagement with innovation or difficulties in generating ideas for quality improvement, so the challenges were in integrating quality improvement with business as usual rather than being seen as a separate initiative, and in aligning quality improvement work with the organisation's strategic direction and external challenges. This chapter describes the introduction of Lean methods in the context of earlier use of quality improvement to bridge these gaps.

Context

The Icelandic health service is government funded with universal coverage. There are also private non-profit and private for-profit providers. Like many other European countries, there are financial pressures on care costs because of an ageing population and the cost of managing long-term conditions (Sigurgeirsdóttir et al., 2014). Landspítali is the National University Hospital of Iceland located in Reykjavik and is the country's largest public organisation. It was formed by the merger of Reykjavik's three acute hospitals in the year 2000 (Landspítali, n.d.). The hospital has around 640 beds, 6,000 employees, and an annual turnover of €500 million.

Iceland has a population of 370,000. It also has a large transient population with two million tourists visiting every year, before the Covid-19 pandemic. There is a major seasonal component to tourism and visitor numbers can be very high at some times of the year (Gil-Alana & Huijbens, 2018).

Landspítali worked on quality improvement for many years but found it difficult to maintain progress. A survey in 2011 showed the need for a more innovative approach to change, when only 5% of the hospital leaders at Landspítali were pleased with the previous approach to change management (Figure 8.1). The hospital leaders wanted to use methods that both supported quality improvement and were able to be sustained. After a review of international options, the hospital

SURVEY IN A LARGE MANAGEMENT MEETING IN 2011

LANDSPITALI IS GOOD AT COMING UP
WITH INNOVATIVE IDEAS TO IMPROVE
THE HOSPITAL

LANDSPITALI IS GOOD AT DRIVING
IMPROVEMENT PROJECTS OVER
TIME

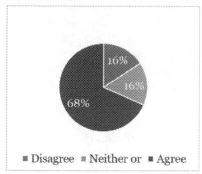

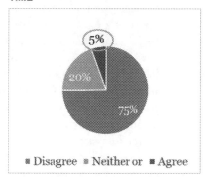

Figure 8.1 Results from a survey of hospital leaders from a large management meeting in September 2011.

management team identified the successful use of Lean at scale in the USA and Europe and decided to use Lean methods and their Lean journey got underway in 2012.

The hospital began to apply Lean with strategic assistance from McKinsey, the Karolinska Hospital in Sweden, and Cincinnati Children's Hospital in the USA. Since 2013, the Virginia Mason Institute in Seattle has been their main Lean consultant. Landspítali's organisational aim was to become self-sufficient and sustaining in Lean training and application. Considering experience with the previous quality improvement initiatives, and the risk of efforts diminishing or even failing over time, the senior leadership team also wanted to identify ways of maintaining efforts over time.

The hospital began by working to develop the ability within the hospital to deliver a Lean training program towards being self-sustainable. While seeking to achieve this, however, it was recognised that maintaining ongoing inspiration and further direction was also vital. Landspítali sought volunteers from the management team to participate in the first three Lean projects in the fall of 2011. These projects were carefully selected, and early work included value stream mapping followed by work to simplify patient flow. The projects were all successful which gave the Lean journey substantial support and energy within the hospital. One of the projects, on reducing the haemolysis of blood samples from the Emergency Department, is outlined in the 'Case Studies' section later in the chapter. From the previous experience, the senior leadership team knew that initial successes are not enough and that more was required to build on these first steps.

Our Strategic Priorities

Landspítali, supported by the Virginia Mason Institute, developed a clear strategic direction. This work included staff engagement and produced a visual product that could be shared easily. The visual representation of the strategy is now on the hospital website and therefore is one of the first things that patients and current and prospective staff access. Ten years on from its initial development the strategic triangle that was developed has changed very little. This is in marked contrast to the experience of previous initiatives that came and went and which contributed the poor staff feedback in 2011.

The top of Landspítali's strategy triangle is 'Patient first'. It is underpinned by work on safety culture, service, people, and continuous improvement. Increased quality and less waste are the foundations of the model, supporting the other components (Figure 8.2).

Active participation of all employees in the process and quality improvement was encouraged with managers' support. In previous initiatives the focus had often been only on clinical services. Understandably this had contributed to a feeling that quality improvement was an activity for clinical services alone and that it was not relevant to support services.

The senior leadership team was determined that the hospital's quality vision would be for all staff. Excluding staff groups had not been intended in the earlier initiatives but had been an unanticipated consequence of the direction of efforts into clinical service work. Delivery of healthcare depends on an integrated network of services. Support services may not always deal with service users directly, but their efforts are essential in producing the conditions that enable clinical staff to provide the best service possible to patients. If all work goes into direct clinical services, this loses the opportunity to make improvements in crucial services and may result in support staff feeling undervalued and excluded. As a result, the management team placed attention on support services including medication management, linen and supplies, and preventive maintenance. All hospital leaders now participate in shaping strategic priorities for the next year with no distinction between clinical and non-clinical services.

Since 2012, Landspítali has seen improvements in financial sustainability. As part of the ethos of Lean, the hospital is also developing an integrated care network with other healthcare organisations in Iceland. This network approach reflects the complex nature of the delivery of modern healthcare. It also reflects the changed nature of healthcare in countries with ageing populations where long-term conditions are an increasing part of the work. Episodic hospital care is required but decreasing the risk of readmission and supporting discharge cannot be done by an acute hospital alone. Equally, actions within an acute hospital can inadvertently make things more difficult

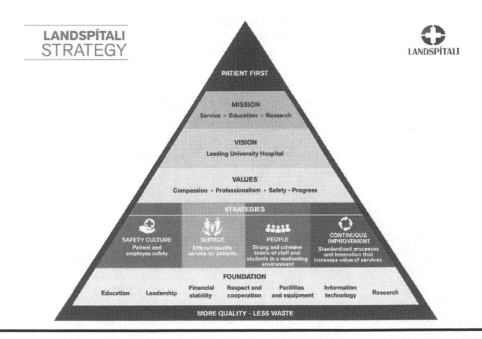

Figure 8.2   The strategy triangle of Landspítali.

for community services. Understanding the whole patient journey is essential. Improvements to the portion of the patient journey within a hospital are important, but being aware of how components of care connect is even more important and is part of Landspítali's current approach.

The Improvement School

Landspítali has an emphasis on Lean education and training. It established a Lean school in 2012 which has been one of the key factors for the success of their Lean journey. The hospital has trained many Lean coaches and a large part of staff members in the basic components of Lean and waste (Figure 8.3).

Several chapters in the current volume discuss the importance of embedding quality improvement and scientific thinking. The Landspítali approach seeks to make quality improvement thinking part of the repertoire of all its staff, and to support this by training managers and executives in how to support Lean thinking. The chapter on Kata in this book (Chapter 11) describes an approach to the same issue of making Lean practice ingrained.

The training Landspítali offers includes Lean tools and approaches and places this in the context of quality improvement science knowledge on change management and teamwork. There is an emphasis on experiential learning with support for method fidelity through coaching. An ongoing relationship with the Virginia Mason Institute helps to provide injections of the latest ideas, and to provide coaching support on consistency of method over time.

The contrast with previous shorter-lived initiatives at Landspítali is marked. The hospital has focused on investment in training and staff knowledge and has maintained this over a decade. The improvement school is still a strong part of our improvement work and has developed into a more comprehensive school on quality management, lean, and change management.

Our Lean Journey

The Landspítali Lean journey started with the three improvement projects referenced in the 'Context' section above. In advance of these events, colleagues from McKinsey trained the improvement groups and provided advisory support on the progress of the events. These improvement projects were also supported by a Kaizen Promotion Office (KPO) which was created in the

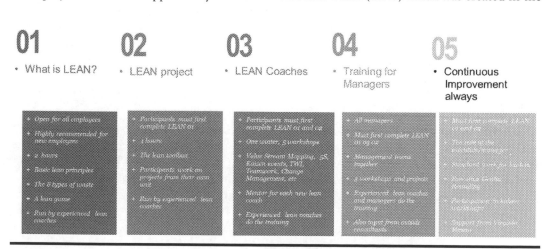

Figure 8.3 Overview of Landspítali's Lean school in 2017.

hospital. The early success of these projects gave the Lean approach to improvement substantial support and energy within the hospital.

The next tool implemented was 5S (Stark & Hookway, 2019). Chapter 2 provides a detailed description of 5S application in Scotland. In Landspítali, the staff participating in 5S events had a short training session on Lean thinking, including discussion of waste. This was followed by implementing 5S with the frontline staff and assisting them in changing their workstations and workrooms to support the processes they deliver. These events also started to spread quality improvement thinking throughout the hospital and with a greater understanding in Lean thinking.

Landspítali has since used various other tools from the Lean toolkit to implement Lean thinking such as kaizen events, 3P, gemba, improvement boards, Rapid Process Improvement Workshops (RPIWs), and more. Integrating them into a system so that they are more than tools has been an important part of the Landspítali approach.

Examples highlighting the hospital's use of Lean tools in the work over the last decade are captured in the following short case studies.

Case Studies

Initial Project-Based Work

One of the initial three Lean projects was on blood samples from the main Emergency Department. Some samples were unusable because they were haemolysed and so could not be analysed. The rate of haemolysis was over 12% and previous measures to improve this process had not been successful. This caused delays for patients and staff and had patient safety risks. Using Lean methodology, a multidisciplinary team managed to bring the rate of failed samples down to 2%–3% (Figure 8.4).

The reduction in the haemolysis rate began in January when the project started in 2012. It is not uncommon in projects that when a process is in the spotlight it may initially improve but slides back when the spotlight is off – commonly known as the Hawthorne Effect (Purssell et al., 2020). Making sure that effects continued over time by embedding methods and practices was an important aim of the project. The group tested some methods for blood sampling and in February the staff tried a particular method for 24 hours and the haemolysis rate dropped down to zero. The results from this pilot were the '*A-ha*' moment for the staff. They implemented the new process in March with sustained results. Haemolysis rate is still one of the indicators on the Emergency Department board ten years later.

Kaizen Events

Kaizen events, which last for four to eight hours, were tried out early in our Lean journey. With good preparation, value stream mapping, data analysis and a narrow scope, these short events were remarkably successful. This began to move the quality improvement work beyond individual projects to accessible methodology that involved large numbers of staff over time.

One kaizen event focused on the process for patients coming to the Emergency Department (ED) with a Transient Ischemic Attack (TIA). A multidisciplinary and hospital-wide team designed a new process for TIA patients in the ED and outpatient care in a four-hour-long kaizen event. The pathway was simplified and standardised, with follow-up care in outpatients the next weekday after the ED visit. In between the patient had some tests done, like Holter, MRI

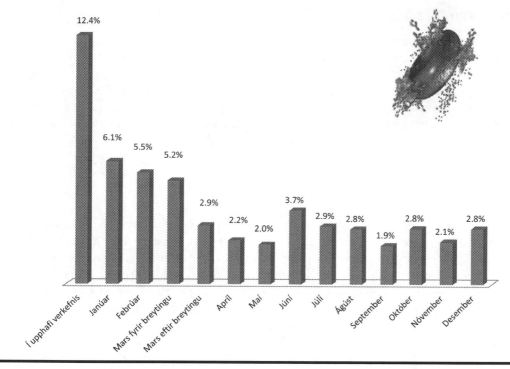

Figure 8.4   Haemolysis rate in blood samples from the Emergency Department in 2012.

scan, and blood work. This led to a shorter stay in ED for patients arriving with TIA, less waiting time for radiology both in the ED and during outpatient care and a dedicated and often shorter wait for follow-up in outpatient care. Patient safety was also improved because there was standard work on the assessment ensuring that best practice was followed every time and was not person dependent.

Daily Huddles

Daily management is an important aspect of Lean management (Kenney, 2011; Mann, 2015; Toussaint & Adams, 2015). In 2012 Landspítali decided to implement huddles in all departments, focusing on safety and daily management. The first department to implement a daily morning huddle was the Emergency Department. Through this process staff realised the need for a huddle at the beginning of every shift.

It was successful and a hospital-wide huddle started on 28 December 2015. The reason for starting on that day was a history of severe incidents happening after the Christmas holidays and a need to be more proactive to improve what was now predictable. This huddle has been held every day since at 11:15 am. In these short huddles, the spotlight is on incidents, infection control, and other safety issues, and on the flow of inpatients. The hospital-wide huddle is a strong part of daily management and supports Landspítali's priorities on safety and quality.

This move from projects and kaizen events to a daily management structure was a key step in integrating Lean practices into the day-to-day work of the hospital. Daily management had been part of the follow-up of projects and events, but this began to spread attention to processes across the hospital system.

Production and Improvement Boards

Visual management is an important part of Lean management (Japan Management Association, 1989). The early production boards were later developed into electronic boards, making it easier to add visual signs of risk factors, like falls and nutrition. Landspítali later developed improvement boards as a tool to put an emphasis on improving, better quality and safety. The boards align the work of staff in each department with organisational aims and priorities while also empowering staff to produce improvements. Improvement meetings are held every second or third week to review departmental metrics, monitor progress on initiatives and identify new areas requiring work.

Gemba

Daily management includes technical and human dimensions of change, such as the use of production boards, improvement boards, and the regular presence of managers on the frontline. In Lean, the Gemba refers to the place where work is done. The executive team with the chief executive in the forefront schedule Gemba visits on the floor to follow up on improvement work and innovations. Together, these components make continuous improvement a daily expectation. This also allows the senior staff to coach on Lean methods and the importance of scientific thinking with problem identification and testing of solutions using Plan-Do-Study-Act cycles. This regular presence also helps to demonstrate to staff that there is continuing organisational commitment to the methods and that the quality improvement activity is aligned with priorities. A similar approach is described in Chapter 11 'Applying Kata in Healthcare'.

The Communication Compact

A communication compact was developed at Landspítali in response to root cause analyses of various incidence reports (Landspítali Hospital, 2019). The purpose of the compact was to make patients feel safer and improve staff well-being through clear, effective, warm, and positive communication. It applies to all those working at the hospital, irrespective of position or profession, and was based on around 900 cases of personal interactions reported by c700 employees of the hospital at fifty development meetings in the spring of 2018.

These cases included both positive examples and thoughts on what could be improved in communication at the hospital. They involved professional channels of communication such as personal interactions, and conduct, as well as communications between hospital staff.

The specific content of the cases examined is presented in eight sections, which make up the text of the communication compact. The sections include welcome, respect, professionalism, care, understanding, responsibility, honesty, equality, and responses (how to respond to breaches of the protocol).

The compact was published on Landspítali websites both internal and external, through social media (Facebook and Twitter), demonstration videos, and posters. Awareness was also heightened by producing tags and buttons for the staff to wear. In addition, news releases and articles are produced on a regular basis. This focus on respect is both a recognition of a core tenet of Lean and an acknowledgement that poor communication is at the root cause of many patients' safety issues. Our focus on equality and on treating staff well helps to embody the values that should permeate our care for our staff and colleagues, and our care for our patients.

Using Social Media to Influence Patient Flow

An example of a project that reflected growing confidence was the increasing use of social media to communicate directly with the public. The purpose of the project was to create a better experience for patients by improving flow through the Emergency Department (ED). There was an average of 25,000 attendances in the ED. Looking at case mix, the department discovered that many people were attending for conditions that could be appropriately and safely assessed and treated in other settings, such as Iceland's municipal health clinics for minor injuries or illnesses. This caused delays for patients with minor injuries or less serious conditions when attending the ED compared to the wait they would have had in the municipal clinics. It also increased risk by diverting attention in the ED from more serious conditions that required a specialist response.

A range of communication approaches were developed to increase public awareness of assessment and treatment options. The communications department assisted with ideas for improving information flow by preparing news releases, and public awareness campaigns that went viral in Iceland.

In close cooperation with staff in municipal health clinics, staff in the department produced 12 videos and campaigns for social media, all highlighting core messages of the opening hours and good service provided in the clinics. Videos were circulated on Landspítali social media accounts, intranet, websites, and throughout the workplace. Directors in the clinics were also active in Icelandic media to discuss their local service.

The campaign reduced attendances by about 2,500 patients a year (10%). In the peak months of this project the reduction was up to 30% which indicates that there are further improvements that can be made.

Communicating with Patients and the Public

It is essential for Landspítali, a modern high-tech healthcare facility, to communicate about vital developments and current affairs such as during the Covid-19 pandemic to the staff and the public. The heavy stream of information coming from the hospital since 2016 when the Communications Team in its current shape was founded has been beneficial. It has helped to shape a positive view of the hospital services by the public towards its operations and importance for society. Providing people with better information is key in helping to improve healthcare, particularly with the increase in long-term conditions and the importance of self-management. Helping people to navigate the hospital system is important and reduces distress and increases confidence.

The Communications Team consists of two reporters, a photographer, a filmmaker, a graphic designer, a webmaster, and two programmers. The last two are outsourced from the software developer Advania. The team was developed to function as a small but robust news agency as well as managing and producing content for the external and internal websites and social media of Landspítali. The output of the team has been prolific. In 2020 they produced 300 news stories in video format, around 900 stories in print format and recorded about 100 podcast episodes. Add to these some 200 posters, reports with infographics and brochures for patients and staff. They also prepared several streaming projects each week. Through this coordinated and proactive approach, population of Iceland is much better informed about the hospital than just a few years ago.

Annual surveys by the market research company Gallup show that trust in Landspítali is at a peak in 2020 among workplaces in the country, both governmental and private. Indeed, it is only toppled by the revered National Coast Guard and the current President of Iceland who is popular in the country. The aim of the work was to improve communication and information for patients and staff, but the inadvertent impact on public confidence has also been a valuable consequence for the hospital.

3P: Production Preparation Process

Landspítali is currently undertaking a range of work to modernise its estate including building a new 70,000m² treatment centre; a 17,000m² central laboratory building at its main campus in Reykjavik; additional technical buildings; and car parks. A patient hotel has already been completed.

Application of Lean methodology has played a key part in preparations for these buildings and related operations running six-week-long 3P workshops in 2015 and 2016 with support from the Virginia Mason Institute.

3P workshops have included:

1. Operation Room, Intensive Care Unit and Cardiac Catheterisation Laboratory.
2. Emergency Department.
3. Patient Wards.
4. Support Services.
5. Laboratory Services.
6. The Campus ('rest of campus').

There were between 30 and 55 employees in each workshop representing all related specialties and services. The chief designers for these new buildings also participated in all six workshops.

The focus of 3P is initially to establish a vision and then create an implementation plan. All participants had to focus on the journey of the patient and all the hurdles they experience. In preparing for these workshops the seven flows of medicine were mapped out for patient groups undergoing treatments, intervention, radiology etc. Figure 8.5 shows the Icelandic summary used in the hospital. 3P events are also discussed in detail in Chapter 9.

Service lines were also mapped out. These maps revealed opportunities and the teams worked on ideas for improvements both in the new build and in the existing hospital.

The first workshop was focused on the third floor in the new building with Operation Room, Intensive Care Unit, and Cardiac Catheterisation Laboratory. The workshop team rearranged the layout of the floor to reflect the flow of patients, separating acute and elective patient flow.

On the last day, each group or team presented their results in the hospital auditorium. These presentations gave other staff members ideas for improvement and generated substantial energy within the hospital. Ideas and solutions from these workshops have been a vital input for the design of the treatment centre and central laboratory and are also opportunities for improvement in our work today.

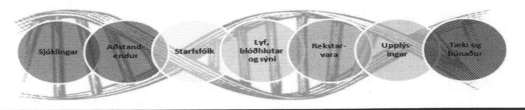

Figure 8.5   The seven flows of medicine.

The events also produced benefits to clinical care. One example of an improvement idea from one of the first 3P workshops was when the staff saw that preparation in the Operation Room for hip and knee replacement was longer than the surgery time. There are long waiting lists for hip and knee replacement and only three procedures could be performed each day. A multidisciplinary and cross-functional team used Lean methodology to change this process so that now they can now undertake four hip or knee replacement procedures each day, an increase of a third.

Rapid Process Improvement Workshop on a Medication Process

The Rapid Process Improvement Workshop (RPIW), sometimes known as a Rapid Process Improvement Event, is another method that Landspítali has incorporated into its quality improvement activities. An RPIW is a three- to five-day-long workshop with a focus on a particular process. In the workshop, the people who do the work are empowered to eliminate waste and reduce the burden of work. The workshop is designed around the Plan-Do-Study-Act method. Another Rapid Process Improvement Event is described in detail in Chapter 6.

One example focused on the medication preparation and administration process on one ward at Landspítali. This also linked to the services' efforts to include support services in quality improvement work. A multidisciplinary team from the ward, the pharmacy, IT department, and Kaizen Promotion Office worked on this process for a week.

The following week, a new process was tried out. One-piece-flow to avoid batching was implemented with nurses preparing and delivering medicines at the patients' bedside and verifying patients' identification with scanning. Implementing this new way of working took many slight changes in medication preparation from the pharmacy and in the ward. Patient safety was utmost in all the participants' minds and the integrated working along the medication value stream was an essential component of the work. The new processes reduced delays and increased safety.

Landspítali's Tips for Success are summarised.

BOX 8.1   LANDSPÍTALI'S TIPS FOR SUCCESS

In our experience key components for successful implementation of the Lean methodology include:

■ Dedicated support and active participation from the chief executive and executive directors.
■ Building a strong central KPO that supports training and guiding key projects.
■ Extensive training – 'Lean journey is a learning journey'.
■ Careful selection of the first projects. They must deliver positive results (early, easy wins).
■ Don't go too fast too soon. Building an improvement culture takes time.
■ Present and spread reliable results.
■ Celebrate success.

Conclusion

Implementation of Lean methodology in Landspítali has been a challenging but rewarding journey. The service has accomplished much in the last decade, but there is no shortage of future work. From finance to facilities to clinical care, there are endless improvement opportunities in healthcare. Our recent work on the communication compact and on public communication demonstrates our learning that we also need a commitment to change the culture in our organisation.

Our improvement training is a vital part of changing the culture and enhancing improvements in our daily work at the hospital. Our communication compact was a milestone that changed our culture, with executives leading the work on the compact. Landspítali is a large organisation, and our Lean approach has not permeated all of it yet.

The support from the chief executive and the executive board of the hospital has been critical to making implementing lean a success. Work is ongoing to continue to embed new principles for this cultural change to survive. Embracing a belief in continuous quality improvement while focusing on respect for people and improving communication with staff and public are our key concepts and commitments. Our mantra is to improve quality and reduce waste, day in and day out. Through this methodology, we hope to continue our improvement and make our services safer and more pleasant for our patients and staff.

Learning Points

- Context and history are important. Few organisations begin a new quality improvement approach with a clean sheet: there are usually previous quality improvement initiatives and pressures on its implementation that must be considered.
- Engaging staff from the beginning is essential. Early successes that can be celebrated and shared are valuable in encouraging support.
- Events and projects are important and can deliver value for patients and staff. To move beyond projects, a Lean approach must be embedded in the organisation and aligned to strategic priorities.
- Senior leadership engagement helps to signal commitment. Leaders should be supported to be able to coach quality improvement on their time on the gemba.
- Daily management is an effective way of promoting organisational alignment and spreading ideas of standard work. It also shares experience of visual controls and helps to identify areas for improvement.
- Training in Lean ideas should not be confined to a narrow group. Wide appreciation of the approach and of the reasons for it is essential.
- External coaches are especially useful in supporting early development. They also have a longer-term role in supporting maintenance over time and sharing current ideas.
- At Landspítali, the development of an infrastructure was unbelievably valuable including a Kaizen Promotion Office and a communications team.
- If you commit to a new improvement method, be prepared to stick with it to obtain maximum gains for your staff, patients, and organisation.

Acknowledgements

Oscar Boldt Christmas from McKinsey.
Chris Backous from Virginia Mason.

Bibliography

Gil-Alana, L. A., & Huijbens, E. H. (2018). Tourism in Iceland: Persistence and seasonality. *Annals of Tourism Research*, *68*, 20–29. https://doi.org/10.1016/j.annals.2017.11.002

Japan Management Association. (1989). *Kanban: Just In Time at Toyota* (Revised ed.). Productivity Press.

Kenney, C. (2011). *Transforming Health Care: Virginia Mason Medical Centre's Pursuit of the Perfect Patient Experience*. Productivity Press.

Landspítali. (n.d.). *Landspítali- The National University Hospital of Iceland*. Landspítali. Retrieved 17 Feb 2022 from https://www.landspitali.is/um-landspitala/languages/landspitali-the-national-university-hospital-of-iceland/

Landspítali Hospital. (2019). *Communication Compact*. L. Hospital. https://www.landspitali.is/library/Sameiginlegar-skrar/Gagnasafn/Um-Landspitala/English/Samskiptas%c3%a1ttm%c3%a1li_B%c3%a6klingur_A5_Enska.pdf

Mann, D. (2015). *Creating a Lean Culture: Tools to Sustain Lean Conversions*. CRC Press.

Purssell, E., Drey, N., Chudleigh, J., Creedon, S., & Gould, D. J. (2020). The Hawthorne effect on adherence to hand hygiene in patient care. *Journal of Hospital Infection*, *106*(2), 311–317. https://doi.org/10.1016/j.jhin.2020.07.028

Sigurgeirsdóttir, S., Waagfjörð, J., & Maresso, A. (2014). *Iceland: Health System Review (Health Systems in Transition, Issue 16(6):1–182)*. World Health Organisation. https://www.euro.who.int/__data/assets/pdf_file/0018/271017/Iceland-HiT-web.pdf

Stark, C., & Hookway, G. (2019). *Applying Lean in Health and Social Care Services*. Routledge.

Toussaint, J., & Adams, E. (2015). *Management on the Mend*. ThedaCare Center for Healthcare Value.

Páll Matthíasson, MD, PhD, MRCPsych, FRCP, FRCPEdin, is a consultant psychiatrist, and immediate past chief executive of LandspítalI – The National University Hospital of Iceland. Matthiasson currently leads work for the Icelandic government on a 2030 strategy and action plan in mental health. Following graduation in medicine from the University of Iceland, he trained in psychiatry at Bethlem and Maudsley Hospitals and completed a PhD in Neuropsychopharmacology at the Institute of Psychiatry. He worked as a consultant psychiatrist and quality lead within the NHS and independent hospitals in London before taking up the post of clinical director and then executive director for mental health in Iceland. From 2013 to 2021, Marthiasson was chief executive of Landspítali The National University Hospital of Iceland, a 700-bed, 6,000-staff hospital. Throughout his time as chief executive, he brought the health service on a quality and improvement drive, to reduce harm and improve outcomes. He has been an honorary senior lecturer at the University of Iceland and has in recent years a particular research interest in the user/patient experience and equal access.

Benedikt Olgeirsson is an engineer from the University of Iceland with a MA in Construction Engineering and Project Management from the University of Washington at Seattle. Benedikt has worked in several industries such as construction, transportation, logistics, and investments. He was the deputy chief executive of Landspítali from 2010 to 2015 and then the executive director of development until 2021. He currently works as a consultant and is the chairman of Vordur Insurance. In all of his management positions, Benedikt has focused on building a clear strategy for the organisation with a strong emphasis on continuous improvement.

Gudrun Björg Sigurbjörnsdottir is a registered midwife, with a BSc in Nursing from the University of Iceland, and an MPH from the Nordic School of Public Health. Gudrun has worked at Landspitali – the University Hospital of Iceland for a long time, first as a midwife in the labor ward and ultrasound clinic, later as a manager and director in the Women's and Children's clinic and in the economic department of the hospital. She has been a manager for the Project Office or KPO (Kaizen Promotion Office) of Landspítali since 2009. As a manager of the KPO, Gudrun has been leading the implementation of Lean in the hospital and the improvement school. The focus has been on quality, patient safety, and the participation of patients in continuous improvements in the hospital.

Chapter 9

Improving Learning Disabilities Services with Lean Design: A Case Application of the 3P Method

Iain Smith and Steven Bartley

Contents

DOI: 10.4324/9780429346958-9

Aims

■ To describe the role and purpose of the production preparation process (3P).
■ To explain the steps of 3P using a case example from National Health Service (NHS) England.
■ To demonstrate how 3P links product and design process.
■ To identify the value of co-production and collaboration between facilitators, architects, building specialists, service users, and clinical staff.

Introduction

The chapter presents a case study of a Lean design process known as the 'Production Preparation Process' (3P). The 3P method is a cross-functional, participatory workshop-based approach to Lean design (Coletta, 2012; Smith et al., 2020). It condenses the elements of Lean's approach to product design into an intense workshop-based format that encourages innovation and collaboration with key stakeholders in a framework linking product and process design (Black & Miller, 2008; Coletta, 2012; Smith et al., 2020).

Typically, a 3P workshop is a "five-day event in which a team focuses on building a production system for a new facility, product or process" (Plsek, 2014). It differs from the more well-known Lean rapid process improvement workshop (RPIW). Whereas RPIWs focus on incremental improvement to existing processes, 3P workshops focus on breakthrough improvement through innovative design (Smith et al., 2020). The 3P Lean design process encourages collaboration between key stakeholders early in the design process. As it is used during the conceptual design stage, it can impact committed costs and the overall performance of the solution (Hicks et al., 2015). It utilises the Lean principles (Womack & Jones, 1996) of understanding user value, mapping value-streams, creating flow, developing pull processes and continuous improvement to help maximise quality, minimise costs and avoid future problems (Black & Miller, 2008; Coletta, 2012; Smith et al., 2020).

3P was first adapted for use in healthcare by Virginia Mason Medical Center (VMMC) (Black & Miller, 2008; Kenney, 2011; Miller, 2005). Based in Seattle, USA, VMMC is an integrated medical centre that has adopted Lean as its management method to dramatically improve the quality and safety of the healthcare services they provide. In 2006, the NHS in North East England established a learning partnership to transfer knowledge from VMMC. Training in VMMC's Lean improvement methods began for northeast NHS organisations in 2007 (Erskine et al., 2009; Hunter et al., 2008). The case study presented in this chapter describes an early example of the northeast NHS's experience of applying 3P to design healthcare facilities and services.

The case describes how 3P engaged multiple stakeholders in the co-design of a new assessment and treatment unit for adults with learning disabilities. The work took place between 2010 and 2012 and was chosen for several reasons. Firstly, the case represents what the authors believe to be the first application of VMMC's adaption of Lean 3P to healthcare facilities in the UK's NHS. Second, service user involvement in healthcare often involves only a narrow group of individuals. Minority groups, including those with mental health or learning disabilities, tend to be excluded even though they may have greater health needs (Ocloo & Matthews, 2016). Health services have been criticised for not considering how to include such minority groups in more democratic relationships that help develop models of healthcare that are more co-designed by all stakeholders. Evaluating methods of involvement that can move beyond narrow, tokenistic approaches is required (Ocloo & Matthews, 2016). The case example illustrates the potential for participative, co-design methods in mental health and learning disabilities service contexts. Finally, although the initial design work took place a decade ago, the lessons learned remain relevant to current policy which promotes the need for improved services for people with a learning disability, autism, or both to support them to live happier, healthier, longer lives (NHS England, 2019).

Case Example

Background

There was an identified need for an assessment and treatment unit for adults with learning disabilities that would improve their service provision. The facility, delivered through a capital development scheme, was to provide a purpose-built, state-of-the-art inpatient facility aiming to provide community-based treatment services with a strong community focus.

The project was undertaken by a large foundation trust in North East England providing mental health, learning disability and eating disorders services. The trust employs over 6,500 staff and has an annual income of over £300 million. It serves a population of around two million people across three localities. The trust provides a range of adult mental health services; older people's services; children and young people's services; adult learning disabilities and forensic mental health and learning disabilities services.

The original facility opened in 1984 comprising three departments, two residential units and a short-term care unit. In 1993, the facility was modified. Service users of one of the residential units moved to other community provisions freeing up space. This space was utilised to provide local inpatient assessment and treatment services for adults with learning disabilities who previously would have had to travel out of the area. The facility's first inpatient assessment and treatment unit opened in 1994 with a second unit following in 1996. Three years later in 1999, a further development took place with the opening of 'The Lodge' – a rehabilitation unit to assist with client discharge to community provision.

In 2010, the facility required updating and redesign. It was poorly laid out and assessment units were deemed to be out of date and no longer appropriate to meet clients' needs. There was a lack of therapeutic spaces and interview rooms. There were also no quiet rooms for clients and no ensuite bathroom facilities. Although the existing facility offered individual bedrooms, bathroom and toilet facilities were communal. Furthermore, the existing facility lacked activity space for clients, and this had been identified by staff as a needed development.

An outline business case had been prepared for re-providing the services in a new, purpose-built facility. The trust held discussions with its local commissioning group about the plan which proposed to replace and recommission the assessment and treatment units as well as the rehabilitation unit. With the support of the commissioning group, the trust proceeded to prepare a full business case which required architectural plans and costings. Clearly, agreeing with the architects, a design brief that would meet the needs of clients and staff was important. With the support of the trust's finance director, it was agreed that the 3P method would be used to achieve this.

Design Space

Space was made available on the existing site for a new build. An old management suite was due to be demolished and it was agreed that the space made available would be used for the proposed

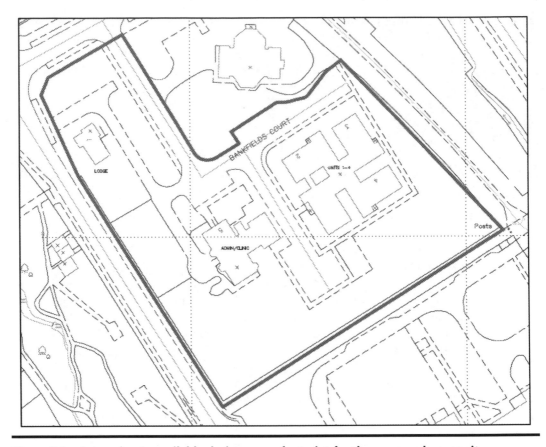

Figure 9.1   Approximate available design space footprint for the proposed new unit.

unit. The available space within which to design the new unit was approximately rectangular as shown by the dashed black line in Figure 9.1.

As the new unit was to be built on the existing site, there was an element of demolition and associated decanting of services and staff. Management was decanted first followed by clinical and therapies.

Experience of Lean

At the time of the 3P workshop, believed to be the first of its kind in the UK, the trust was three years into its Lean journey with VMMC. The trust had established a Kaizen Promotion Office (KPO) charged with training and coaching staff in the application of Lean improvement methods and coordinating activities across the organisation. Thirty-three rapid improvement workshop leaders had been trained and certified (mostly directors, the KPO team and some senior managers) and approximately 300 trust staff had taken part in RPIW activities.

From the unit being designed, none of the staff (clinical or administrative) had yet received any training in Lean. Therefore, for the team selected to attend the 3P event, the approach and methodology were new, and for most, it was their first exposure to a Lean workshop.

The Head of KPO, who led the 3P workshop, had not received formal training in the 3P method from Virginia Mason; however, they had been introduced to some of the core concepts (such as rapid prototyping) on a visit to VMMC in Seattle. The Head of KPO had also undertaken a learning visit with VMMC to Japan and participated in 3P activities facilitated by Shingijutsu consultants in production plants visited on the tour. VMMC had shared a '3P manual' which provided a guide to the structure and tools of the method (Black, 2002).

> It was an experiment. It had never been used before … it was way out of the box for us as facilitator.

> **(Head of KPO)**

Intervention (Lean 3P)

The design process comprised three phases centred around a time-out participative design workshop (Smith, 2016a, b). The first phase focused on scoping the problem, setting the workshop aims and planning the workshop logistics. The second phase was the design workshop which brought together stakeholders to create design options applying the Lean principles of value, value-streams, flow, pull and perfection (Smith, 2016a). In the third phase, the outputs from the design workshop were translated into operational plans (Kenney, 2011; Smith, 2016a, b).

Scoping and Planning

The 3P event began with a scoping, planning and information gathering phase. This was used to understand the situation in the current unit in detail and to measure the 'as is' state before attempting to design a future state. The trust's KPO team coordinated and carried out data collection including:

- Demand data to predict how many patients would use the new unit and implications for diagnostic and care provision for the client group.
- Value-added and non-value-added process time data collected manually via observation in the unit.
- Visual data of the current condition via photographs of the existing unit.
- Interviews with staff to secure their views on the current condition and opportunities for improvement.
- Best practice guidance for provision of learning disabilities services.

Throughout the scoping and planning phase, regular meetings were held to share data with staff and to plan for the time-out design workshop. Planning meetings were attended by the director and the team leaders (who would be the managers of the unit) as well as the KPO team members who would lead the 3P workshop. The Trust board member (executive director), acting as senior sponsor for the event, also participated.

Time-Out Design Workshop

The 3P design workshop took place over five consecutive days and was attended by 25 participants. Participants represented a multi-disciplinary team comprised of the unit's consultants, qualified staff health care assistants and allied professionals. The event was also attended by the trust's estates and capital developments team and, crucially, service users and their carers who all acted as part of the design team.

Orientation of delegates – Before undertaking introductory training in Lean techniques, workshop participants were first briefed on the 3P approach. This included an overview of what 3P was, its origins in Lean automotive production and how it had been used to design clinical facilities by VMMC. Ground rules for creativity and innovation were discussed and agreed with participants using standard 'participant contracts' based on the 3P practices of VMMC and Shingijutsu consultants (from whom VMMC had learned the method). Ground rules included, for example, commitments such as:

■ I will not judge (good or bad) another person's idea.
■ I will make every effort to overcome the hurdles in my own thinking to generate useful ideas.
■ I will not think in limited ways but will make every effort to look at the problem from many angles.
■ I will make every effort to express my ideas openly.

Delegates were then engaged in training activities in Lean. A series of presentations giving an overview of core Lean concepts were shared by the KPO staff leading the workshop. The presentations covered topics and tools that would be used in the workshop including: an introduction to Lean; value and waste; flow; error proofing; visual management and workplace organisation and layout.

Before starting to develop designs, delegates were briefed on the functional requirements of the new unit and engaged in developing criteria and attributes against which emerging designs would be evaluated. Functional requirements included the number of single-person bedrooms (five), single-person flats (three) as well as the clinical and communal spaces required to provide the service. Ideally, functional requirements would be satisfied in a flexible way to accommodate variety in client mix (such as intensive clients, clients with autism and client rehabilitation). To help shape the vision of the new unit, participants (staff and service users) were asked what they would value and want from it (Table 9.1).

Building on the feedback, participants were facilitated to develop criteria and attributes against which the appropriateness of proposed designs would be assessed. The group specified what the future facility should possess in terms of design principles, standards, qualities, features and characteristics to deliver against their vision and requirements. These criteria and attributes were subsequently used by the workshop participants to iteratively assess and score successive designs.

[The attributes and criteria] were essentially the group's statements of truth.

(Head of KPO)

Table 9.1 Summary of Staff and Service User Feedback on What They Wanted from the Design

Staff		Service Users/Clients	
• Workable	• Appropriate	• Personal	• Pleasant
• Comfortable	• Contemporary	• Feel safe	• Tidy
• Innovation	• Multi-functional	• Equal	• Caring
• Practical	• Effectiveness	• Friendly	• Homely
• Modern	• Usable	• Clean	• Comfortable
• Flexibility	• Spacious		

Design cycle 1 – In the first cycle of design, the workshop delegates were split into smaller groups of three to four (seven groups in total) and asked to start thinking about the new unit, what it would be like and how it would be laid out. This involved multiple design concepts being produced using a tool that was new to the trust – the 'seven designs' tool. This tool involved participants creating pictorial representations of their envisioned designs rather than textual narratives. As the name suggests, participants were encouraged to each produce seven (or more) alternative designs. This acted as a means of pushing participants' thinking out of the box and generating ideas beyond the expected norm. The tactile, visual nature of the seven designs tool particularly resonated with service users and facilitated participants to develop almost one hundred visual graphics (Figure 9.2).

At this stage, each of the small groups shared with the wider team their ideas and design concepts they had generated. The numerous ideas facilitated discussion between participants which was encouraged before assessing the ideas using the agreed criteria and attributes. Assessment was undertaken via a nominal group voting process (Smith, 2016a, b). Each group scored each other group's designs against the criteria and attributes. Participants voted using a pro-forma criteria and attributes template. Group scores were determined by taking the mode of participant scores and calculating an average (weighted to account for the number of group members). This provided both a quantitative, democratic decision-making process as well as qualitative feedback to groups on the strengths and areas for improvement of their design concepts. Based on the feedback, the number of design concepts to take forward was reduced.

Design cycle 2 – In this cycle, to develop the preferred design concepts, participants were re-formed into three groups. The new group composition aimed to ensure that good ideas from lower-rated overall design concepts were not lost and could be carried forward and incorporated to further improve higher-rated designs. Each team developed their designs and incorporated features and ideas from their earlier discussions. Additional materials were introduced in this cycle of design. This included cardboard cutouts and paper, used to create more detailed 2D designs, and plastic building bricks, used to create 3D representations of design options (Figure 9.3).

Teams started to discuss early ideas on how they envisaged the pathway working and how service users and staff would move, or flow, through the new unit. One key concept that emerged was that of 'zoning'. The zoning concept aimed to improve the delivery and experience of care by limiting interruptions in the client care area. To achieve this, the concept proposed separate zones for client care (such as therapy) and support activities (such as administration). The zoning concept

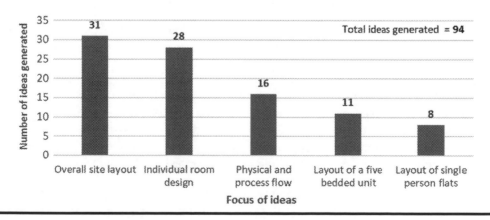

Figure 9.2　Number and focus of initial 2D design ideas.

Example of Group working on Flat design	Example of Flat design
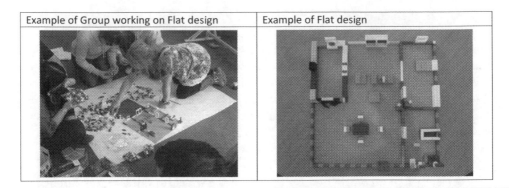	

Figure 9.3 Example of group working on initial 3D detailed designs.

Example of Group 1's Single Person Flat design	Example of Group 2's Five Bed Unit design
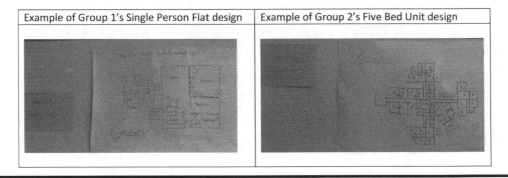	

Figure 9.4 Examples of detailed 2D layout designs.

was therefore influential on both the facilities' layout designs produced and the envisioned flows of patients, staff, equipment and supplies required to make the layout designs work effectively.

> [W]e wanted to keep the care zone separate from all of the support activities, all of the things that would interrupt people's therapeutic environment.

(Service Manager)

The design cycle concluded with another round of presenting designs to the wider group and assessment against criteria via nominal group voting. Two preferred designs were selected to take forward and further develop.

Design cycle 3 – Participants were again re-formed, this time into two groups to further develop the front-running designs. The teams developed their designs adding further detail to the overall facility layout as well as its constituent components. Teams added greater detail to the design of functional requirements such as the five-bedded unit and single-person bedrooms, the single-person rehabilitation flats, communal spaces and staff/management areas. Teams also paid attention to the service user and staff flows that would contribute to the effective and efficient operation of the overall facility (Figure 9.4).

Designs were again presented to, and discussed by, the wider group before undertaking a final round of assessment and nominal group voting. This identified a preferred overall design concept and layout to be taken forward for refinement.

Design cycle 4 – To size key design features, participants used a large, exterior lawn area at the design workshop venue. Full-scale layouts of the single-bedded units and the single-person rehabilitation flats were constructed. The layouts helped staff to identify that the sizing they had initially proposed was inappropriate and that adjustments were required.

> We drafted out actual sizes on the lawn. This allowed staff to see that the sizes they were initially thinking of were not appropriate.
>
> **(Head of KPO)**

In addition to room size appropriateness, the full-scale layouts helped resolve differences of opinion over design concepts such as individual ensuite vs communal bathroom facilities. Participants were facilitated to lay out both alternatives and vote on their preferred layout by standing within it. This voting process highlighted a clear separation between management, who preferred the communal bathroom design, and the staff and service users, who preferred the ensuite design. However, it also illustrated the participative and democratic power of the 3P approach as management who were clearly, and visibly, in the minority accepted the group decision (Figure 9.5).

> You become accustomed, through 3P, in being part of a wider group – and even though you may have a strong view, if you're in the minority I think you have to go along with … the majority decision … otherwise the system wouldn't really work.
>
> **(Service Manager)**

Design cycle 5 – In the final design cycle, participants worked on developing final 3D detailed models of the preferred facility design. What was learned from previous cycles was incorporated to refine and develop the design, particularly sizing and detailed room layouts from the full-scale mock-ups (Figure 9.6).

Following completion of the final design models (Figure 9.6) the participants then worked on preparing a final report-out presentation. The presentation followed a standard format that the trust was familiar with and typically used to conclude RPIWs. The report-out presentation was led by the workshop facilitators and included contributions from all participants. Participants reported out to their wider team of colleagues and the senior sponsor for the 3P design workshop.

| Example of a full-scale single bedroom layout | Example of democratic decision making |

Figure 9.5 Example of full-scale layout designs.

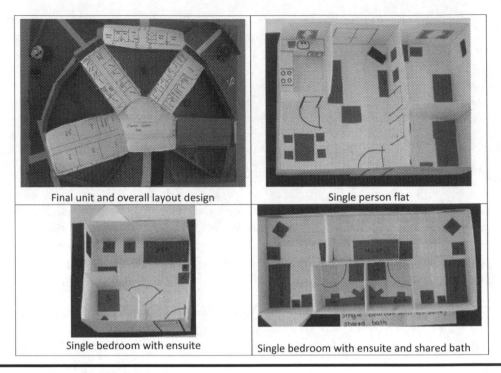

Final unit and overall layout design	Single person flat
Single bedroom with ensuite	Single bedroom with ensuite and shared bath

Figure 9.6   Final 3D detailed facility design.

Follow-Up

Following the 3P workshop, the proposed design was presented to the architects appointed to prepare the plans for the build. The challenge was to achieve an architectural plan that accurately reflected the design created by the team during the event. In the meeting, the architects fed back their initial impression that the design the 3P participants had produced was a 'buildable' scheme. Architectural layout drawings for the new facility were developed and reflected very closely the final model constructed in the workshop. This demonstrated that the final design proposed by the 3P team could be developed as a workable architectural plan (Figure 9.7).

A project group was established and tasked with carrying the capital project through to completion. It included members who had participated in the 3P workshop who knew the details of the proposed design and could act as champions for its realisation.

The initial draft of the architectural drawing was examined in detail by the project group to verify that patient and staff flows would be able to operate as intended in the 3P design. The project group identified a problem relating to the absence of a separate staff entrance. To deliver a workable architectural blueprint, the staff entrance had been omitted. However, this created a constraint to staff flow through the central management hub thus limiting the practicality of the proposed zoning approach. By identifying this in the final stage of design, it was possible to amend the plans to include additional doors opening into a planned central courtyard to achieve the desired flow.

The project group also worked with the architects on softer aspects of the design including colour schemes and décor.

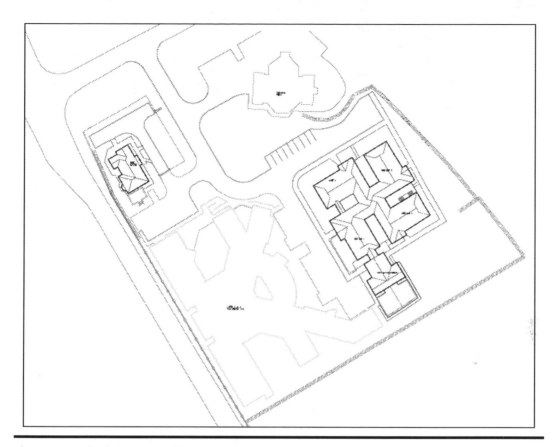

Figure 9.7   Final design (architect's drawing).

> We worked with the architect around a number of different colour schemes and then
> we involved people in choosing which they thought was best.

(Service Manager)

In addition to achieving homely environments for clients, colour schemes were also used to support the zoning concept. For example, the colour scheme helped to differentiate the communal and 'care zone' spaces from administrative 'support zone' as well as personal private spaces. Different coloured doors were also used to differentiate between client and staff-only access. Staff-only doors used neutral colours that blended with the walls whereas client access doors used more prominent colours – though all colours were fairly subtle to minimise risk of sensory overload for clients (Brand, 2010).

Outcomes

The design outcomes from the Lean 3P project were a proposed servicescape for an assessment and treatment unit for adults with learning disabilities that informed the architect's project brief. Architects subsequently developed the 3P design into a workable architectural plan which informed the business case for the new unit. Following business case approval, the design for the new unit progressed to construction.

Proposed Servicescape

The servicescape designed in the 3P workshop refers to the role played in the service user's overall experience by the physical environment in which services are delivered (Bitner, 1992). Staff and clients were involved in designing the servicescape which comprised not only layout and flows but also décor and ambient conditions, such as heat and light.

Space, layout and flow – The Lean 3P design workshop facilitated participants to develop a layout and flow for a learning disabilities assessment and treatment unit. The service system adopted was also highly innovative, based on a 'zoning' concept and using a 'hub and spoke' design. The administrative 'support zone' or 'hub' acted as a control centre for staff, but with only minimal staff congregation space. This design concept aimed to maximise staff time in the clinical 'care zone' areas (the 'spokes'). By the end of the 3P design workshop, participants had achieved their aims and developed a workable layout plan and pathway within the available space.

Ambient conditions – This refers to lighting, temperature, sound, air quality and odour (Bitner, 1992). Ambient conditions are important considerations for clients with learning disabilities and/or autism where appropriate lighting, acoustics and ventilation can help minimise sensory overload (Brand, 2010). Furthermore, in this case, maintaining a home within the community and proactive encouragement of independence and recovery had been highlighted as important. The adoption of the single bedrooms with ensuite design provided greater overall privacy and dignity for patients as well as control of their personal space.

Signs, symbols and artefacts – This refers to signage, wayfinding, personal artefacts and style of décor (Bitner, 1992; Sahoo & Ghosh, 2016). For clients with learning disabilities and/or autism, colour schemes and private spaces that can be personalised have been identified as important considerations to help reduce triggers that may cause agitation (Brand, 2010). Colour schemes were used to help differentiate communal, therapeutic, personal and administrative spaces. Colour was also used to facilitate wayfinding by distinguishing client access from staff-only access doorways.

Project Brief

The project brief captures the requirements and needs of the client and end users. It collates information expressing the goal of the design and users' requirements that set the parameters for professional designers (Elf et al., 2011, 2012). In this case, the design parameters and user requirements were surfaced through the 3P workshop and captured in the artefacts produced. The final design was developed as a detailed 3D scale model (Figure 9.6) which informed the project brief for development into architectural blueprints (Figure 9.7).

Construction and Post-Build

The new unit commenced building in 2010. Following completion of the build, but prior to occupancy, a rapid process improvement workshop was run focusing on the operational working of the unit. This RPIW engaged the unit's Service Manager and staff in designing and specifying new, detailed standard work processes for the unit. The team also created standards and processes for

Figure 9.8 Exterior of new facility.

maintaining organisation of the workplace and the visual management of operational tasks. In the spring of 2012, the new unit was occupied and the vision of the staff, clients and carers who had contributed to the 3P workshop was realised (Figure 9.8).

> The flats and two assessment units were built very close to the design the staff came up with and this really gave the staff the ownership that what they now had was what their design looked like in the 3P event.

> **(Head of KPO)**

Upon occupancy, the same clients moved into the new building as had been receiving care in the previous facility. The Service Manager reported noticing a reduction in episodes of disturbance.

> [W]hen we moved into th[e] building, there was an initial decrease in the number of untoward incidents that we had and episodes of disturbed behaviour.

> **(Service Manager)**

Whilst the evidence is anecdotal, and acknowledging that incidents can be dependent upon the admission pattern and reason for admission, the unit's Service Manager took this as a potential early sign of improved client experience.

Following completion of the project to redevelop and modernise the unit's inpatient facilities for clients with learning disabilities, a further phase of redevelopment was undertaken focusing on new short-term care facilities. The 3P method was again deployed to produce a design brief for a new building to include an eight-bedded short-term care unit and several flats to support the individual care of clients with autism. The business case for this second phase of development was completed in late 2012 with the new facilities opening to clients in 2014.

At the time of writing, the latest inspection report from the Care Quality Commission (published 8 January 2014) found that the facilities met the required standards relating to safe and appropriate care and protection from abuse.

Lessons Learned

Learning can be extracted from the case in terms of the Lean principles and how they were applied in the 3P workshop. How each of the Lean principles was manifested in the case is described below. Also described is how the 3P workshop facilitated application of the Lean principles through its participative approach and use of prototyping and pathway modelling.

Lean Principles

Value – The 3P workshop provided a forum for discussion and debate between stakeholders which facilitated communication of their experiences and requirements. The 3P workshop helped participants to share their various value perspectives and balanced clinical and operational views with the experiential preferences of patients.

> It was critical to hear their [service users] opinions so we ensured we engaged with them as much as we could and utilised the opinions of their carers fully.

(Head of KPO)

Value streams – The process facilitated stakeholders working in cross-functional teams to make their ideas tangible to communicate, test and develop a layout and pathway (value stream) for an assessment and treatment unit for adults with learning disabilities. Scale model prototypes of the unit provided a platform for participants to communicate and test pathway assumptions.

Flow – Service user, staff and support service flows were considered by participants to describe the pathway.

> Mocking up a room or interior space and allowing the group to investigate the interrelationships between people, functions and understand how the designed space flowed was fantastic.

(Head of Capital Design)

Thinking about staff and client flow helped participants to realise their 'zoning' by developing practical routines for the flow of staff between the administrative and care zones.

Pull – The Lean concept of pull is typically described in terms of manufacturing logistics (Bicheno, 2004). In this case, visual management and workplace organisation introduced participants to the concept of using visual cues (5S) to manage equipment and supplies. Using simple Kanban cards and tactics, participants worked on systems to pull equipment and supplies as needed to ensure there was always sufficient on hand. A further innovative take on the pull concept was to ensure the maximum availability of staff and contact time with clients and service users. Clients can 'pull' help as needed due to the accessibility of staff in the 'care zone'. The focus on improving the service user experience led to a more health-care service-oriented implementation of pull (Westwood et al., 2007). The 3P workshop helped participants to create a pathway (value stream) that directed service flows towards the clients.

Perfection – Participants were facilitated to pursue perfection through multiple cycles of design. Each cycle provided stimulus for debate and exchange of information within and between multi-disciplinary teams. This allowed participants to refine their designs and add increasing levels of detail over the course of the workshop. The 3P approach helped participants to develop and iteratively improve their service model and facility layout trying to deliver the highest possible client experience and best practice care.

Participation

Arnstein described participation as escalating rungs on a ladder (Arnstein, 1969). The lower rungs are characterised by non-participation. The centre rungs are formed of various degrees of tokenism, such as informing and consultation. The upper rungs represent various degrees of power such as partnership working and delegated authority in which participants are responsible for decision making.

The Lean 3P design workshop was characterised by high levels of participation. The workshop comprised 25 delegates from various clinical, managerial and corporate roles as well as service user representatives. Participants worked together in multi-disciplinary teams to co-design concepts for the new facility which were informed by their various experiences and perspectives.

> By using the [3P] approach we not only designed a unit but also, through engaging staff in the design of the unit, undertook staff consultation too.
>
> **(Head of KPO)**

However, the participation went further than mere consultation. The workshop participants had an influential role in the design process that differed from the usual designer-led approach.

> As an approach 3P was different due to the fact that rather than using architects and presenting a design to staff … it was clearly the staff who were doing the design and then giving it back to the architects.
>
> **(Head of KPO)**

Furthermore, the workshop included service user representatives and their carers. Such voices are often either excluded from design processes, or included in only narrow or tokenistic ways, particularly those with mental health or learning disabilities (Ocloo & Matthews, 2016). The case presented here illustrates that such minority groups can be involved in more democratic relationships to co-design healthcare services with other stakeholders.

Prototyping

Prototyping is a key tool of design. Through prototyping, ideas can be brought to life and made tangible before they are built (Sanders, 2013). The goal is to help participants learn about the various strengths and weaknesses of ideas. Developing prototype models of various scales and levels of fidelity made design concepts tangible and helped both staff and patients to visualise and understand proposals.

> A key moment was the mocking up of a room on 1:1 scale and seeing staff, service users and carers doing a dry run of using the space as intended.
>
> **(Head of Capital Design)**

Building prototype models facilitated communication between participants of different disciplines. The models, and full-scale mock-ups, helped create a shared understanding of proposed designs and stimulated debate about how to improve and proceed towards a preferred outcome.

Pathway Modelling

Prototype models also facilitated participants to develop and model pathway options. This involved virtual walk-throughs being presented on the proposed pathways of model and design. The approach made clear the intended process and flow routes which could be tested against clinical, operational and regulatory requirements as well as compatibility with service user preferences.

Summary and Implications

Applying the Lean principles using the 3P method helped stakeholders to create an innovative design to meet healthcare staff and service user requirements. The 3P workshop used an iterative approach to apply the Lean principles to: consider value to clients and carers; develop a care pathway (value stream) for clients; consider and model the flows of people, equipment and supplies that interacted in the pathway; use pull as a concept to draw care towards clients through the concept of a 'care zone' and pursue perfection through repeated cycles of design that built and improved upon the best features and ideas from earlier cycles.

The case provides a practical example of stakeholders applying the Lean principles to a learning disabilities context. After completion of the case build, NHS England, together with the Local Government Association and Directors of Adult Social Services, established a vision and national plan to "ensure that all people with a learning disability, autism, or both can live happier, healthier, longer lives" (NHS England, 2019). For people with a learning disability and/or autism, the vision reaffirms their right "to the same opportunities as anyone else to live satisfying and valued lives, and to be treated with dignity and respect" (NHS England, 2015, p. 4). To be able to develop and maintain relationships, and get the support they need to live healthy, rewarding lives, the vision identifies that "[people] with a learning disability and/or autism … should have a home within their community" (NHS England, 2015, p. 4).

The national plan and service model recognises that, in times of crises or potential crises, inpatient accommodation is needed to provide a place people can go. This can be to prevent avoidable admission to hospital settings or to be admitted for assessment and treatment. Furthermore, people presenting an immediate risk to themselves, or others, may require admission for assessment or treatment that cannot be provided safely and effectively in the community. However, services should always focus on proactive encouragement of independence and recovery and minimising lengths of stay (NHS England, 2015). Therefore, the case remains relevant and demonstrates the potential applicability of the Lean 3P approach to design healthcare services in line with policy requirements.

In addition to recording what is believed to be the first event of its kind in the NHS in the UK, the authors hope that the case provides useful learning of benefit to healthcare managers and staff.

Learning Points

- The production preparation process (3P) links service requirements and design to a final product by applying Lean principles.
- It is a collaborative process which engages service users, clinical and non-clinical staff and design and construction teams.
- Visual design tools promote untrammelled thinking and support teamwork.
- Key techniques include participation, pathway modelling and prototyping.
- The organisational context with current investment in Lean, an existing Kaizen Promotion Office (with specialist staff and significant senior engagement from directors and managers), all combined to provide an environment that supported the application of Lean principles at scale.

Acknowledgements

The authors would like to thank Keith Appleby, Paul Foxton and Mark Gray (Tees, Esk and Wear Valleys NHS Foundation Trust) who provided information for the chapter.

Bibliography

Arnstein, A. R. (1969). A ladder of citizen participation. *Journal of the American Institute of Planners, 35*(4), 216–224.

Bicheno, J. (2004). *The New Lean Toolbox: Towards Fast, Flexible Flow* (3rd ed.). PICSIE Books.

Bitner, M. J. (1992). Servicescapes: The impact of physical surroundings on customers and employees. *Journal of Marketing Management, 56*(2), 57–71. https://doi.org/10.2307/1252042

Black, J. (2002). *Production Preparation Process (3P) Doer's Manual.* Shingijutsu America LLC.

Black, J., & Miller, D. (2008). *The Toyota Way to Healthcare Excellence: Improve Efficiency and Improve Quality with Lean.* Health Administration Press.

Brand, A. (2010). *Living in the Community: Housing Design for Adults with Autism.* Royal College of Art.

Coletta, A. R. (2012). *The Lean 3P Advantage: A Practitioner's Guide to the Production Preparation Process.* Productivity Press.

Elf, M., Engström, M. S., & Wijk, H. (2011). Development of the content and quality in briefs instrument (CQB-I). *HERD: Health Environments Research & Design Journal, 5*(3), 74–88.

Elf, M., Svedbo Engström, M., & Wijk, H. (2012). An assessment of briefs used for designing healthcare environments: A survey in Sweden. *Construction Management & Economics, 30*(10), 835–844.

Erskine, J., Hunter, D. J., Hicks, C., McGovern, T., Scott, E., Lugsden, E., Kunonga, E., & Whitty, P. (2009). New development: First steps towards an evaluation of the North East transformation system. *Public Money & Management, 29*(5), 273–276. https://doi.org/10.1080/09540960903205857

Hicks, C., McGovern, T., Prior, G., & Smith, I. (2015). Applying lean principles to the design of healthcare facilities. *International Journal of Production Economics, 170*, 677–686.

Hunter, D. J., Erskine, J., Hicks, C., McGovern, T., Scott, E., Lugsden, E., Kunonga, E., & Whitty, P. (2008). *The North East Transformation System: A Scoping Study of the Background and Initial Step*. Durham University Business School.

Kenney, C. (2011). *Transforming Health Care: Virginia Mason Medical Centre's Pursuit of the Perfect Patient Experience*. Productivity Press.

Miller, D. (2005). *Going Lean in Health Care* (IHI Innovation Series White paper., Issue). Institute of Healthcare Improvement.

NHS England. (2015). *Supporting People with a Learning Disability and/or Autism Who Display Behaviour that Challenges, Including Those with a Mental Health Condition: Service Model for Commissioners of Health and Social Care Services*. NHS England.

NHS England. (2019). *The NHS Long Term Plan*. www.longtermplan.nhs.uk

Ocloo, J., & Matthews, R. (2016). From tokenism to empowerment: progressing patient and public involvement in healthcare improvement. *BMJ Quality and Safety*, *25*(8), 626–632. https://doi.org/10.1136/bmjqs-2015-004839

Plsek, P. (2014). *Accelerating Health Care Transformation with Lean and Innovation: The Virginia Mason Experience*. CRC Press.

Sahoo, D., & Ghosh, T. (2016). Healthscape role towards customer satisfaction in private healthcare. *International Journal of Health Care Quality Assurance*, *29*(6), 600–613. https://doi.org/10.1108/IJHCQA-05-2015-0068

Sanders, E. B. N. (2013). Prototyping for the design spaces of the future. In L. Valentine (Ed.), *Prototype: Design and Craft in the 21st Century* (pp. 59–73). Bloomsbury Publishing.

Smith, I. (2016a). Operationalising the Lean principles in maternity service design using 3P methodology. *BMJ Quality Improvement Reports*, *5*(1), u208920.w205761. https://doi.org/10.1136/bmjquality.u208920.w5761

Smith, I. (2016b). The participative design of an endoscopy facility using lean 3P. *BMJ Quality Improvement Reports*, *5*(1), u208920.w203611. https://doi.org/10.1136/bmjquality.u208920.w3611

Smith, I., Hicks, C., & McGovern, T. (2020). Adapting Lean methods to facilitate stakeholder engagement and co-design in healthcare. *BMJ*, *368*, m35.

Westwood, N., James-Moore, M., & Cooke, M. (2007). *Going Lean in The NHS*. NHS Institute for Innovation and Improvement.

Womack, J. P., & Jones, D. T. (1996). *Lean Thinking: Banish Waste and Create Wealth in Your Corporation*. Simon & Schuster.

Iain Smith, PhD, PGC, BSc, is an Associate Researcher at the Newcastle University Business School. With over 25 years of experience in England's National Health Service, Iain has worked in local, regional, and national roles as a quality improvement leader. He has trained in quality improvement methods with the Institute for Healthcare Improvement and trained as a Lean leader with Virginia Mason Medical Centre. Iain has applied these methods across many sectors of healthcare including in acute hospitals, primary care, and mental health services. As a mathematics graduate, he also holds postgraduate qualifications in innovation and transformational change and a PhD in the application of Lean thinking to design healthcare facilities and service systems.

Steven Bartley is the associate director of Improvement and Design at Tees, Esk and Wear Valleys NHS Foundation Trust (TEWV). Steven has over 25 years of experience in quality improvement, first in the automotive sector and then in the public sector. He has worked across healthcare and Local Authority service provision. He was head of TEWV's External Kaizen Promotion Office, providing training and coaching across many organisations. Steven was the head of quality improvement at TEWV before taking up his current post.

Chapter 10

Co-Producing an Organisation's Quality Improvement Method: No Decision about Me, without Me

Nathan Clifford, Sarah Curtis, and Karl Marlowe

Contents

DOI: 10.4324/9780429346958-10

Aims

- To explain why co-production is core to any Quality Improvement methodology.
- To show the fit with Lean principles.
- To demonstrate how co-production can be achieved.
- To share some of the positive outcomes for an organisation.

Introduction

Southern Health NHS Foundation Trust (SHFT) is part of the National Health Service (NHS) in England. The organisation provides community physical health services, primary care including General Practice, and outpatient and inpatient mental health services across the county of Hampshire. In 2021, its annual budget was £350m, with a workforce of approximately 6,500 staff, comprising 2,250 nurses, 295 doctors, and 1,600 healthcare support workers. Staff serve a population of 1.75 million across 300 different sites and care for 215,013 people annually.

SHFT was regarded as a high-performing organisation before a series of adverse events between 2013 and 2016. The organisation's mental health services were repeatedly criticised by external regulators and by users of services leading to a breakdown in trust and resulting in staff having a lack of pride in their work.

The Trust management realised their approach had to change and early in 2018 decided to develop a Quality Improvement programme. The Trust Board decided to use Lean methodology. This was influenced by a budding arrangement with Cumbria, Northumberland, Tyne & Wear NHS Foundation Trust and the international reputation of Lean in healthcare associated with organisations such as the Virginia Mason Medical Center in the USA. The local work was initially focused on staff engagement at all levels. While patients were invited to participate and share their side of the story, this was a secondary consideration at first.

It was within this context that the journey that led to co-producing our approach to Quality Improvement (QI) got underway.

Setting the Scene for Co-Production

The term co-production refers to a way of working where service providers and users, work together to reach a collective outcome. The approach is value-driven and built on the principle that those who are affected by a service are best placed to help design it.

(Involve, n.d.)

Initial Projects

With the benefit of hindsight, SHFT should have co-produced our approach to QI from the start. Individuals are experts in their own experiences, and this adds narrative to any project. But co-production goes far beyond people sharing their experiences; at its core co-production aims to tap into the diversity of thinking and perspectives.

Patients, carers, and other stakeholders from outside of SHFT came in with a distinct perspective. To be able to challenge, question, and think differently has such strength in the initiation of any QI work. External stakeholders are often in the best position to naturally use the '5 whys' techniques (Stark & Hookway, 2019, pp. 135–138). To question why something is the way it is, contrasts with the status quo, *this is the way it has always been*. Benefits also come from differing perspectives and ways of thinking. While individuals who have worked in healthcare for years will often see and frame things from their historical training or current practice, patients and other external stakeholders will view things as their own experiences.

Patients and carers are far more than their diagnoses. People have their own mindset and skills, and direct experience of service use. This holds real value for any QI project. Over time, the SHFT QI programme invested more resources to bring external stakeholders around the table as equals. As the value of diversity was recognised, more stakeholders were included; patient advocacy groups, commissioners, families, referrers to services as well as anyone who was calling for change.

By mid-2018, SHFT realised they could take co-production much further than the original plan for staff inclusion. A new executive leadership team with previous QI experience joined the Trust Board. Building on their previous QI experience, the new leadership team concluded that an immersive experience of co-production would have the greatest impact in helping to move the organisational culture away from a defensive posture. The Board decided that a patient/carer should be allocated to each of the QI training cohorts. This allowed the patient voice to be part of the work on the ground and helped to shape SHFT's emergent QI strategy. The QI Steering Group decided that patients would be a partner in the training process and in initial events. There was initial staff concern about patient and carer involvement. This reflected previous relationships with external groups that were sometimes adversarial and concerns that unreasonable demands might be made.

Building Confidence and the Role of the Expert by Experience Coordinator

The success of the initial QI project on staff engagement was reported to have been due to the aspects of co-production. Patient and carer involvement added further depth to the training and to work in projects, especially with the provision of personal insights. This kept people's feet firmly on the ground and away from abstraction. The contributions made by patients/carers in the initial projects were central to the change processes and were celebrated by the staff, who had felt so threatened at the beginning of the QI programme.

As the QI programme went through its own Plan Do Study Act (PDSA) cycle in the first 12 months, the leadership team decided that co-production would be the focus of the future QI strategy. Early experience indicated that co-design, co-delivery, and co-production do not happen by accident, but need a systematic approach. To deliver consistent co-production there must be an organisational will, an emotional attachment to its importance, and commitment and leadership from the senior levels of the organisation.

As the QI programme evolved, the steering group made the decision to create a role of an Expert by Experience Coordinator. This was someone who had completed their Quality Improvement training and had lived experience of mental illness. They could see both sides: how hard it can be to engage with the organisation, but also the huge benefits that QI can bring to improve care. Such a coordinator can mentor the patients/carers in QI projects so that their voice truly reaches exactly where it is needed. This role can champion co-production in a way that it starts to become part of the organisation's culture and challenges the organisation when it falls short of this.

A good description of the strengths of this co-production approach can be found in the work of Edgar Cahn (Cahn, 2004). Cahn, the founder of the Timebanks movement, envisaged people as assets, identified the need for partnering between professionals and clients, and saw a new role for service users as co-producers of outcomes (Boyle & Bird, 2014; Cahn & Gray, 2015). These principles echo the arguments of Nobel Prize–winning economist Elinor Olstrom on the advantages of democratic participation in areas of shared resources (Tarko, 2016). Olstrom's ideas have been applied in healthcare including the planning, design, delivery, and evaluation of healthcare improvements. Robert et al. contend that applying Olstrom's principles to co-design allows healthcare organisations to '(bring) together relevant stakeholders throughout a health(care) system to pool resources (e.g., experiential knowledge, labour, funding) in creative and constructive interactions' (Robert et al., 2021) (p 3).

Cahn and Timebank use *The Parable of the Blobs and Squares* to make the point that true co-production does not require one group's views and experiences to be preferred over another (No More Throw-away People, 2014). Professionals bring many process skills to the co-design of improvements while members of the public, or in the case of patients and carers, bring great contextual knowledge which allows better solutions to be identified. The Lean quality improvement provides a framework for this type of active collaboration. It is possible that someone in the coordinator role could over time become 'indoctrinated' by the organisation and start to lose objectivity, and so there must be a constant reflection of how this role evolves through a QI journey.

The role of the coordinator is also to empower others (both patients and staff) to have their voice heard and this formed a key part of the Trust's QI Strategy. By 2019, the organisational culture had shifted from a defensive position to staff wanting to make changes in collaboration with patients/carers and feel empowered to do so. This is evidenced in the Annual NHS's Staff Survey over four years (Figure 10.1) and the Annual Community Mental Health Survey over eight years (Figure 10.2).

Involving Patients and Users of Service in QI Training

From conception to delivery, the voice of patients and carers is essential to any project or service design. Co-production must go far beyond QI and be seen as organisation-wide business as usual. To embed co-production at SHFT, the organisation has committed to increasing the opportunities for peer support workers and patient/carer participation across all services. It has become part of the culture. To truly be an organisation that lives by 'no decision about me, without me'.

These peer support workers, carers, and patients have been trained in QI, and deliver on projects alongside colleagues. They also coach new cohorts of QI-certified leaders. They are part of the centrally resourced team that provides internal QI developing delivery training and coaching to the 60+ certified QI leaders. It is at this training stage that co-production is taught and instilled as mandatory. It is made clear that in any improvement work no matter the format, co-production is not an afterthought – it is planned and built in.

The Expert by Experience Coordinator coaches and supports people from all over the organisation to ensure that patients and carers are involved in anything and everything they do. The Coordinator supports and coaches the certified leaders and practitioners as part of the organisational QI programme, with co-production competency embedded in the training (Figure 10.3).

The Expert by Experience Coordinator is not there to have their voice heard alone – they are there to support and empower others to bring their views, experience, and thinking to the QI

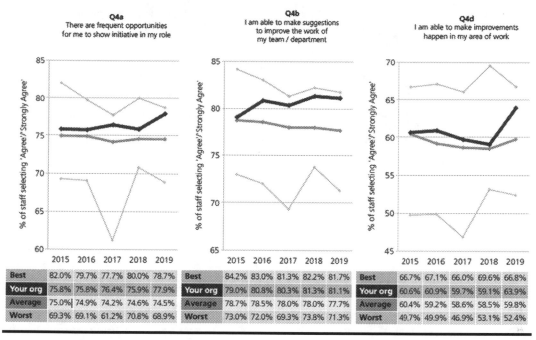

Figure 10.1   Questions showing the change in staff QI culture, between 2015 and 2018 with national comparison.

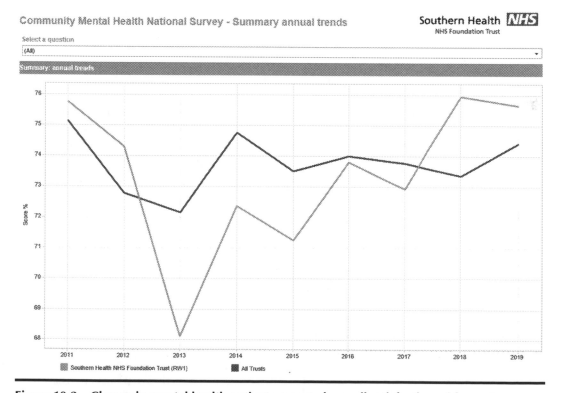

Figure 10.2   Change in mental health patients reported overall satisfaction with services.

- Experienced and practising certified leader
- Develops other certified leaders and practitioners
- Develops and champions organisation strategy

- Experienced quality improvement practitioner
- Leads quality improvement projects
- Develops practitioners

- Actively participates in quality improvement activity
- Completes training in quality improvement

- Involved in improvement activity led by others
- Awareness of some quality improvement techniques

6 Coach
60 Certified Leader
600 Practitioner
6000 Foundation

Emerging Competency Framework

Figure 10.3   Emerging competency framework.

process. From the QI steering committee to delivery of Rapid Process Improvement Workshops (RPIWs), they are there to bring stories and examples of how decisions have an impact on lives.

The turning points that happened during early RPIWs often resulted from patients and carers telling their stories. These moments must be supported with sensitive facilitation. As the QI programme developed, the importance of having a good balance of facilitation skills and theoretical QI skills became clear. Not everyone trained in QI is a natural facilitator, so work is necessary to ensure that each training cohort, as they learn to apply their new QI skills, also develop as skilled facilitators. Facilitation can be enhanced via training in coaching skills. There should be at least one patient and/or carer in every cohort of QI facilitators. This is not necessarily something that is easy to do. The weeks are intense, and patients/carers need to be supported by the organisation's QI programme.

For the patient and carers, to have these opportunities to sit side by side with staff is also valuable. While learning new skills and ideas, it is also an opportunity for them to see and understand the work that goes on internally to improve services. While this may not always be felt or seen from the outside, this supports transparency and the building of trust with an organisation. Small decisions that go on behind the scenes can have a profound impact on patients and carers.

Not everyone wants to become a QI facilitator, but still wants to learn some of the skills and lessons that QI has to offer. One of the ways that SHFT tackled the intensity and time commitment for training was the introduction of 'Bite Size QI training'. This provides training in QI skills in bite-size sessions making it more accessible, for patients, carers, and staff. The addition of these smaller sessions provides skills for participants to take away and equip them to take part in QI work. This commitment is the gateway to going beyond co-production and starting to reach levels of co-delivery. This is to have patients and carers at the helm of all improvement, and this should be the goal for sustainable continuous improvement. This goes a long way to realise SHFT's declared values of: 'Patients and people first', 'Partnership' and 'Respect'.

Coming along for the Whole Journey: Tailored Patient and Carer QI Training

Some of the most important and game-changing moments came when patients felt they were able to share their story and/or challenge what was being said. To facilitate this, the organisation worked to create psychological safe spaces to hear differences and share emotions, within the QI methodology. As the approach to co-production evolved, SHFT created a preparatory stage to support those that wanted to be involved. In partnership with patients and carers, a training package was developed that any patient, carer, or indeed any staff member could attend to find out about the 'ins and outs' of QI and to know what to expect.

The training covers everything participants can expect when attending a workshop or helping with a piece of improvement work. Anything that can help is relevant, from understanding terms such as '5S', 'Just in Time', and 'A3', to the practicalities of where workshops are held, where participants should go on day one, and what transport arrangements are available.

The intention is to empower the patients and carers to be on a level playing field with staff. This training allowed patients and carers to understand the complete process of QI. This includes what is said and done in the workshops, or the design stage, and to be confident that there is a place for them throughout the process. It meant that they were not coming from a disadvantaged position, and so allowed them to feel able to have their voices heard and their stories valued. But it went further than that. It also helped to ensure that the diversity of thinking was utilised. Patients and carers can be a part of the development and be a critical friend throughout the delivery. They can hold the process to account and help to ensure that what is being delivered is a true reflection of the original intent. This added to the 'full QI' and the 'QI Bite Size' training programmes to create a suite of training options that can be adapted to fit the needs of the user.

Building in Involvement at the Beginning, During, and on Evaluation of a QI Project

No matter in what industry the tools and principles of QI are applied, there is always discussion of organisational processes and policies versus the needs and perspectives of patients or customers. In a meeting of only staff conversations, it can too easily become focussed on bureaucratic processes. The real-life stories, experiences, and challenges from carers and patients can bring these conversations back to and define the real value. A wonderful example of this was in a project looking at instances of violence and aggression in a mental health inpatient unit which turned out to be a turning point for co-production at Southern Health NHS Foundation Trust.

RECOGNITION OF SHARED PURPOSE

In a breakout session in an RPIW, the staff were asked to write down administrative and office-based tasks that they carry out on every shift. When the room came back together and the A3 sheet was shared it got quite a reaction.

One of the carers immediately stood up and said, 'no wonder you don't have the time to care for my daughter'. This was a profound moment. While the system problems that had led to the event remained unacceptable, the carer participant saw that staff were trying their best but the system needed to be changed.

For staff, it illustrated how the system made it more difficult for them to care for and support patients. This changed the atmosphere in the room to one of togetherness with a shared intent to change the system and processes to improve care.

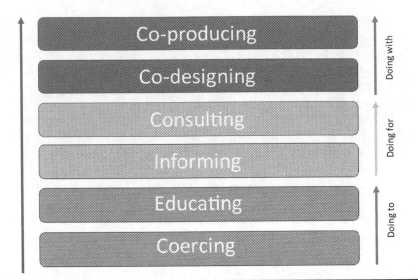

Figure 10.4   The engagement ladder.

This example highlights how to bring reality back into the conversations and help to keep people's feet firmly on the ground.

Co-production benefits all participants. In working together, honestly, and transparently, patients and carers will come away with a newfound appreciation and understanding of what happens behind the scenes. And while not always palatable, it brings out areas to really focus on. There is bravery in making oneself vulnerable and open to change or shift in thinking. We are reminded that expression of vulnerability makes us all human and levels the power imbalance. The more partnership working there is, the more person-centred care can be achieved.

What is vitally important is that patients and carers, as well as staff, are taken along for the whole journey of design, development, and delivery. It is not enough to have patients and carers come along to a workshop for it to simply end there. They need to be at follow-up meetings for the review of action plans. There will be times when things do not go as planned and when this happens, patients and carers must be part of the problem solving. Everyone that invests time in quality improvement is a partner and should be enabled to work together throughout the co-production process (see Figure 10.4).

This understanding of the entire process of co-production came later in the QI journey at SHFT.

Building the Will

The aim of QI should be to meaningfully invest in as many people as possible. That is not to say go out and find anyone to be involved indiscriminately, but really engage and work with people from all walks of life. Pay particular attention to seldom heard voices, so that the QI work becomes a bottom-up empowerment culture.

Ensuring co-production is meaningful is not easy and should not be underestimated. Simply sending out a bulk email and seeing who replies is not an appropriate way to ensure involvement. True involvement involves being proactive and going out to meet people where they are. This is particularly true when projects involve individuals or communities that are harder to reach. These are often overlooked people, but their stories and experiences are equally valid and important. From formal QI projects to changing an information leaflet, seeking views and involvement is core to quality improvement delivered through co-production.

The whole spectrum of staff including frontline staff, managers, and board members should always strive for more engagement. This should make up part of people's jobs, and not be seen as an added extra if time permits. It should not be a tick box exercise where the bare minimum is done to be seen to be engaging. Staff of all levels should see and understand the true value of co-production and respect what it can do for the services they provide. Co-production can become business as usual if there is a will.

Communication Plan

> We believe there is a case for formalising, integrating, and expanding the role of communications within the design of any improvement intervention. The dividend is radically to extend scope and longevity of effect. Too often we see communications being done as an afterthought by folk who are expert in other fields, or it is the preserve of specialists who are isolated from clinical work.
>
> **Alan Wilson, The Health Foundation (Wilson, 2015)**

Both internal and external communication played a key role in the QI journey at SHFT. Communication with patients and carers externally is more complex and heterogeneous than staff communication. But the content was similar with regards to how people could become involved. The personal stories of all parties involved describing their experiences bring co-production to life and help to promote and reinforce engagement.

In SHFT, promotion of the QI programme and recruitment of patients and carers to get involved began on an ad-hoc basis. The Expert by Experience Coordinator was able to approach people they had met on their journey and ask them if they would like to be involved. It almost had the nature of 'friend of a friend'. Another example of this would be a manager of an acute mental health ward being approached by the Expert by Experience Lead to ask a patient, and carer, to be involved in a Rapid Process Improvement Workshop (RPIW). The ward manager used 'local' knowledge to approach those individuals; a patient she knew, and happened to have the email address of, who had had an admission to the ward, and a carer she knew from a colleague who had attended a carers' group. Whilst this approach did achieve its purpose of recruiting patients and carers to become involved, there was a feeling that there was a wider group of individuals who had expert knowledge that was being missed and who would have been hugely valuable to the process.

The Expert by Experience Lead understood the need to adapt their method of communication according to whom they were speaking to make participating in QI accessible. They were prepared to speak to patients and carers in whatever format they chose. This ranged from face-to-face meetings, telephone conversations, emails, and text messages.

As awareness of QI grew in the Trust, patients and carers began to get involved in the process through referrals from other sources, such as service managers who had received, and were investigating, complaints from patients and carers. This approach had two benefits: a wider group of those with lived experience sharing their encounters with services and, for those people, a feeling that they were not just complaining in vain, but they could be part of the solution to make changes. It also demonstrated the will from the Trust to use those complaints to improve in a structured way, using QI and co-production.

At the beginning of the QI journey at SHFT the team had access, on a very part-time basis, to a communications manager who was responsible for the general spreading of awareness through various media channels and development of some website pages. A year into the QI journey it became apparent that the QI team, and the process itself, needed its own dedicated communications manager and a member of the Communications team was seconded to the team. Their role was to promote QI via the further development of the website, social media channels, and at local events with other stakeholders in healthcare in line with findings on integrated QI communication (Cooper et al., 2015). There was a clear distinction between the communication manager's role and the Expert by Experience Lead, which was to recruit patients and carers to QI projects.

The wider QI team still had a role to play in the communication by advocating for QI and recruiting staff and patients who they perceived might like to become involved. To promote the work a twice a year conference was started. Up to 150 Trust staff, patients, carers, and other interested parties such as third-party organisations attended. Patients and carers are invited to speak at these conferences to communicate their experience of being involved in QI. These conferences are planned very carefully so that they did not have a corporate feel with an executive speaker, but with patients and carers centre stage. The ethos, and emphasis, is on welcoming patients and carers to the day, having an inclusive environment, and showing respect in terms of both their experiences and their willingness to share those experiences with a wider audience.

A month after the secondment of the communications manager to the team, an additional Expert by Experience, who had been involved in QI projects from the start, was employed on a part-time basis. They had a dual role of supporting the communications manager, whilst also continuing to share lived experiences of mental illness and supporting other people to share their experiences. An opportunity then arose for them to become involved in a United Kingdom (UK) 'Communications in QI Collaboration' that meets monthly to share ideas about how QI can best be communicated and promoted both within Trusts and to a wider audience.

The methods of communication used to promote QI at SHFT have been successful with over 100 patients and carers now involved within two years of starting the QI programme. However, the Trust recognises that there is more to do, by recruiting further individuals to take part and in the wider communication of QI.

Feedback from Participants

Feedback from patient and carer participants is included below. These contributions give a good feel for the range of experiences, including initial apprehension and the importance of the processes put in place to support participants.

Carer A

I took part in a Southern Health QI project, initially, in my role as a carer, although, as a result, I became an official volunteer. I was asked to participate in a weeklong workshop, which was investigating how aggression could be reduced on Melbury, a mental health inpatient ward. Much fruitful discussion emerged from the ideas we identified as being the most likely to cause patient and carer frustration, on the ward, and therefore, could lead to aggression. I felt very much accepted as part of the team – there was absolutely no hierarchy – and valued for my opinions as a carer. The changes, instigated by this project, were implemented on the ward, making it possible for staff to spend more quality time with patients and improving everybody's well-being. I think my experiences as a carer influenced the decisions of what needed to change, for patients and their families to feel more in control of their care.

Patient A

I am a long-term patient at Southern Health NHS Foundation Trust. A while ago now I was approached to be involved in a piece of Quality Improvement work happening in my local area. Since I have had both particularly good experiences and bad, I was excited by the opportunity and keen to see what I can do to help.

I had never thought about getting involved in this sort of thing before, so did not know what to expect. I knew little about Quality Improvement and the journey that SHFT was going on. I was extremely nervous at the beginning, worried I would feel like I was there as the 'token patient', and anxious about seeing people that had treated me when I was at my worst. I was made to feel welcomed and, more importantly, valued. While there were clearly efforts made to make myself and others feel this way, it was not over the top and I did not feel singled out, something about which I was worried.

What was important was that I felt like my thoughts and experiences mattered and that I was involved in the bigger discussions and decisions. I felt like I was helping shape changes and the future. I felt like I was making a difference in the outcome of the project which was incredibly rewarding.

Carer B

I am passionate about improving mental health services for patients and their families, as a mental health carer, our family have seen and experienced good and poor services.

I was told to be available for a week, I had no idea what Quality Improvement was and had absolutely no idea what to expect! After the nerve-wracking introductions, it began to make more sense and proved to be a very intense but worthwhile week. I have been part of two more QI projects since that initiation.

Reflecting on the whole experience there were big differences in the projects, but my main impressions were how small improvements can have a big impact. How important it was to have the staff and users/carers together to generate ideas and try to help solve the issues. How the Trust needs to buy into QI for the long term and develop the culture of continuous improvement.

Patient B

When I was first approached to take part in, what I now know, was one of the first QI projects run by Southern Health, I was extremely nervous. I was saying to my mum, up until the Sunday night before, that I was not going! I had had the opportunity to meet two of the facilitators beforehand, which I had found helpful but, as to be expected I guess, the nerves remained. This was a new experience for me.

On the first morning, the consultant who had cared for me when I had been unwell and with whom I did not get on during my admission, came and sat next to me. I remember it so well. It was awkward for all about five seconds and then it all fell into place. I felt totally accepted by the group and there was a real sense of equality in the room.

By Friday, I did not want the week to finish. I had so enjoyed going in each day and sharing my experiences of care and having those experiences heard and taken for what they were was so powerful. I remember saying to the wider group: 'It's an amazing feeling, I wish I could bottle it!'

Taking part in the QI week was a real turning point for me. I started working as a volunteer with the Trust and this has slowly progressed into a paid role. It is particularly important not to underestimate the power of QI. It can have a huge ripple effect.

Carer C

I am the proud mum of a patient; I got involved in the QI project as my son had attended a workshop. As a mum, I am a strong advocate for my son to have access to the best support from SHFT and this had sometimes been challenging. I was impressed at the way that the QI team were keen to have the full involvement of services users and carers in any of the decisions that were made. We were actively encouraged to put our thoughts and suggestions forward. I felt comfortable voicing where I felt SHFT had failed my son and was equally comfortable in offering practical solutions.

The workshops were exhausting, frustrating at times, but by the end of the week, by working collaboratively, we were able to develop some worthwhile suggestions for service improvements for not only the patients and carers but also the staff.

Further Development

Twenty-four months into the QI programme, the first wave of the Covid-19 pandemic affected our population and the NHS. The QI programme was in the process of transitioning from the Phase One stage of building internal staff and external population engagement to making larger-scale local service improvements. This desire to improve, grows energy and engages others, and we have seen this momentum in SHFT. After the challenges of Covid-19, Phase Two now looks to embed the QI methodology as part of an organisation Quality Programme. This is summed up in the four interlocking quadrants of Figure 10.5. The Quality Programme enables the co-production to move beyond the QI methodology and into planning, assurance, and measurements.

Conclusions

Co-production can combine process expertise, QI expertise, and lived experience to make a whole that is greater than the sum of the parts. The context in which the work was commenced was challenging with criticisms of the service, and diminished trust in the quality of service provided.

SHFT harnessed the power of quality improvement and co-production to help it to move beyond defensiveness to an open willingness to learn from experience. Using Lean processes allowed the organisation to engage the people with the best knowledge of services – staff, and the people who use the services as patients or as relatives and carers of patients.

Focusing these efforts on co-production followed from SHFT's values of partnership, respect, and putting patients and people first. To make this possible, the organisation had to develop appropriate training provisions and support arrangements. These approaches were developed over time in response to learning in a quality improvement process coordinated by a steering group and overseen by the Trust Board. Although progress was challenged by the Covid-19 pandemic,

Quality Improvement (QI) model

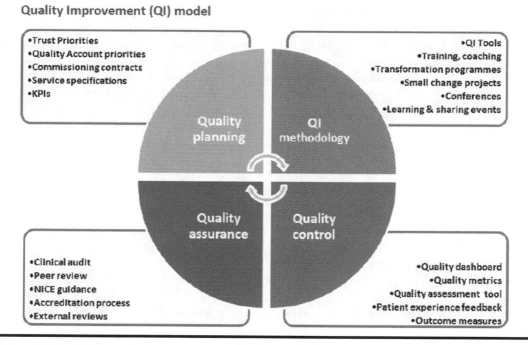

Figure 10.5   SHFT Quality Programme, with the expanded role for co-production.

the will in the organisation was sufficiently strong to maintain progress. This put the organisation in a good position for further development with core inclusion of co-production across all the organisation's quality functions.

Southern Health NHS Foundation Trust will never finish their Quality Improvement journey. At every stage of a QI programme, particular care and attention will be made to ensure that all the excellent work that goes on gets embedded into the organisation and becomes 'business as usual'. In this report, we have described Phase One, intended as a two-year journey, interrupted by the worldwide pandemic. We have described a wider Phase Two, where co-production starts to become embedded beyond the QI methodology.

Co-production has been the breakthrough we did not see at the beginning of our QI journey. It is the patients and carers that understand what their needs are and how services should look, and it is the frontline staff that know how to deliver this. These are the people that should be working in partnership in any service design or Quality Improvement approach.

When people with lived experience and the organisations share power – working together as equals – then improvements can be made. It is only when this happens that true, person-centred care can be delivered. The alignment that comes from co-production with patients, carers, staff can elevate our voices, and the barriers that often constrain us come crashing down!

Learning Points and Tips

In this collation of our learning, we have suggested some tips for co-production. Some we have learnt along the way from what went well and not so well, and some from having external peer review.

- It is important to spend time ensuring that staff also feel that they can share their stories and can challenge. The QI facilitator should allow true equity in the room and equal opportunity between staff, patients, and carers and ensure that all participants feel psychologically safe.
- It is best to instil the ethos of co-production early in the stages of training new certified leaders and practitioners, and not as an afterthought.
- Co-production does not happen by accident; it is not something that can be tagged onto someone's job role. Dedicated resources and time need to be allocated, e.g., employing an Expert by Experience Coordinator.
- Include costs for employing expertise beyond the normal healthcare staff groups. Patients and carers should be employed as part of a QI team. Budget for patient/carers attending workshops, improvement weeks, and visiting services.
- Make accessing the workshop or the logistics for involvement as easy as possible, e.g., taxis, travelling buddies, or respite for carers to allow them to attend.
- Good facilitation allows patients' voices to be heard, e.g., writing ideas down, sitting next to someone to express their views, etc. It will also ensure that individuals do not dominate the floor, even if there is passion and conviction.
- Remember The Parable of the Blobs and Squares – relying on one or two individuals (users of services) is not the way to go. There must be a will to continuously empower and encourage as many different people to get involved as possible to really understand the diversity of a population.
- Develop an all-encompassing 'Introduction to Quality Improvement' for patients and carers, covering anything from the 5 Whys to jargon busting. Allow staff of all levels to attend these sessions.
- In each project, have a point of contact for any patients and carers. Beginning, middle, and end. This is important to remember, as small oversights can make an enormous difference. E.g., at lunch, staff sitting with people they know and not leaving a patient sitting alone. Without this point of contact, when the work goes forward to become business as usual, it can be easy to lose sight and forget about those people that helped throughout the project.
- Communication is key. For co-production to happen you need to be able to communicate with a wide variety of people. At the instigation of a QI programme, put resources into co-production and 'no decision about me, without me', e.g., websites, social media, letters, or leaflets. Quality Improvement is fast moving and so your communications need to be up to date and accurate all the time.

Learning Activities

- Try to picture yourself or a family member receiving these services. As a patient or carer, would you feel that your views are taken on board?
- When it comes to change, how far up the engagement ladder would you say that your organisation goes? Too often organisations only reach the 'doing for' stage (Figure 10.4).
- Are there any opportunities in your organisation for you to co-produce change? And what would you hope to achieve from this?
- What would you perceive to be the barriers to co-production internally and externally? Do you have the resource and commitment to break down these barriers?
- Do your staff feel able to share their views and experiences? Are they encouraged and supported to challenge the senior team?

Acknowledgements

Huge thank you to Cumbria, Northumberland, Tyne and Wear NHS Foundation Trust. In particular to Ian Railton, Laura Woodward, Sarah Keetley, and Stuart Gee for their wisdom and guidance and helping us at the start SHFT's journey and training us all initially in Lean.

Thank you to the board of directors and non-executives as well as the governors for constantly pushing the QI programme and holding them to account, with Dr Nick Broughton, chief executive, sponsoring the QI programme. No stone was unturned. Thank you to Sara Courtney and Rachel Anderson for their clinical leadership and to Dean Garrett for his overall leadership and support. Thank you to everyone that gave so much to the programme, both time and energy – working on the front line – to deliver what was set out.

And of course, a huge thank you to all the service users, patients, carers, friends, and family that gave their time and shared their stories. Without their generosity to the organisation, none of this would have been possible.

Bibliography

Boyle, D., & Bird, S. (2014). *Give and Take: How Timebanking is Transforming Healthcare*. Timebanking UK.

Cahn, E. S. (2004). *No More Throw-Away People: The Co-Production Imperative* (2nd ed.). Essential Books Ltd.

Cahn, E. S., & Gray, C. (2015). The time bank solution. *Stanford Social Innovation Review, 13*(3), 41–45.

Cooper, A., Gray, J., Willson, A., Lines, C., McCannon, J., & McHardy, K. (2015). Exploring the role of communications in quality improvement: A case study of the 1000 lives campaign in NHS Wales. *Journal of Communication in Healthcare, 8*(1), 76–84. https://doi.org/10.1179/1753807615y.0000000006

Involve. (n.d.). *Co-Production*. Involve. Retrieved 07 Feb 2022 from https://www.involve.org.uk/resources/methods/co-production

No More Throw-away People. (2014). *The Parable of the Blobs and Squares*. James Mackie. https://vimeo.com/42332617

Robert, G., Williams, O. L. I., Lindenfalk, B., Mendel, P., Davis, L. M., Turner, S., Farmer, C., & Branch, C. (2021). Applying Elinor Ostrom's design principles to guide co-design in health(care) improvement: A case study with citizens returning to the community from jail in Los Angeles County. *International Journal of Integrated Care, 21*(1), 1–15. https://doi.org/10.5334/ijic.5569

Stark, C., & Hookway, G. (2019). *Applying Lean in Health and Social Care Services*. Routledge.

Tarko, V. (2016). *Elinor Ostrom: An Intellectual Biography*. Rowman & Littlefield.

Wilson, A. (2015, 08 Feb 2022). Exploring the role of communications in quality improvement. https://health.org.uk/blogs/exploring-the-role-of-communications-in-quality-improvement

Nathan Clifford is the expert by experience lead for Southern Health NHS Foundation Trust in England. His role involves using his own lived experience to affect change within the Trust. He is a strong advocate to ensure that patients' voices are heard in a meaningful and effective manner as part of quality improvement in healthcare. He has also undergone quality improvement methodology training.

Sarah Curtis is the expert by experience lead for NHS Hampshire, Southampton and Isle of White Clinical Commissioning Group.

Karl Marlowe, FRCPsych, is a consultant psychiatrist and currently the chief medical officer at Oxford Health NHS Foundation Trust. He has extensive training and experience in Quality Improvement methodologies (e.g., Improvement Science in Action; Lean) having led Quality Improvement projects in England: at East London NHS and Southern Health NHS Foundation Trusts. He holds post-graduate qualifications from University College London, Kings College London, and Oxford's Said Business School.

Chapter 11

Applying Kata in Healthcare

Ann Hill and Graham Canning

Contents

Aims

- To identify reasons why success in project-based applications of Lean may not result in organisation-wide gains.
- To describe Toyota Kata, a term coined by Mike Rother, and to distinguish between Improvement Kata and Coaching Kata.

DOI: 10.4324/9780429346958-11

■ To explain the importance of scientific thinking in Lean and in being aware of areas where knowledge of underlying causes is limited.
■ To describe the application of Toyota Kata in a large project in the English National Health Service and to share the lessons from its implementation.

Introduction

There are examples of the successful use of Lean in the UK Health Sector from as early as 2002 (de Souza, 2009), and well-used and familiar Lean tools underpin many Lean training workshops in National Health Service (NHS) improvement programmes. Lean has been applied in many healthcare environments worldwide, yielding positive results not only in the quality, safety, and productivity of service delivery but also in-patient and carer satisfaction along with staff morale and retention.

Lean is successful in healthcare environments because it 'tackles the heart of the matter: how the organisation's work gets done' (Jones & Mitchell, 2006, p. 7). However, whilst there are numerous successful examples of Lean projects in UK healthcare, sustained whole organisational Lean transformation is much less common.

One hypothesis lies at the heart of how Lean has been understood and applied within healthcare. Like many other industries the health services are proficient at using the tools of the Toyota Production System, but miss the less visible thinking patterns, enshrined in the way Toyota manages (Spear & Bowen, 1999).

This also occurs in other settings, where the tools and techniques typically adopted by Lean practitioners do not have the impact as they do within Toyota. Mike Rother, a long-time management researcher, explored why this might be so. He identified a pattern of thinking within Toyota designed to deliver organisational goals through systematically overcoming obstacles to success (Rother, 2009). Rother adopted the term 'Toyota Kata' to describe the use of a systematically applied set of steps within Toyota. 'Kata', a term used in martial arts, describes a sequence of steps practised and applied consistently (Augustovicova et al., 2018).

At the heart of Toyota Kata are practice routines based on principles of scientific thinking which include rapid experimentation and learning and which are applied to achieve challenging goals in unpredictable and changing circumstances. Establishing local goals that are linked to organisational goals, and then experimenting toward them, is done by teams at the heart of making products or delivering services, coached by their line managers.

Kata involves everybody from senior executives to frontline staff. It challenges traditional preconceptions of Lean and its adoption within some organisations. It is an activity to be practised, rather than a tool to be copied. Systematic practice results in the development of an instinctive scientific thinking meta-skill. This allows practitioners to overcome their own problems where the path to success is unclear. It is applicable in both personal and professional settings.

At the start, Kata takes discipline, commitment, and practice. Kata moves organisations from directionless activity to improvement being aligned to strategy delivery and making quality improvement part of everyday business as usual. It creates a habit or practice routine which ensures improvement effort is incorporated into daily activity, in both predictable and unpredictable times. By design, staff are practically involved to continuously learn and improve. Anecdotal evidence from work in the NHS so far has demonstrated that staff feel more engaged in their work for exactly this reason.

Context

The Vital Signs programme was launched in NHS England in 2018. It offers support to NHS Trusts that want to use Lean methods. The programme provides executive coaching support to senior trust executives. This coaching is provided by former trust chief executives who have delivered transformation in healthcare using Lean-based principles. The programme offers support with establishing trust continuous improvement teams and help in securing clinical engagement. To promote learning, the programme offers workshops, events, and networking opportunities and a peer learning network. Training programmes, tools, and materials are provided by the central team (Lean Transformation Programme Team, 2020).

In the first wave of the programme, seven NHS Trusts joined the programme (NHS England, 2018). These Trusts cover a wide range of service provision including university teaching hospitals, regional and local hospitals, and community health services. The programme includes a partnership with Livewell Southwest. Livewell Southwest is a social enterprise in the South of England which provides integrated health and social care services.

The chapter authors are part of the global Kata community and have worked at programme, organisational, and individual levels. This chapter introduces the underpinning principles and concepts of Kata. Early learning from adoption of Kata across an English healthcare national programme is shared along with tips for success based on this experience. The wide coverage and the range of services and contexts in the first cohort of Trusts allow enormous opportunity for learning.

What Is Kata?

In essence, Kata broadly translates as a way of doing things, or a predefined, choreographed, sequence of movements (Rother, 2009). With Kata, every step forward is effectively an experiment or a short Plan-Do-Study-Act (PDSA) cycle. Each step is a hypothesis, and what is learned from testing it provides a learning opportunity that informs the next step.

Rother's original book on Toyota Kata was a summary of research conducted between 2004 and 2009. He sought to understand the unseen managerial routines and thinking that lie behind Toyota's continued success with continuous improvement and adaptation, and to identify how others can develop similar routines and thinking in their organisations.

It became clear during the research that Toyota's management approach involved leaders at all levels teaching their team members a scientific approach and mindset, rather than jumping to conclusions. This skill and mindset can be applied to an infinite number of different challenges and objectives. The practice does not have a name in Toyota, it is just how managers manage.

For other organisations to benefit from this practice, Rother argues that they must build a model or system to help them to develop the thinking and routines that Toyota does habitually. This includes building a set of routines for both learners and coaches to practice, to develop a habit of scientific thinking – Improvement Kata – and habits to become an effective coach – Coaching Kata.

The Improvement Kata

The main feature of the improvement Kata pattern is that it gives a model for practical, everyday scientific way of thinking and working, which, in turn, is a disciplined approach to achieving organisational challenges. It is a series of four steps and corresponding practice routines for both an Improvement and a Coaching cycle. The steps are tested. That is, each step is framed by the previous step. There are practice routines, called Starter Kata, for each step.

Step One – The challenge. This sets the direction or purpose for the improvement. Typically, these are passed down from senior leadership. The challenge is usually aligned with the strategic goals within Toyota. It may come directly from a policy deployment exercise or be part of a wider improvement focus. A challenge at the local level, then, will typically be a subset of an overall organisational challenge.

Step Two – Grasp the current condition. This step is the analysis of local processes, reviewed in the light of the challenge set in Step One. The purpose is to get a direct fact-based understanding of the situation. This step allows a team to see and understand how a process currently operates, without judgement. It is essential to spend time doing this well as it provides the foundation, or frame, for the next steps.

Step Three – Establish your next target condition. Challenges are meant to be challenging! They can intimidate and be daunting. The next target condition provides a description of a goal on the way to delivering the challenge. It describes where you want to be next. Some coaches will describe it using the analogy of a time machine – 'If you could travel two weeks into the future, what would you want to see?' This is a description of conditions rather than a single isolated numerical target. A good target condition will have a clear outcome and process metrics. It will also have a desired working pattern, which is a kind of hypothesis. If the focus process were to function this way, we expect this outcome as a result.

Step Four – Conduct experiments to get there. This phase is about finding a path between the current state to the target condition. It is here that the obstacles standing in the way of achieving success are successively discovered. The team should consider what things are preventing success. It is common for a list of solutions to be given here, but this is not the point. The obstacles show the way by providing focus for the experiments that will be carried out, thus aiding successful movement to the target condition.

In the Kata approach, the ongoing improvement story is told via the Kata storyboard (Figure 11.1).

The constantly updated storyboard contains the Starter Kata templates used to capture thinking, progress, and learning. Figure 11.2 shows a Kata storyboard in use at Livewell Southwest, a social enterprise providing integrated health and social care services for people in the southwest of England.

The Coaching Kata

The Coaching Kata is the set of actions that coaches can use to support successful development of scientific thinking skills, practised on delivery of organisational challenges. The coaching routine is designed to keep the learner clearly focused on the steps of the Improvement Kata, and carry them out thoughtfully and with discipline. Coaches can ask five questions (Rother, 2018):

1. What is the target condition?
2. What is the actual condition now?
3. What obstacles do you think are preventing you from reaching the target condition? Which one are you addressing now?

Focus Process:		Challenge:	
Target Condition Achieve by: _____	**Current Condition**	**Experimenting Record**
		Obstacles Parking Lot

Figure 11.1 Storyboard Format. Source: Toyota Kata Practice Guide. Copyright: Mike Rother, used with permission.

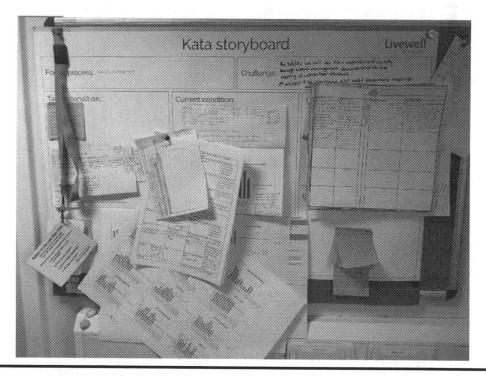

Figure 11.2 Photo of a working storyboard. Source: Rhian Slattery, Livewell Southwest. Used with permission.

4. What is your next step? (Next experiment) What do you expect?
5. How quickly can we see what we have learned from taking that step?

The use of the two Kata – the Improvement Kata and the Coaching Kata – supports a transition to a new culture. The Improvement Kata trains a way of scientific thinking and acting that helps to ensure that people do not make judgements based on previous experience or assumption. The Coaching Kata trains a way to support people using the Improvement Kata. Coaching is done consistently, and people are encouraged to develop self-motivation and resilience.

Kata and Lean

There has been a misinterpretation or even an intentional disregard of the thinking processes behind the development of the Toyota Production System. Jeff Liker identified the principles of Lean management as philosophy, process, people, and problem-solving (Liker, 2004). He updated his model in 2020 to include the underpinning principle of scientific thinking (Liker, 2020).

The umbrella term 'Lean' was coined to describe this approach and the tools of the Toyota Production System. The application of scientific thinking to industrial processes predates both Lean and Toyota. The tools we recognise now as the Lean tools were developed through scientific thinking to overcome problems experienced in Toyota's continual quest to achieve their vision.

A lack of recognition of the core role of scientific thinking has resulted in many organisations deploying Lean in a mechanistic fashion (Liker, 2020). This is characterised by having a focus on tools, having a preconceived road map of deployment, a top-down imposition, and the need for return-on-investment analysis before every stage. This usually results in low levels of engagement, weak patterns of learning, and a separation of Lean from daily business.

It is far better to see Lean deployment as an organic process, which establishes a clear goal or direction, and then (through experimentation) improves iteratively towards that goal. This approach to Lean is typified by traits such as leaders leading by example and then becoming coaches; a culture of learning, and Lean being seen as a journey towards a vision where the path is not yet clear.

To illustrate the difference, Rother notes that Kanban, discussed in Chapter 2, are used at Toyota as a Target Condition towards single-piece flow (Rother, 2009, p. 99). He argues that the implementation of a Kanban system without the team members understanding why it is a step to a long-term goal would miss a vital point:

> It is the striving for Target Conditions via the routine of the Improvement Kata that characterises what we have been calling 'Lean Manufacturing'.

> **(Rother, 2009, p. 101)**

Liker and Hoseus describe Toyota as a unique blend of Japanese culture, the Aichi prefecture where Toyota was founded, the influence of the Toyoda family, and the great leaders in its history (Liker & Hoseus, 2008). Toyota was extraordinarily successful at adaptation and experimentation to suit changing circumstances. In an internal publication Toyota stated:

> We continue to search for breakthroughs, refusing to be restrained by precedent or taboo.

> **(Liker & Hoseus, 2008)**

Kata describes the thinking, the mindset, which resulted in the Toyota Production System and the tools that have become synonymous with it. Diligent and systematic practice of scientific thinking is required and is a foundation for Lean. A very narrow range of tools is required to deliver improvement when this approach is applied. It may be as simple as being able to effectively use tools such as run charts and block diagrams, in Step Two of the Improvement Kata. The Starter Kata templates provided by Rother guide practice activity (Rother, No Date), so an improver does not need to be well versed in PDSA cycles (Rother 2018).

Documentation of obstacles is critical, i.e., question three of the Coaching Kata – Which obstacles are preventing you from reaching the target condition? If, for example, being unable to find key equipment is an obstacle to successfully achieving the target condition, those versed in 5S may reach for this tool from their toolbox (see Chapter 2). Those not, may solve the problem in a different way.

Similarly, if the obstacle is described as a variation in process outcomes, creation of standard work may underpin the experiment to overcome it, while others may use a different approach. Kata relies on the creativity of the improver not technical knowledge of established tools from any improvement methodology, not just Lean.

Learners often ask, 'When do we use A3 thinking and when do we use Kata?' It is more important to appreciate that Kata develops a meta-skill – a structure that supports scientific thinking that can be applied in multiple situations and at any level.

Both Toyota Kata and A3 problem-solving are 'thinking' approaches. Many successful organisations can deploy Lean using A3 without explicitly using Kata, but A3 thinking also has a core component of scientific thinking (Sobek & Smalley, 2008). The methods to support scientific thinking that underpin Kata should be applied at every stage of development of an A3 project. The Toyota Kata Starter Kata are easily combined into PDSA and A3, to make them more effective for practice and learning.

Thinking about understanding the current state, there is a risk that Lean practitioners will map the current conditions but that this will be affected by unknown biases and assumptions. Kata confronts this by being explicit about the threshold of knowledge, where the current state map moves beyond facts and data, to areas of uncertainty. The greater the unrecognised knowledge threshold, the more unreliable other elements of a typical A3 will be.

Fishbone diagrams are a common tool used to highlight issues and enable teams to identify root causes (Stark & Hookway, 2019, pp. 136–138). Many fishbone diagrams are completed in a classroom or improvement workshop setting, without meaningful facts and knowledge to underpin the assigned root cause, driven by a timetable. Similarly, the 5-Why technique may be used for brainstorming rather than as a problem-solving approach for which it is intended (Rother & May, 2013). The resulting 'root causes' are prone to be based on assumption and bias at individual and group levels. For true problem solving, there is a need to be comfortable with ambiguity and to recognise it. Asking 'why' to get to a threshold of knowledge, then take a scientific approach and see further through experimenting, not conjecture. Kaschak and Roche (2019) describe moving away from asking 'why' in the 5-Why technique, to asking, 'What obstacles are preventing us from meeting our target condition?', to then asking, 'Why is that an obstacle?', thus moving the threshold of knowledge.

Being conscious of the knowledge threshold allows for a combination of 'just do it' actions with experimentation to learn (Kaschak & Roche, 2019). When understanding is within the threshold of knowledge, it is appropriate to assign actions in an A3. Where the desired future state is beyond the threshold of knowledge, then the next step is to use a series of rapid cycles of experimentation to achieve it, fully involving frontline staff during this process.

Applying Scientific Thinking

Healthcare is by necessity built on patterns of scientific thinking and use of knowledge obtained by scientific method. Clinical staff are educated as scientific thinkers, and many are trained scientists.

A course of treatment is set with a plan to review its impact. Different drugs and interventions are tested, predicting but never being fully certain about the outcome. Another review will be done to determine whether the patient's condition or their symptoms are improving, and based on this another course of action will be planned.

However, experience suggests that even trained scientific thinkers, when stepping outside the consulting room, may act on unproven assumptions of the nature of a problem and implement untested solutions. A challenge is how to embed scientific thinking into how we manage healthcare. Many coaches have heard the frustrated retort of 'we are not Toyota, and we don't make cars': the challenge is to emulate the principles and habits of scientific thinking which have made Toyota successful. What is required in healthcare is the need to create an environment where staff can solve the problems in front of them and work toward challenging goals every day.

Case Study: Practising Kata in an Organisation Getting Started

Vital Signs is a Lean transformation programme offered by NHS Improvement in England. At the very start of the programme, we were developing our approach. We were fully aware of the experience of delivering Lean in healthcare, and the risks of focusing on tools rather than a management approach. With the Toyota Kata Practice Guide (Rother, 2018) recently published, we decided to contact Mike Rother to seek his advice. A video call with him was the first step to us adopting Kata.

As a team, we had all read Toyota Kata (Rother, 2009) and some of us had read the Toyota Kata Practice Guide (Rother, 2018) and seen Mike's YouTube site. It became clear early on, however, that our knowledge did not mean that we understood the true nature of Kata.

Mike Rother advocated deliberate practice as the path to understanding. The first step was to determine our direction, underpinned by the principle of what do you want to achieve, where do you want to be? From a personal perspective, this was the most uncomfortable few weeks in my improvement career. I needed to be able to describe where we wanted to be in the simplest way possible, with no real understanding of Kata. Eventually, our concept document was developed, with coaching from Mike and served to focus our activity towards achieving our goal. Much improvement activity and precious staff resources are often not directly aligned to the bigger goals of an organisation. Therefore, top level impact is not seen. This leads to staff dissatisfaction and the perception that 'improvement' is a separate or even niche activity that happens on top of already busy day jobs.

Mike's, and latterly Beth Carrington's, coaching continually took us back to our initial challenge: where do we want to be two years from now?

Our previous experience had shown us we were not going to learn Kata from the books or the widely available videos. Two of the Vital Signs team attended The Kata for Daily Improvement workshop offered by the University of Michigan as the first step to developing our knowledge. This trip also provided us with the opportunity to see Kata being practised and deployed in both healthcare and manufacturing settings. This learning was invaluable in informing the Vital Signs approach.

While in the US, we visited a retail setting with high volume, high variation with large yet predictable seasonal spikes in demand. Maurene Stock of Mercy Health, Muskegon, Michigan, also facilitated visits to different clinical settings within her organisation, from acute medicine to post-acute rehabilitation. The videos we made of her staff describing their experience and learning have been powerful in our programme. Maurene has been invaluable in her support. As we developed our coaching capability, her team shared their knowledge with ours.

A reflection on our trip was the importance of seeing Kata in action. We were able to observe applicability across many settings and at all grades of staff, relevant to the NHS. It was useful to learn how others had overcome obstacles within their own organisations. The most startling reflection was their conscious and deliberate move away from firefighting and knee-jerk problem solving. They have adopted a continued check with organisational direction and using PDSA to overcome the obstacles preventing achievement. The questions for healthcare executives are:

- What behaviours do they want to see to ensure the organisation successfully delivers its goals?
- How do executives want themselves and their managers to lead?
- Is Kata the right approach for their organisation?

Kata as a Modifier of Culture

Culture can be described as the sum of common behaviours and thinking patterns. Every organisation has a culture, which has been invented or developed over time to cope with problems, and that has worked well enough to be valid.

Schein suggests that organisational culture can be broken down into three levels (Schein, 2004):

- **Artefacts** – The way people do things (organisational routines, physical layouts, etc.).
- **Values and beliefs** – The way people think. The accepted rules and behaviours.
- **Underlying assumptions** – The way people think and act. The mental patterns that unconsciously steer perceptions.

The complex relationship between all three levels makes changing organisational culture exceedingly difficult to achieve. Our US visits demonstrated the way line managers, supervisors, and shift leaders were deliberately teaching a way of thinking and well-practised action.

For culture modification to be done successfully, it needs to start at the most visible level and change the way that people 'do' things. Culture can be altered using routines, that then establish new behaviours, which over time form new habits, leading eventually to building new organisational values and beliefs. Management and leadership behaviours are hugely influential in shaping how people think and act when applied intentionally (Tsui & Girard, 2019). Therefore, establishing supporting management behaviour through consistent daily coaching is vital. Leaders need to encourage their team members to practise Kata, provide procedural feedback via coaching cycles and recognise the success that practice of Kata brings.

Developing a Cohort of Learners

Our first three-month Kata challenge was to develop a cohort of learners at each of the sites across our programme. Working with Beth Carrington and Mike Rother, we created a series of four short modules to guide development of the Kata 'advance party' on each of the participating Vital Signs organisations. The modules, delivered over two days, provided background knowledge and an opportunity to practise being a coach and a learner through practical simulation. Beth observed and gave feedback to the coaches, a role termed 'Second Coach'.

Each delegate chose their own challenge, using this to continue to practise in the weeks following the workshop. Early challenges are to provide learners with a reason to practise and learn the improvement and coaching routines. They can be personal or professional but should provide an opportunity to experiment regularly, ideally at least once per day.

Following their initial practice, each of this first group was required to deliver the modules themselves, within their own organisation and to create their own organisational cohort, known as an Advance Group. The purpose is to develop familiarity with the subject and how it works through practising the Improvement Kata.

It was difficult and frustrating using Kata to create the first development block. As experienced improvement facilitators having developed numerous workshops and training materials using a new thinking pattern felt time-consuming and awkward. Without Beth's guidance, we may well have resorted back to our well-practised approach.

The pressure was compounded by the fact that the entire development block was run as coached experiments where our learning was unfolding to the audience as well as ourselves. It was a reminder of the vulnerability felt by new learners and coaches. Standing in front of a group, describing Kata moves initial knowledge towards greater understanding. It is daunting and exciting, and a true learning experience.

As facilitators, we witnessed a range of responses. Some of our cohort were willing to experiment, with varying degrees of scepticism. We also witnessed point-blank refusal of some to experiment ('I don't need a coach') or too much time spent attempting to codify Kata as a tool. Many Lean programmes have replicated the visible artefacts of Lean (i.e., the tools) but not the invisible management routines that Kata is capturing. In organisations where seniority is attained on being perceived as a Lean expert, and this has been built on the application of tools, introducing a whole new paradigm can be perceived as a threat.

Kata coaching capability is learned through consistent coached practice to improve skill, and consciously choosing the coaching model as a way of behaving. An observation from our own personal reflections, and that of others, is that becoming an effective coach is independent of seniority. A barrier to senior leaders' development as Kata coaches is the tendency to tell improvers the answer or instruct them what to do. This is addressed directly in the first development block.

We delivered the blocks on consecutive days, thus giving learners a chance to reflect overnight before coming back to the next session. The first development block was designed to give delegates the knowledge required to practise the initial four steps of the Improvement Kata and the 5-Questions Coaching Kata pattern, without development or augmentation, within their own organisation. These components are termed 'Starter Kata' and are the basis on which all else is built.

Subject areas covered in each module were:

■ Module 1 – Introduction to Toyota Kata – Awareness of the Improvement and Coaching Kata.
■ Module 2 – Grasping the current condition. Participants are able to undertake a basic, unbiased data- and fact-based analysis in relation to a challenge.
■ Module 3 – Establishing a good target condition, an ability to correctly describe obstacles.
■ Module 4 – Participation and observation of coaching cycles. Planning for organisational deployment.

When run as four two-hour sessions held on consecutive days, participants have time to think about what they have learned and formulate questions before moving to the next area of knowledge. The conversations are much richer and become aligned to the context in which learners are working.

Development block workshops have been attended by executives, management staff, senior and junior clinical staff across medical, nursing, and allied health professional groups. Lean training is often tailored for different staff groups based on their seniority, e.g., Lean for Leaders. This is not the case with Kata. Kata is about practising a new routine to create a thinking pattern that is universal and therefore the approach must be the same for everybody.

Rother advises against fighting well-established neural pathways and habits, and to build new habits through practice (Rother, 2018). Our learning has been that we must convince people to give it a go, and to just practise. Practise until the routine becomes more natural; many learners describe an 'a-ha' or 'penny drop' moment. In our work, the experience was that it happens after anything from 20–50 coached improvement cycles.

For that to happen, coaches need to be able to create the conditions for learners to get to that point. There are some practical considerations ranging from ensuring learners and coaches get the time and opportunity to practise in often busy clinical environments to the location and style of Kata storyboards. Storyboards may contain confidential information and need to comply with local infection control standards.

Establishing Coaching Capacity and Capability

Success and spread of Kata within an organisation are determined by the number and quality of coaches in an organisation (Rother, 2018; Rother & Aulinger, 2017). A typical assumption, driven by incomplete knowledge of Toyota Kata, is that it can be taught in a classroom. This is not the case. Development Block 1 is designed to establish the very first learner capability, and this Advance Group will become the organisation's first coaches. The purpose is to grow coaching skills quickly and effectively. There is no shortcut to this. Effective coaches first need to be skilled learners and this skill can only come from repeated practice and coaching.

The coach is responsible for the learner's success. Where we have seen poor practice spread can come from coaches who are not thoroughly skilled in each of the Starter Kata practice routines. This often results from deviating from the Starter Kata before it is understood fully. It can be very tempting to print coaching cards and give them to every senior manager to use. This will not create effective coaching skills within an organisation.

Our second programme challenge was to create coaching capacity and capability within each of the Vital Signs organisations. In the first level, the coach supports learners in their skills development. The second level is being able to act as a second coach, who trains and mentors new coaches. The second coach role enables an organisation to develop new coaches independently and to develop the skills of existing coaches (Legentil et al., 2018).

We worked with our mentors to create a training block that included:

- Demonstrating and evaluating existing learner skills.
- Practising the role of coach and second coach.
- Evaluation of learner, coach, and second coach competency.
- Organisational deployment of Kata.

To attend this development block, delegates had to show their practice through their storyboards. The initial focus was to coach core elements such as challenge, target condition, and obstacles. Our learning and advice are to focus on the quality of coaching from the very beginning of their practice. The opportunity to observe learner skills at the beginning of this second block highlighted the need for excellent quality and continued coaching to support learner skills development.

A question-and-answer session with colleagues from Mercy Hospitals was invaluable in sharing coaching experience. The coaching development block focused on bringing the key elements of good coaching to life and practising them in a safe and fun environment (Rother, 2018). We emphasised sharing experience and learning the trials and tribulations of coaching. These ranged from overcoming obstacles such as how to display storyboards in a clinical area through to learning how to schedule coaching sessions to ensure they happened every day as planned.

Our experience is that to develop effective Kata coaching skills, we need to bring together the principles of psychological safety, verbal and non-verbal communication learned in traditional coaching with the Kata steps. A key principle of the NHS People Plan in England is 'we must all make sure our people feel valued, and confident that their insights are being used to shape learning and improvement'(NHS England, 2020, p. 28). This is a core tenet of Lean and fits well with the application of Kata.

As with the Improvement Kata, Coaching and Second Coaching Kata have their own routines thus embedding scientific thinking within each Kata role. The consistency and the predictability of each of the Kata create a 'safe' space for both learner and coach. The concept of humble enquiry, and asking questions to understand rather than telling, underpins the Coaching Kata (Schein, 2014).

EXPERIENCE OF KATA COACHING

The NHS traditionally is used to command and control (as can be seen in the way managerial hierarchies are split into divisions in most NHS trusts). The learner coacher dynamic is different in Kata. The coach supports them through learning by experimentation and provides mentorship support rather than giving the learner direct commands to carry out.

Kata coaching is more aligned to relationship of learner pupil and Mr Miyagi relationship in 'Karate Kid' films rather than Darth Vader and Emperor Relationship in 'Star Wars' films!

(Dr Aklak Choudhury, Consultant Respiratory Physician, University Hospitals of Derby and Burton Foundation NHS Trust)

Feedback from coaches is that the burden of assurance reporting has been reduced. Managers coaching at the frontline coaching can see real-time progress. Previously, they would have asked for a report to be presented at a weekly or monthly committee. Relationships have improved and the rigour and safety of the coaching questions mean security and predictability are provided through the coaching conversation, guided by the Coach and Second Coach following the appropriate Kata routine. The close relationship people have or are creating with their line managers, enabled by coaching, makes it safe to experiment.

At the heart of every Kata deployment programme must be a clear development and assessment plan for coaches. As learner capability is the bedrock for great coaching skill, development and assessment begin with the learner. There will initially be neither coaching or learner skills. The role of the Advance Group will be to overcome this obstacle, in a way that works in their organisation.

Scaling Kata across an Organisation

When early success is seen, executives are often keen to ensure this is replicated quickly. The Development Block 1 format provided the temptation to train large numbers of learners. In our

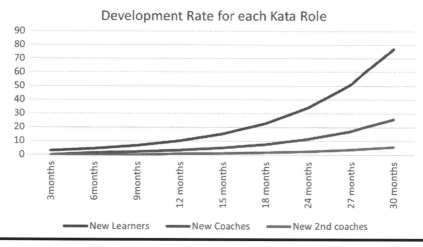

Figure 11.3   Development rate for Kata roles.

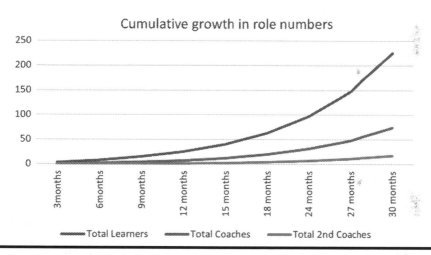

Figure 11.4   The cumulative growth in role numbers. Copyright Mike Rother used with permission.

experience, this approach led to pockets of poor practice, both in learner and coach skills development. The pace of effective Kata deployment is dictated by the amount of available good quality coaching capacity, and this takes time to develop.

We modelled the rate at which new learners, new coaching, and second coaching capacity can be achieved (see Figures 11.3 and 11.4).

ASSUMPTIONS UNDERPINNING THE MODELLING OF THE RATE AT WHICH NEW LEARNERS, NEW COACHING AND SECOND COACHING CAPACITY CAN BE ACHIEVED

The following conservative assumptions, to make projections for Kata role development across an organisation, have been made:

Assumption 1 – Approx. 60 coached/coaching cycles are required to move from a new learner to a new coach – typically this would take three months, based on one cycle per day on a five-day week working pattern.

Assumption 2 – 50% of learners become coaches.

Assumption 3 – Each new coach has three new learners every three months.

Assumption 4 – 50% of coaches become second coaches.

Assumption 5 – Second coaches coach three to six coaches at any given time.

Success Factors for Applying Kata

Choosing Kata as a management approach needs to be a conscious decision by the leadership within an organisation. This will not necessarily happen at the beginning of the Kata journey. It may take a small group of enthusiasts to demonstrate the power and impact of the approach before it becomes formally adopted. However, the conditions required for success can only be achieved when senior leadership fully engage to create them.

Strive for rapid cycles (several per day is possible). Change, at both individual and organisational level, requires repetition and practice. Daily practice on both Improvement and Coaching Kata is a desirable cadence. Organisations should beware of falling into the trap of a weekly 'cadence' of coaching cycles. The times when the new habits and behaviours are not being practised, you are engaging in the default behaviour. If the new habits are marginal, they will easily become overpowered by the default condition in the space between coaching cycles.

When deploying Kata in an organisation, care needs to be taken to ensure that there is a basic level of competency with the Improvement Kata pattern before moving on to become a coach. Typically, this is a minimum of 30 cycles of experimenting and attaining three successive target conditions. To achieve a basic level of Kata Coaching competency, expect coaches to need to conduct 60 or more coaching cycles, of which at least 20 have been observed by a second coach.

A successful deployment of Kata should start small with a Learning Group and then grow slowly and fractally from the core group. This Learning Group would ideally contain members of the senior leadership team who are open to practising and applying new skills to meeting challenges and solving problems. They will also need to show the necessary behavioural approach to coaching in the Kata style of being solution open, but highly precise on method.

Where possible, it is recommended to link a team's 'challenge' to the cascaded objectives set by the leadership team to support strategic alignment. This challenge sets the direction, and then, Kata gives a structure to support teams in running rapid experiments that iterate towards the challenge. This policy deployment or hoshin kanri system also supports the fractal nature of Kata deployment.

Organisations should see Kata as key to developing a learning culture, where individuals and leaders adopt growth mindsets – where they believe they can develop new knowledge and skills through focused effort. They recognise that what they know and can do today is not what they need to know and be able to do in the future. Such an approach to developing a growth mindset helps to evolve and adapt to change, and Kata provides a method and structure to help get started.

When starting out on a Kata journey, there is often a constraint in that there just are not enough experienced coaches and second coaches in an organisation. External support can help here, but only in so much that they support the internal development of coaches and second coaches and provide shepherding support to the rollout of Kata across the whole organisation.

Risks and Barriers to Success

The most common mistake in the deployment of Kata is that it is seen as just another Lean tool or that it is positioned as an alternative approach to other problem-solving tools such as A3 or the PDSA cycle. If Kata is seen as a tool and the Five Coaching Questions are seen as a miracle cure, the essence and ambition of scientific thinking will be lost. Kata supports the use of Lean tools and tools from other improvement philosophies to overcome obstacles standing in the way of success. More importantly, Kata opens team and individual minds to think creatively about fresh solutions and adaptations that might meet a specific challenge in a better way.

Another potential barrier is that coaching is done based on organisational seniority rather than an individual's experience in the use of the Improvement and Coaching Kata patterns. Staff members may want to be a coach without having developed the discipline and understanding that comes from being a learner. A leader cannot become a Kata Coach without experience as a learner or improver themselves. Conversely, experienced improvers at any level can become coaches to other improvers.

To maximise the likelihood of a successful culture shift through adoption of Kata, some of the senior leadership team must be involved from the start. Starting to develop an Advanced Party at too low a level of management, or confined to the Lean or Quality Improvement function, runs the risk that Kata is seen as a marginal activity, or only for specialists.

If an organisation's previous culture is one of developing detailed plans of action and multiple objectives, then there may be some resistance or disbelief when the Kata approach seeks only to develop a series of 'challenges' to set the organisational direction, not to spend time at the outset developing solutions and detailed plans.

In organisations where the culture is not open to experimentation in a controlled environment or does not provide the psychological security for staff to be able to admit that they do not know the answers, then the Kata approach will not sustain. Similarly, if the prevailing leadership does not want to commit by act as well as thought and to the engagement of team members in solving organisational challenges then Kata will fail.

Top Tips for Getting Started

Be curious. A good place to start is the Toyota Kata Website (Rother, Undated). You will find links to resources in many media formats. Try 'Kata in the Classroom', a short exercise designed to demonstrate the key principles of Kata. There are also some useful links in the resources section at the end of this chapter.

Get a coach, be a coach. The most experienced Kata practitioners still have coaches. An experienced coach will ensure good quality and deliberate practice of the Kata thinking patterns. So, as a coach becomes more experienced, they will move to be a second coach thereby ensuring the organisation develops its coaching capacity. The goal is to become self-sufficient in second coaching capacity and capability.

Connect with others. The organisations outlined in this chapter have real and lived experience of developing Kata, the experience from other industries is applicable to healthcare. Follow their social media activity, look for presentations they are giving online. Many will be free to access.

Just do it. Scientific thinking is a skill developed through practice. Reading all the academic material will most certainly give you knowledge but true understanding comes with practice. The more practice you can do, the better.

Coaching. For the best chance of success, the Advance Group needs to have executive and senior leadership members who have practised both as learners and coaches. Skilled coaches can come from any area of the organisation and be of any grade.

Use Kata to develop the Kata. Keep focused on the aim, to systematically overcome obstacles that are hindering progress. Remember though the pace of rollout will be dictated by the availability of experienced coaches.

Conclusion

It is our belief that Toyota Kata develops a 'meta-skill' that supports the adoption of new habits of thinking scientifically to meet challenges and solve problems. Our experience, and those who have shared their experience with us, has shown that new thinking patterns can be applied in many contexts, and at many levels of an organisation. Successfully moving an organisational culture towards Kata takes practice, and careful and considered development of leaders as coaches.

We also strongly believe that the supporting principles of Kata, through the engagement with frontline staff to work at a rapid pace, using a structured and scientific process of experimentation, gives Toyota Kata tremendous synergies with the existing and emerging culture within the NHS. These will apply in many organisations.

The debate about how Kata fits with existing Lean activity and initiatives misses the point. They can, and should, co-exist and complement one another. Scientific thinking must be the prevalent approach that underpins all work. A tool-led deployment of Lean will not meet all organisational challenges and will deprive people of the opportunity to gain experience and develop potentially even better solutions to challenges. This can present a problem to Lean method experts. Lean experts need to focus on coaching the development of solutions by the team involved in that area rather than imposing tools and solutions.

Where there is no pre-existing Lean programme, Kata can be used to develop scientific thinking to meet challenges without a parallel Lean implementation. This will take courage and persistence on the part of senior leaders but will result in a management system and culture that is uniquely attuned to meeting organisational challenges. We would argue that that is exactly what Toyota has done and is still doing. Above all else, Liker's personal challenge to those of us responsible for improving our organisations is to 'learn from the Toyota Way's principles, rather than simply copy Toyota's practices' (Liker, 2020).

Learning Points

- Scientific thinking underpins all improvement activities.
- Application of Lean tools, or any Quality Improvement tools, without understanding the reasons they are used, and the aims of the actions being undertaken, will be unsuccessful.
- Toyota Kata teaches ways of thinking that when applied at scale can make enormous differences to how an organisation works.
- Improvement Kata is relevant to all staff and should not be restricted to specialist staff.
- Coaching Kata is designed to support the teaching and spread of Improvement Kata.
- Senior engagement in the introduction and use of Toyota Kata is essential. While there should be alignment with organisational aims, all staff develops solutions.

Acknowledgements

The authors would like to thank and acknowledge the following people for their help, encouragement, and inspiration.

Mike Rother, who in articulating scientific thinking as Kata, has inspired a global movement.

Beth Carrington for her coaching and support to begin the NHS Kata journey, and Alan Martin, whose idea it was in the first place!

The global Kata community, of which we are privileged to be part. It is a constant source of shared learning, experience, and new connections.

Finally, special mentions to Mike Denison, Dr Joy Furnival, Professor Sylvain Landry, Jeff Liker, Tilo Schwarz, Maurene Stock, Betty Gratopp, and every one of our colleagues at the Vital Signs Sites for accepting the challenge and helping us to learn.

Bibliography

Augustovicova, D. C., Argajova, J., Garcia, M. S., Rodriguez, M. M., & Arriaza, R. (2018). Top-level karate: Analysis of frequency and successfulness of katas in K1 Premiere League. *Journal of Martial Arts Anthropology*, *18*(4), 46–53. https://doi.org/10.14589/ido.18.4.6

de Souza, L. B. (2009). Trends and approaches in Lean healthcare. *Leadership in Health Services*, *22*, 121–139. https://doi.org/10.1108/17511870910953788

Jones, D., & Mitchell, A. (2006). *Lean thinking for the NHS*. NHS Confederation.

Kaschak, G., & Roche, O. (2019). *Toyota Kata meets A3*. https://www.youtube.com/watch?v=bimOyQ3IZVU

Lean Transformation Programme Team. (2020). *Vital Signs: An Improvement Practice*. NHS England. Retrieved 14 Feb 2022 from https://www.england.nhs.uk/vital-signs/

Legentil, J. M., Legentil, M. O., & Schwarz, T. (2018). *The Toyota Kata Memory Jogger*. GOAL/QPC.

Liker, J. (2004). *The Toyota Way: 14 Management Principles from the World's Greatest Manufacturer*. McGraw-Hill.

Liker, J. K. (2020). *The Toyota Way: 14 Management Principles from the World's Greatest Manufacturer* (2nd ed.). McGraw-Hill Education.

Liker, J. K., & Hoseus, M. (2008). *Toyota Culture: The Heart and Soul of the Toyota Way*. McGraw-Hill.

NHS England. (2018, 11 April 2018). *Seven Trusts Take Part in Our Lean Programme*. NHS England. Retrieved 15 Feb 2022 from https://www.england.nhs.uk/2018/04/seven-trusts-take-part-in-our-lean -programme/

NHS England. (2020). *We Are the NHS: People Plan 2020/1: Action for Us All*. http://www.england.nhs.uk /ournhspeople

Rother, M. (2009). *Toyota Kata: Managing People for Improvement, Adaptiveness and Superior Results*. McGraw-Hill Education.

Rother, M. (2018). *Toyota Kata Practice Guide* (Vol. 2022). McGraw-Hill Education. http://www-personal .umich.edu/~mrother/Supporting_Materials.html

Rother, M. (n.d.a.). *Toyota Kata Practice Guide Supporting Materials*. Retrieved 14 Feb 2022 from http:// www-personal.umich.edu/~mrother/Supporting_Materials.html

Rother, M. (n.d.b.). *Toyota Kata: A Way to Practice and Develop Scientific Thinking in Everyday Work*. http:// www-personal.umich.edu/~mrother/Homepage.html

Rother, M., & Aulinger, G. (2017). *Toyota Kata Culture: Building Organizational Capability and Mindset Through Kata Coaching*. McGraw-Hill Education.

Rother, M., & May, C. (2013). *Are We Doing it Wrong?* https://www.slideshare.net/mike734/five-whys- 27172177

Schein, E. H. (2004). *Organizational Culture and Leadership* (3rd ed.). Jossey-Bass.

Schein, E. H. (2014). *Humble Inquiry: The Gentle Art of Asking Instead of Telling*. Berrett-Koehler.

Sobek, D. K., & Smalley, A. (2008). *Understanding A3 Thinking: A Critical Component of Toyota's PDCA Management System*. Productivity Press.

Spear, S., & Bowen, H. K. (1999). Decoding the DNA of the Toyota production system. *Harvard Business Review, 77*, 96–106.

Stark, C., & Hookway, G. (2019). *Applying Lean in Health and Social Care Services*. Routledge.

Tsui, K., & Girard, A. (2019). Driving an intentional culture change through an enterprise-wide mentoring program. *Nurse Leader, 17*(3), 197–200. https://doi.org/10.1016/j.mnl.2019.03.010

Ann Hill is a certified Kata coach, and her Lean experience has been predominantly within healthcare across several different settings. She specialises in leadership development and executive coaching. Ann has led national, regional, and organisational programmes and worked as an international consultant. Her improvement journey began as a biomedical scientist, combining the operational delivery of five services into one.

Graham Canning, BEng (Hons), MSc, is the managing director of consultancy firm Lean FSL Associates, and a partner in the training company People-Centered Excellence. He has worked in improvement consultancy roles for 17 years across many sectors including healthcare. His experience is built on 15 years of working in the manufacturing sector for companies such as Toyota, Black & Decker, and Pilkington Glass. He recently presented a paper on Toyota Kata at the European Lean Educators Conference in Portugal and is certified to Level 3b in Cardiff University's Lean Competency System (LCS). Graham is an experienced Kata coach and a founding member of the Kata School, UK. He lectures part time on the Executive MBA programme at Cardiff Business School and leads a research workstream for the Lean Enterprise Research Council (LERC) on the successful use of Kata to grow scientific thinking in organisations.

Chapter 12

Executive Leadership in Sustaining Lean Transformation

Kim Barnas

Contents

DOI: 10.4324/9780429346958-12

Aims

The aims of this chapter are to:

- Provide healthcare executives and leaders with an understanding of how to develop meaningful, lasting system-wide improvements using Lean systems.
- Understand the value of a clear vision and strategy for the organization.
- Describe how a Lean management system helps to produce and maintain progress.
- Give examples of the methods applied in practice.
- Offer exercises to reinforce learning.

Introduction

In my decades of experience applying Lean thinking to improve how hospitals function and collaborating with hundreds of healthcare leaders to help implement system-wide Lean healthcare initiatives, I have come to understand one thing: The challenge is not about creating short-term change. The challenge is creating *sustainable* change. Lean leaders must have the infrastructure and support to create and make continuous improvements.

The basis for every lasting Lean healthcare implementation is having the full support of the organization's leadership – the board, the chief executive, and the executive team. The goal is to change how the entire hospital system functions to improve results and enhance patient outcomes. If the hospital's top leaders do not support Lean principles and apply the tools to their day-to-day activities, the full benefits and anticipated improvement will never be realized.

Healthcare executives must take specific measures to ensure their Lean initiatives will last for the long haul. Most importantly, to sustain Lean momentum during periods of organizational change, leaders must commit to the development of a Lean operating system. Without this commitment, the life expectancy of Lean could be dramatically shortened.

Like the latest fad diet, health system leaders are in a constant lurch to seek fast, system-wide fixes that will:

- Provide better patient care.
- Enhance employee engagement.

- Improve operations.
- Reduce costs.

Typically, flavor-of-the-day improvement systems are not built to last and rarely produce sustainable improvements.

I maintain a strong commitment to Lean principles – applying not just the day-to-day tools and practices but creating an explicit Lean management system. This system will have sub-systems several of which I will talk about in this chapter and will change and improve over time. The foundation is that Lean is a proven improvement methodology. In the past, it has been applied as a set of tools sometimes without regard to the human component around foundational principles and behaviors. This led some to think that "Lean is mean." I have considered not using the term "Lean" to see the principles and philosophies in a more comprehensive light. The reality is, no matter what you call it, Lean produces lasting results that change the system. Through my work and collaboration with many colleagues, I have seen first-hand the success that hospitals achieve when leaders commit to change the culture and use Lean as their preferred system for improvement.

"One of the biggest barriers to our implementation of Lean was dispelling some of the myths about the methodology," said Jeff Mainland, executive vice president at the Hospital for Sick Children in Toronto, Canada. "Medicine is highly evidence-based. Once we were able to show that Lean is based on good evidence and highlight some of the outcomes other organizations had when implementing Lean, we were able to implement more successfully."

Mainland also said it is important not to underestimate the heavy demands of change management. "The journey is long. We are now six years into our journey, and we still have a long way to go. Yes, we have achieved impressive results but there's much more to do."

When properly implemented, Lean management systems will deliver results long term and hospital leadership can sustain the change if it is rooted in a clear vision and strategy that is communicated and embraced by all who are involved.

Providing Organizational Leadership

American educator and author, Reed B. Markham, said, "If you are standing still, you are also going backward. It takes significant effort to maintain forward movement."

Leading people through complex organizational change, creating new management systems, and improving processes every day, while empowering each employee on the team to act requires diligence and constant attention.

Organizational change only works when leaders have a shared desire to improve and make improvements stick – all the way to the frontline and each individual employee.

In this system, the chief executive officer provides a vision that is supported by the strategic engagement of the entire board and executive team. Focused strategies are deployed through the organization using Lean breakthrough tools and methodologies. The Lean management system comes into play to help identify and remove waste, manage strategic priorities while engaging all staff in daily continuous improvement. This system becomes the way we improve our business and is used for improvements both big and small.

Unfortunately, many healthcare leaders who attempt to implement change quickly stumble on a large hurdle that separates strategy and action. Perhaps the entire leadership team is not on board. The anticipated "quick" results do not happen, or a crisis gets in the way that demands attention and sucks momentum away from the plan.

An important first step to successful Lean implantation is the creation of the organization's True North (the vision, mission, and priorities that support these statements). True North is the way we see the overall health of the organization and the success of the systems. Often the True North metrics include the development of measures around customer experience, people, quality, safety, and financial stewardship. These priorities are then translated by the leadership team through strategic and breakthrough initiatives that cascade to staff throughout the organization.

With True North metrics in place, organizations can move forward with a Lean management system that is centered around a Strategy Deployment System – a process designed to ensure that every staff member understands the strategic priorities, how this impacts the True North metrics, and how the work they do connects to what leaders have identified as being most important. Strategy Deployment helps executives focus and align their organizations around the most important goals. Goals and plans are cascaded down and up in an organization – senior leadership to middle management to frontline staff and back up – for repeated review, input, actions, and revisions using Plan-Do-Study-Act cycles. While senior leaders may focus on True North metrics and high-level strategies, the rest of the organization collaboratively translates these goals into specific plans, targets, and actions. And unlike traditional planning, it is not an annual exercise but an iterative approach for transformation and continuous improvement.

With True North and Strategy Deployment in place, senior leadership can learn and stay focused on sustaining improvement and supporting the cultural transformation. The leadership behaviors they will need to develop will be supported by leader standard work and help them to better understand their role in leading and supporting the Lean transformation.

When I spoke with Marianne Griffiths, chief executive officer of Western Sussex Hospitals NHS Trust (Sussex, England) and chief executive officer of Brighton and Sussex University Hospitals NHS Trust about the overall success of the patient-first program, she shared that in addition to the daily continuous improvement focus, the need for an aligned strategy deployment process was an important element in their overall transformation.

"One of the keys to our success is the ability to focus on the most important priorities," Griffiths said. "Strategy deployment or SDR as we call it (Strategy Deployment Review) and the conversations it prompts are critical to our success. This process requires that we deeply focus on the most vital strategic and breakthrough initiatives."

Of course, finding success starts with some significant change to traditional leadership behavior. An article published by McKinsey & Company (Jenkins, 2017) makes it clear: Leaders need to know not only what they need to do differently, but *why* changing their behavior matters. What is more, leaders typically have years of old habits that must be unlearned to adopt the Lean behaviors needed to achieve results. Most leaders, therefore, need coaching and support to master this new way of leading.

Let us look at how hospital executives, leaders, and employees can make dramatic – and lasting – organizational change within their healthcare systems using Lean methods.

Tools and Much More

A Lean management system is not a box of tools leaders can cherry-pick from to make quick, organizational change. The focal point should be the management system. Lean, in effect, is more than a management system and becomes a driver of the *operating system* for the organization itself.

However, tools are an essential part of an integrated management system. The problem-solving tools related to A3, Value Stream Analysis, and Kaizen remain relevant in breakthrough process improvement systems.

With that said, there are eight key elements, or additional tools, integrated into a Lean management system:

1. Status Reports – used to assist in helping individuals learn the business, see trends, and proactively plan and develop reports for their teams.
2. Team Huddles – used to help elevate problems or defects in daily flow and problem solve during Gemba.
3. Managing to Established Standards – creating Standard Work for processes and the use of the Kamishibai process observation calendar to ensure progress.
4. Problem Solving – use of A3 thinking with robust root cause analysis to understand the problem and to create countermeasures to solve problems.
5. Transparency – communicate with frequency to direct reports, managers, and staff to ensure everyone understands expectations. Use of visual management wherever possible.
6. Advisory Teams – these unit-based teams see performance issues and own metrics. Understand problems and implements timely responses.
7. Scorecard – used at all levels to cascade and prioritize drivers, "know the numbers," and create countermeasures to respond to performance issues.
8. Leadership Standard Work – used to reduce variation and improve performance, support and develop direct reports, and "model the way."

Each of these elements is linked to create a system as they work together to become interlocking gears that move an organization forward (Figure 12.1).

The critical step for any leader interested in Lean is to look beyond the tools described above and, instead, consider the following four core elements designed to help an organization and its leadership team effectively implement a sustainable Lean management system.

Core Element Number One: Lean Methods and Systems Start at the Top and Are Rooted in Values, Principles, and Behaviors

Commitment to behavior change and to Lean practices begins with the chief executive. If he or she is not fully committed, the organization will quickly reach a plateau. What is more, when this plateau is reached, many organizations abandon the system entirely, saying Lean does not

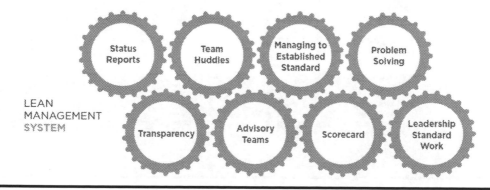

Figure 12.1 Eight key elements integrated into a Lean management system.

work. But if department heads, managers, and frontline workers see a commitment from those they report to, they will embrace the change and make the system work at every level of the organization.

When the president or chief executive officer makes the commitment to support system change using Lean methods, he or she is ready for the next step. They must look inward and identify the personal principles and behaviors that need to be adjusted to implement change. This step cannot be delegated and becomes a commitment that the leadership team must be able to see and understand. The chief executive sets the tone and expectation for organization-wide transformation. Only then can the leadership team agree to create a new operating system based on Lean principles and behaviors to guide the organization.

This Shingo model highlights the behaviors and principles that leaders, managers, and frontline employees must embrace (Figure 12.2) (The Shingo Institute, 2021).

Importantly, leaders must develop a vision with systematic thinking – setting high but reasonable targets. Next, they must inspire and enable their teams, leading with humility and energizing those around them to overcome hurdles. Finally, leaders must stay focused on process improvements and adjusting plans through constant listening and observing. These behaviors can be further broken down into key behavioral indicators (KBI) that are observable and measurable as leaders learn to lead differently.

In addition, John Toussaint and Karl Hoover have developed a self-assessment that identifies five behavioral traits or dimensions required for leaders to build a culture of continuous improvement: willingness, humility, curiosity, perseverance, and self-discipline (Toussaint & Ehrlich, 2017). These dimensions have specific reinforcing and observable behaviors to help leaders improve their ability to support the culture of improvement. Examples of these reinforcing

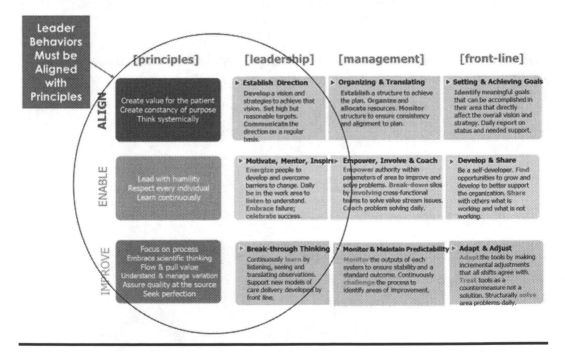

Figure 12.2 Shingo model of leadership principles and behaviors.

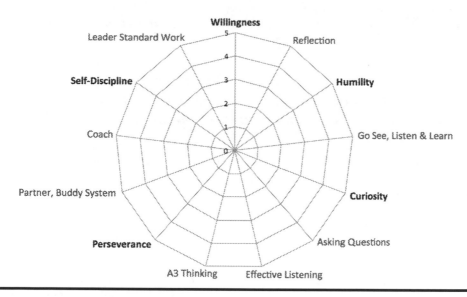

Figure 12.3   Reinforcing behavior for leaders.

behaviors include: Reflection; Go See/Listen and Learn; Asking Questions; Effective Listening; A3 Thinking; Partner/Buddy System; Coach, and Leader Standard Work (Figure 12.3).

These behaviors are measured on the spider diagram (Toussaint & Barnas, 2020) and leaders are asked to develop a plan to work on one or two of them that appear to have the most opportunity. Many leaders include these changes in their personal development plans and leader standard work.

Core Element Number Two: Effective Leadership, Lean Principles, and Tools Combined with a Lean Management System Become the Foundation for This Transformation

An executive with a clear vision will be able to use Lean to support both strategic initiatives and daily operations. System change requires a decisive plan involving Lean methodologies and practices. This plan includes the critical steps needed to connect vision and values with the principles and behaviors that will support transformation. To connect all of this, a clear definition of how to manage becomes critical, i.e., a Lean management system.

Providence Little Company of Mary (PLCOM), a 450-bed hospital in Torrance, California, quickly discovered the benefits of connecting its organization's strategy with leadership vision. PLCOM's chief executive officer at the time, Mary Kingston, now an executive for PeaceHealth, shared a common interest in implementing a Lean management system at PLCOM. Step one, and the most important, was sharing her vision with every physician and leader at the health system. Steadily, the cascade and communication of this vision reached every employee. Through visual management, and effective communication strategies, the entire organization understood the vision, strategy, and steps that needed to be taken to create PLCOM's new Lean management system. The result was that leaders and staff worked together to create a culture that today is more adaptable and prepared to face sweeping healthcare change. Their quality measures improved as did customer satisfaction end employee engagement. These results will be shared later in the chapter.

Core Element Number Three: Leaders Set Expectations of Behavior Change at Every Level of the Organization to Support and Sustain the Operating Improvements

At Western Sussex, Marianne Griffiths, her board of directors, and the leadership team created a clear vision of what's important for the organization. As Western Sussex began its Lean journey, leadership focused on a patient-first program to transform the organization. Each employee was asked to make continuous improvements to benefit patients. Initially, using a breakthrough/Kaizen approach, they added a Lean management system they referred to as their "Patient First Improvement System." This served as a framework for service development at the hospital with a focus on redesigning systems to remove waste and reduce errors, and to standardize practices so every patient gets great care and service.

The entire staff at Western Sussex have become an army of problem solvers with the permission and skills needed to make the change that improves service for patients. In April 2016, the Care Quality Commission (CQC), the independent regulator of health and social care in England, gave Western Sussex an Outstanding rating – one of only three acute trusts in England to receive the highest possible grade. In addition, in 2016, the NHS in England asked the leadership team to oversee operational change in a neighboring Trust, Brighton and Sussex University Hospitals, that was not meeting performance objectives. Patient First was foundational in their approach and they were able to move the Trust out of quality and financial regulatory measures over the first two years. In 2019, Western Sussex was the first hospital in England to achieve an outstanding CQC rating in all categories.

Core Element Number Four: Educate the Board of Directors to Generate Long-Term Support for Organizational Change

To create long-term board support for a major initiative such as adopting a Lean management system, the chief executive must also educate each board member about his or her role.

As Joseph Sluka, Don Shilton, and John S. Toussaint noted in a *Healthcare Executive* article (Sluka et al., 2018), many boards typically are composed of community leaders who are accomplished executives. But rather than focusing most of their attention on overseeing processes and outcomes and making changes at the C-suite level if performance goals are not achieved over time, often these well-meaning board members want to apply their business acumen to the operations of the hospital or health system.

At St. Mary's General in Kitchener, Ontario (Canada), Shilton was able to focus his board on governance – putting systems in place to ensure effective performance, succession planning, financial and quality oversight, and board-level improvement using Lean thinking and methodologies.

For a board of directors to remain focused on Lean, three categories of principles must be applied, according to the Shingo Institute at Utah State University. The authors outlined these categories in *Healthcare Executive* and although they apply to executive leaders, they further defined how they also apply to non-executive board members.

> The Align Principles include creating value for the customer, constancy of purpose, and thinking systemically. When applying these principles to governance, the board should first define customer value to determine its role in assuring customer value. For example, if the board defines customer value in the classic way of quality divided by cost equals value, then the

board should determine if they are delivering better quality at a lower cost by looking at such measures at each meeting.

A board that thinks systemically should be interested in more than the organization's finances.

The Enable Principles include respect, humility, and continuous learning. These establish the cultural foundation for the board with "respect for every individual" at the core. This means one board member cannot dominate a board meeting, and that personal agenda must be left at the door. A spirit of consensus should be present, and confidential material should never be shared outside the board room.

The Improvement Principles focus on process, embracing scientific thinking, understanding and managing vision, and seeing perfection.

For example, the board of St. Mary's General Hospital, improved its governance practices using the Plan-Do-Study-act Cycle – a tool for accelerating improvement.

The board began its Lean journey by aligning the organization under a clear and aspirational vision: "to be the safest and most effective hospital in Canada, characterized by innovation, compassion and respect." The vision was then supported by the operational goals of eliminating preventable harm; improving the patient experience; developing, supporting, and sustaining a culture of problem solvers; and reducing the cost of quality healthcare. The result was a board that believed in the organization's vision and strategic direction; and a hospital president who trusted that board members would support his decision-making at the operational level.

The principles board members must adopt to govern effectively are summarized (Sluka et al., 2018) (Figure 12.4).

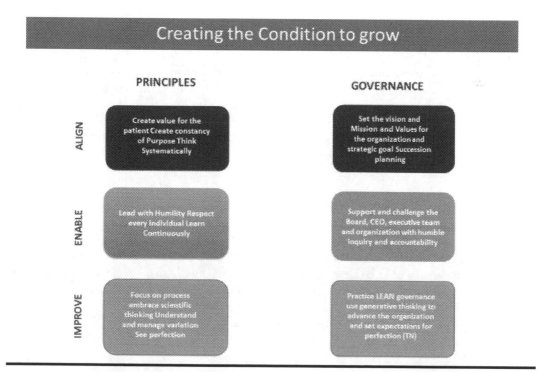

Figure 12.4 Creating conditions: principles board members adopt to support effective governance.

The board of directors at St. Charles Health System in Bend, Oregon (USA), also adopted a comprehensive approach to using the Align, Enable, and Improve principles to guide how they govern the organization.

Sustainability, safety, and engagement were priorities in 2015 when leaders at St. Charles suggested a renewed effort on continuous improvement with system-wide, top-to-bottom adoption of Lean thinking. The board wanted to be supportive, but its members were cognizant that hardwiring organizational Lean thinking takes at least five to 10 years, longer than the average tenure of most trustees and executives. To that end, the board conducted a three-day visioning session, using an A3 problem-solving approach to understand what management meant by Lean transformation. This approach is a scientific method for problem solving those entails exploring gaps between a problem or an opportunity and what a favorable outcome might look like and experiments that might close the gaps. Scientific thinking is discussed further in Chapter 11 "Applying Kata in Healthcare."

One outcome was to initiate a rapid improvement event on the selection of new board members. Board member longevity at St. Charles ranged from three to 10 years, whereas every management executive participating had been with the organization less than three years. This presented an obvious challenge for any sustainable transformation. The board adopted a new, more rigorous selection process in which prospective trustees are vetted systematically for Lean leadership attributes, long-term strategic thinking, and technical or clinical acumen. In addition, new board members receive an orientation that includes A3 education and participation in a rapid improvement event.

Lean thinking becomes the driver for broad operating system change. From board members to senior executives, and from department/function heads to frontline employees – when everyone embraces the vision, success is much more likely to result.

Getting Results with a Lean Management System

The rate of change in the business of healthcare has been extraordinarily fast in the past two decades. The shift to electronic medical records, mergers that create giant health systems, nationwide plans to insure more (or less) people. These transformations get rolled out with a hopeful promise that healthcare will be better for everyone.

These promises have not been followed with meaningful reporting of metrics or noteworthy results. In fact, the lofty claims have raised fundamental questions:

- Can changes in operations management, driven by healthcare administrators, really improve the care patients receive from physicians, nurses, and therapists?
- Can non-medical managers and executives affect patient outcomes with management alone?

Not long ago, as president of hospitals for a large cradle-to-grave health system in Wisconsin, I wrote a book about my hospital's experience implementing a daily management system (Barnas & Adams, 2014). This system, in conjunction with the improvement tools and principles we employed, had a profound effect on patient outcomes, patient satisfaction, and employee engagement. Throughout the hospitals, we improved patient safety, reduced medical and surgical errors, and increased the percentage of caregivers who said they would recommend our hospital as a good place to work.

The daily management system gave administrators and caregivers a method to find the root cause of problems together, every day. Instead of rushing around putting out fires, managers began their day resource planning with frontline staff and addressing issues before they became problems. Quality metrics rose and costs declined.

After I left that health system, I wanted to know if the results of those early experiments were a fluke. In my new role coaching healthcare executives, I would check in frequently with the early adopters to see how time was testing the system. As new hospitals and health systems adopted daily management, I began asking for their results, as well.

The Results

To date, I have gathered data from six very different healthcare organizations in the United States, Canada, and the United Kingdom and the results are eye-opening:

King's County Hospital Behavioral Health, Brooklyn, New York, USA

This system of in-patient and outpatient clinics dedicated to mental health treatment and drug rehabilitation is part of the New York City Health and Hospitals Corporation. It is the largest municipal health system in the United States. With 133 adult beds and 40 beds for children and adolescents, the in-patient unit discharged 4,042 patients in 2016.

In early 2016, leaders here chose to focus their daily management system queries on why some patients were staying in-patient longer than 15 days. Illnesses such as schizophrenia, depression, and bipolar disorders always require long-term treatment. Patients are admitted to the hospital to overcome crises and stabilize, with therapy continuing when patients were discharged. But too many patients stayed well past the usual 15 days and leaders wanted to understand why.

Using problem-solving tools, a team soon found a root cause: providers did not trust that outpatient services were robust enough to help their more fragile patients once they were discharged. Patients often found it difficult to schedule regular appointments and miscommunication was also a common thread to the problem.

So, the gap between in-patient and outpatient services became a daily focus of check-ins and improvement projects at King's County. Within a few months, staff worked to improve communication between providers.

Jordan Vanek, senior director at King's County Hospital Behavioral Health, said:

> By cleaning up the provider templates, standardizing intake times and slots based on a factorial calculation of the demand at different levels, with a no-show probability percentage, to determine true required slots per day, we were able to identify opportunities. The daily management system helped us ensure no available appointments were left unfilled.

In a single month, the average number of days until the third next-available appointment – the measure all outpatient clinics use to assess availability – dropped from a high of 31 to just five. During the next 12 months, the team shifted from paper records to centralized electronic records and the average days crept up to eight before settling at a steady four days.

Leaders also reconfigured staffing to ensure accountability and created oversight triads – with one provider, nurse, and administrator – for each service area. Needs and solutions were identified in team huddles and daily check-ins, and then reinforced and standardized.

"We've hardwired anticipating and solving problems for our patients," said Dr. David Estes, director of primary care. "The metrics we're focused on reflect our goals across the system. And now we transmit information both top-down and bottom up."

Within 16 months, Behavioral Health had reduced by 68% the number of days a patient spent over the 15 days. This amounted to 59,200 fewer bed days during those 16 months and a savings of $2.9 million. At the same time, their 30-day readmission rate dropped from 9% to 6%.

St. Mary's Hospital, Kitchener, Ontario, Canada

At St. Mary's Hospital, leaders selected patient falls and infection rates for their safety and quality metrics. For 12 months, daily check-ins all included questions about falls and infection risks. Unit and area huddles discussed recent cases and gaps in the care process, and then, supported by root cause analysis, a management team chose specific, measurable countermeasures. When standard work procedures were changed, staff members were assigned to teach new procedures, and then follow up regularly to see if the countermeasures were still in place and working.

In 2017, patient falls were reduced by half. Three diverse kinds of hospital-acquired infections had been reduced by 51%, 63%, and 64% across the hospital.

"A key learning for us was to focus on just a handful of improvement measures rather than everything at once," said chief executive officer Don Shilton, retired president of St. Mary's. "We reduced our focus from seven goals, to five and finally four, which served as an ideal number for us."

Western Sussex Hospitals NHS Foundations Trust, England

Western Sussex focused on quality measures on an internationally recognized metric that is notoriously difficult to budge: Hospital Standardized Mortality Ratio (HSMR). This is a mathematical calculation that in England is calculated by comparing actual deaths versus expected deaths in 65 diagnoses that comprise 80% of all deaths. Moving that number requires a hospital to look hard at its weaknesses in a variety of areas and address common problems.

One statistic the team examined was later-than-expected discharges from Intensive Care Units. By investigating problems, applying countermeasures, and then returning to the scene multiple times to make sure they were still in use, staff cut in half the number of delayed discharges from the unit. Correcting problems like this throughout the system all added up to a remarkable 18% improvement in the HSMR and vaulted Western Sussex into the top 20% of all hospitals in the NHS in England.

Hospital for Sick Children, Ontario, Canada

At the Hospital for Sick Children, daily improvement work reduced the number of central-line infections by 45% and reduced the number of time children and parents had to spend in the emergency department by 14%.

Providence Little Company of Mary, Torrance, California, USA

At Providence Little Company of Mary (PLCOM), the team focused on reducing patient harm. Providers and staff worked together to cut the rate of central line-associated blood stream infections (CLABSI) by 50%. And they reduced hospital-acquired pressure ulcers – bedsores – by 92%.

"This reinforced my belief that great leadership can be even better when people connect regularly and discuss day-to-day problems and performance using data," said Mary Kingston, former PLCOM chief executive officer. "They begin to aspire to greater things, and it became contagious."

Of course, health systems are not judged on the quality of patient care alone. Patients must be satisfied with the care they receive, and employees must be satisfied too. These measures are far more alike than quality metrics. So, in most cases, reporting on annual response rates to two questions will suffice.

- For patients: Would you recommend this hospital to friends and family?
- To care providers and staff: Would you recommend this hospital as a good place to work?

Would You Recommend This Hospital to Friends and Family?

- Leaders at PLCOM found that low patient satisfaction scores were strongly correlated with longer wait times in the emergency department. Physicians changed the triage system and reduced wait times between their department and radiology. This increased patient satisfaction scores in the emergency department by 8%.
- At the Hospital for Sick Children in Canada, administrators used patient satisfaction scores to guide improvement work in pediatric surgery. During daily check-ins and huddles, they sought ways to reduce waiting and errors.
- The staff at St. Mary's General Hospital in Ontario improved their patient satisfaction score by 8% in 2016.
- Western Sussex Hospitals reported that patient satisfaction was up by 1% from 2014 to 2015.

Would You Recommend This Organization as a Good Place to Work?

This is the question many health systems, particularly in the USA use to assess the satisfaction of staff doctors, nurses, and support staff. Here are some results available from 2015.

- PLCOM: 8% improvement.
- Hospital for Sick Children: 12% improvement.
- St. Mary's General: 8% improvement.
- Western Sussex: 8% improvement. (Note: In 2019 93% of staff surveyed said they would recommend Western Sussex to others as a place to work. In addition, 97% said they would recommend the hospital as a place to be treated.)

These different health systems attacked their own problems from a variety of directions and found at least one common outcome: steady progress toward a goal over a sustained period. Each health system team chipped away at problems in unit huddles, found root causes, and made changes and it added up.

Dramatic solutions followed by crashing trend lines are not a common feature of a daily management system. The daily nature of the system creates a steady cadence that helps hospitals focus just as much on sustaining past improvement as it does on achieving dramatic results.

Breakthrough improvement projects still give these health systems big bumps in quality improvements and waste reduction.

It is important to note that leadership change does not have to result in the dismantling of a performance improvement team. Instead, with the adoption of leadership behaviors that support a unified management system, and support from a board that ensures new senior leaders have expertise in daily management systems, any health system can keep its momentum moving in the right direction.

This five-year study proved that a daily management system can create better patient outcomes and happier staff and patients. Like all systemic changes, however, we have also seen that improvements will be transitory unless leaders make long-term commitments to supporting the work. As the study continues, we will examine how such initiatives fail as well as succeed.

Lean at Zuckerberg San Francisco General Hospital – A Case Study

While we have pointed to a variety of sustained results following the implementation of a Lean management system, it's important to also share some in-depth details in a case study format to allow you to have educated discussions with your peers, your leadership team, and with board members about the importance of Lean and sustainable transformation.

In this case study, excerpted from an article written and published by Ehrlich et al., examined how Zuckerberg San Francisco General Hospital (ZSFGH) created a culture of continuous improvement starting with the chief executive and senior executives where their behavior is known to be directly related to an organization's performance (Ou et al., 2018). In 2018, the five behavioral traits or dimensions required to build a culture of continuous improvement: willingness, humility, curiosity, perseverance, and self-discipline, were incorporated at ZSFGH in an effort to change leader behavior and produce better patient outcomes (Toussaint & Ehrlich, 2017).

But first, why is leadership behavior so important?

As I explained previously in this chapter, healthcare has been slow to adopt modern management principles (Toussaint, 2015). Most healthcare organizations are still managed in a traditional autocratic style that does not allow for much worker input. The manager or leader makes most decisions and tells everyone what to do. Problems that arise are not managed expeditiously at the front line by people who understand the work. Instead, problems pile up on the manager's desk and most are not solved. This lack of real-time problem solving has led to a terrible performance in the US, where it is estimated that at least 100,000 people die prematurely from preventable harm in hospitals every year (Makary & Daniel, 2016).

Many hospitals around the world are building a different management system to combat this unacceptable medical error rate. Leaders take lessons from world-class manufacturing and software companies to build systems that transfer decision making to those who do the actual work. In software design, it is the software engineer who makes hundreds of decisions each day, none of which are reviewed by management. The engineer simply runs small, rapid experiments of software changes to determine if they can build something the customer wants. Likewise, in manufacturing, frontline workers have clear expectations that any problem identified in quality or workflow is their responsibility. The workers suggest ideas, test them, and make changes in real-time. In healthcare, on the other hand, ideas to improve the patient experience typically go unsaid.

High-performing industries have management systems based on a set of fundamental principles, such as using scientific methods to solve problems at the front line. But for traditional healthcare managers, relinquishing responsibility for problem solving to the people closest to the work is hard to swallow. To overcome this requires a different way of behaving.

Healthcare organizations that have made these kinds of changes demonstrate undeniable results. ZSFGH began to see immediate results when leaders focused on changing their own behaviors.

Goals, Strategies, and Personal Growth

ZSFGH adopted six True North goal areas – equity, safety, quality, care experience, workforce care and development, and financial stewardship – and decided how to measure each performance category. These measures are ZSFGH's must-do, can't-fail metrics for organizational performance. As part of the improvement management system, hospital leaders also defined a few important strategies and deployed them across the hospital in 2017 known as Strategy Deployment.

If organizations are to change, then leaders must change. That was the step ZSFGH took next in 2017. The workforce care and development goal focused on developing principle-based leaders who embrace the five key behavioral dimensions of willingness to change, leading with humility, curiosity about how things work, perseverance, and self-discipline. The observable behaviors necessary to know whether leaders are cultivating the five qualities include practicing self-reflection and going to where the work is done to observe, learn, and coach (Awdish et al., 2018). We call the going to where the work is done "going to the Gemba," which simply means the place where value is created for the customer. Other observable behaviors include asking open-ended questions, listening carefully, and practicing the approach known as A3 thinking.

An A3 is an 11-by-17-inch piece of paper that tells a story about a problem or barrier. The story explains the background and current state of the situation. This leads to the most important step: defining the problem to be solved. As Einstein reportedly said, "If I had 60 minutes to save the world, I would spend 55 minutes defining the problem and five minutes finding the solution."

Thinking this way stops us from jumping to solutions that have no bearing on the actual problem. The A3 process can also be used for personal development. Other observable behaviors include having an established coach for improvement and adopting a set of standards to guide the leader's workday, called "leader standard work." Figure 12.5 shows a photo of an example of A3 forms and Leader Standard Work in use within the Lean Management System at ZSFGH.

In 2017, Dr. Ehrlich focused the 55 top leaders at ZSFGH on the five key behavioral dimensions. For each leader, the plan started with a 360-degree evaluation based on the five behaviors. With

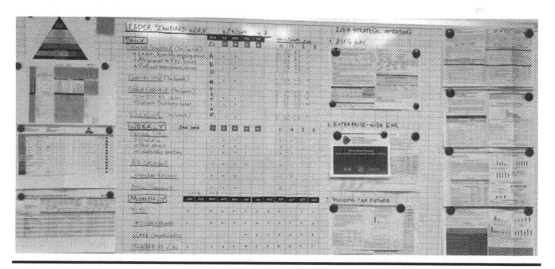

Figure 12.5 An example of A3 forms and Leader Standard Work in use within the Lean Management System.

results in hand, each leader worked with his or her superior to develop a Personal Development Plan–A3 (PDP-A3), focusing on the areas needing improvement. From there, each leader adopted leader standard work, which included daily, weekly, and monthly activities that codified what the leader was going to do to achieve the organization's strategic goals (Toussaint, 2016). The process included reflection to help leaders assess whether they were carrying out their plans.

To promote this deep personal development work, ZSFGH's 55 leaders assembled in small work groups to share their PDP–A3s. Dr. Ehrlich recruited a few leaders who were a bit ahead of the rest to describe their plans and their leader standard work. This peer-to-peer learning exercise was readily accepted. It became a learning journey that everyone experienced together, rather than one more thing they were told to do.

Leveraging a Crisis

As the ZSFGH team worked to ensure the behavioral dimensions were being instilled in the culture, a crisis arose. The hospital experienced the heaviest winter volumes in its history in 2017. The emergency department volume had been increasing steadily by about 5% to 10% per year; in July 2014, ZSFGH saw about 175 patients per day, and in January 2017, during the initial crisis, volumes were about 215 per day. Volumes peaked at 240 per day in January 2018. Patient flow through the emergency department and hospital in-patient services became the number one priority (Somlo et al., 2018), and the biggest source of staff stress. Staff also had to adjust to a new acute and emergency facility that had just come online and required radical redesign of workflows – adding even more stress.

Instead of panicking and trying to solve the crisis at the top, the ZSFGH leadership team viewed the crisis as an opportunity to model its new leadership culture. Dr. Ehrlich worked with the executive leadership team to establish weekly standup rounds, during which the team reviewed metrics related to flow. Then, leaders responsible for addressing issues such as workflow, staffing, supplies, and patient transportation recruited scores of colleagues throughout the organization to help. Leaders dove into the situation and demonstrated their curiosity by going to frontline staff, asking questions, and removing barriers.

In addition, the leaders revisited the True North metrics, established earlier in the year. They selected a handful of new performance metrics: percentage of time on ambulance diversion, mean emergency department length of stay (Skarzynski et al., 2018), and the number of patient days attributable to non-acute patients. Using A3 story papers, they reported the progress of multiple rapid experiments focused on flow-sticking points, including staff ideas to accelerate progress.

Dr. Ehrlich visited the emergency department, in-patient, and ambulatory areas to observe the work and to ask questions of staff and leaders. In this way, she had the opportunity to reinforce the new behaviors at all levels of leadership.

Quality Improvement Results

The following year, ZSFGH dramatically increased the number of leaders adopting the key behaviors:

- 100% of leaders were trained in A3 thinking, up from 81%: a 23% improvement.
- 87% of leaders adopted leader standard work, up from 55%: a 58% improvement.

The behavioral changes had a direct impact on ZSFGH quality results. Although ED volume increased by 13% in 2017:

- Mean emergency department length of stay declined by 9%.
- Ambulance diversion declined by 25%.
- Days attributed to non-acute patients declined by about 35%.

The results in this case study reflect a work in progress, not a finished product. Most importantly, ZSFGH continues to see improvements. Their experience shows that with consistent disciplined practice, leaders can continually focus on eliminating critical problems and get results.

Conclusions for the Case Study

The management system being developed at ZSFGH is based on a common set of behaviors that are proven in other industries. The behaviors are the bedrock of a culture of continuous improvement. Today, leaders believe ZSFGH will see sustained success by reinforcing leadership growth and development. The executive team will do this by cultivating behaviors and by building a set of management standards across the entire organization designed to deliver better patient outcomes (Sadun, 2017).

Learning Activities

Getting started can be difficult. Observing waste and paying thoughtful attention to problems are good ways to start. Two useful activities to help with these points are Silent Observation and Gemba Walks.

Activity 1: Silent Observation

Here is an effective learning activity designed to help leaders see waste in the process.

The key to the "Silent Observation" process is to refrain from offering any solutions during the actual observation (Table 12.1).

1. Silently observe a process in your hospital, accompanied by your coach or performance improvement team member.
2. Let the staff know that as part of your personal development, you are required to observe and learn but you will not make any judgment or take any action based on what you see.
3. Observe for 20–30 minutes, being aware of the "wastes" in the process.

Write your observations on a worksheet. A sample worksheet combining the process and space for notes is provided.

Table 12.1   Types of Waste in Healthcare

Type of Waste	Example
Defects Mistakes that require additional time, resources, and money to fix	Wrong medication is given to the patient
Overproduction Producing something when those who receive their output either are not ready for it or do not need it	Specimens delivered in large batches
Waiting This occurs whenever work must stop for some reason: because the next person in line is overwhelmed, because something broke down, because you are waiting for approval or materials, or because you have run out of something	Patients waiting in emergency department Staff waiting for work to do
Not using talent Not (or under-utilizing) peoples' talents, skills, and knowledge	Incorrect skill mix Poor teamwork
Transportation Waste caused by moving things around	Patients walking long distances between oncology clinic and chemotherapy
Inventory This waste occurs when there is supply more than real customer demand, which masks real production	Expired medications
Motion Any excess movement, whether by employees or machines, which does not add value to the product, service, or process	Nurses walking many miles per day
Excess processing More work or higher quality than is required by the customer	Unnecessary imaging or pathology investigations Excess reporting or recording

Background:

1. Silently observe a process in your hospital, accompanied by your coach or performance improvement team member.
2. Let the staff know that as part of your personal development, you are required to observe and learn but you will not make any judgment or take any action based on what you see.
3. Observe for 20–30 minutes, being aware of the "wastes" in the process.

Write your observations here:

Activity 2: Gemba Walk

When going to the Gemba asking humble open-ended questions is critical. This worksheet will help you practice. Start by only asking these questions (Figure 12.6). We want to avoid blame, fear, and facilitate open dialogue about how a process is working and encourage the team to experiment with the process with encouragement and support of leadership. Helping to remove barriers is an opportunity for leadership to look toward.

Gemba Walk

Example Questions		Observations & Reflections
Purpose	What is the purpose of this process?	
	What problems are you are trying to solve?	
	What are the challenges you face?	
	What is today's priority?	
Process	How do our processes work?	
	How do our patients define value from this process??	
	How do we know how we are doing?	
	What waste is there (DOWNTIME)?	
People	How are the people engaged in the improvement?	
	What challenges are hindering your staff from improving the process?	
	Is there Standard Work? Is it posted? Is it being followed?	
Lean Management	How are problems identified and solved?	
	How many opportunities were identified in the last month? How many improvements were completed?	
	What progress has been made on the driver metrics?	
	What are the next steps?	
	What help do you need to prioritize or remove barriers?	
	What would help make the huddles and the huddle board more effective?	

Figure 12.6 Gemba walk.

Conclusion

Lean is a methodology proven to work in healthcare systems of all sizes around the globe – with lasting results. We know hospitals can achieve success with a Lean Management System when everyone (the chief executives, senior leaders, board members, and staff) commits to change and sticks with their commitment.

With an organization's True North (vision, mission, and priorities) and a shared Strategy Deployment System that every staff person understands, effective change can begin. Throughout the process, keep in mind these four core elements:

- Leaders set expectations of behavior change at every level of the organization to support and sustain the operating improvements.
- Educate the board of directors to generate long-term support for organizational change.
- Lean methods and systems are rooted in values, principles, and behaviors.
- Effective leadership, Lean principles, and tools combined with a Lean Management System become the foundation of the Lean operating system.

Avoid distractions and do not let your plans get derailed. During times of chaos, it is easy to lose focus or abandon Lean methodologies entirely. There is no faster way to sidetrack progress than to let a single event disrupt your weeks, months, and years of planning and execution. As leaders at Zuckerberg San Francisco General Hospital did, apply Lean thinking to the crisis du jour. You will find new strength in managing issues and putting out fires – implementing Lean tools and expertise to solve the problem at hand. While your journey will be long, it will most certainly produce sustainable results when Lean is in place as your guide.

Learning Points

- The first step to successful Lean implantation is the creation of the organization's True North (the vision, mission, and priorities that support these statements).
- Leadership behavior change is often the first, and most difficult, step in creating a sustainable Lean operating system.
- Involve the board of directors by inviting them to see first-hand how other health systems have successfully implemented Lean Management Systems.
- Focus board members on the Align, Enable, Improve principles to keep them centered on their roles throughout the Lean transformation process.
- Strategy Deployment is the process designed to ensure that every member of staff understands the strategic priorities, how these map to True North metrics, and how the work they do every day connects to the strategic priorities.
- Tools (status reports, huddles, A3s) are part of an integrated operating system where leadership, vision, and strategies are connected to daily continuous improvement to sustain and steadily improve the organization.
- An integrated Lean Operating System consists of leadership, vision, and strategies connected to daily continuous improvement to sustain and steadily improve the organization.
- Following these four core elements to effectively implement a sustainable Lean management system:
  - Lean methods and systems start at the top and are rooted in values, principles, and behaviors.

- Effective Leadership, Lean principles, and tools combined with a Lean management system are how we define the Lean operating system.
- Leaders set expectations of behavior change at every level of the organization to support and sustain the operating improvements.
- Educate the board of directors to generate long-term support for organizational change.

Acknowledgments

Susan P. Ehrlich, MD, MPP, chief executive officer, Priscilla Chan and Mark Zuckerberg San Francisco General Hospital and Trauma Center.

John S. Toussaint, MD, chief executive officer, Catalysis (formerly ThedaCare Center for Healthcare Value).

Marianne Griffiths, chief executive officer, Western Sussex Hospitals NHS Trust (Western Sussex), and Chief Executive of Brighton and Sussex University Hospitals NHS.

Mary Kingston, chief executive officer, Providence Little Company of Mary (PLCOM), (now an Executive for PeaceHealth).

Don Shilton, retired chief executive officer, St. Mary's General.

Bibliography

Awdish, R. L., Glenn, D. M., Sharieff, G. Q., Howell Jr., T., & Mohta, N. S. (2018). *Physician Coaching Models: Solutions and Impediments*. NEJM Catalyst. https://catalyst.nejm.org/doi/full/10.1056/CAT .18.0231

Barnas, K., & Adams, E. (2014). *Beyond Heroes: A Lean Management System for Healthcare*. ThedaCare Center for Healthcare Value.

Hunter, J. (2018). *Patient-Centered Strategy*. Catalysis, Inc.

Jenkins, A. (2017). *Advancing Lean Leadership*. M. Company. https://www.mckinsey.com/business-func-tions/operations/our-insights/advancing-lean-leadership

Makary, M. A., & Daniel, M. (2016). Medical error: The third leading cause of death in the US. *BMJ, 353*, i2139. https://doi.org/https://doi.org/10.1136/bmj.i2139

Ou, A. Y., Waldman, D. A., & Peterson, S. J. (2018). Do humble CEOs matter? An examination of CEO humility and firm outcomes. *Journal of Management, 44*(3), 1147–1173. https://doi.org/10.1177 /0149206315604187

Porter, M. E., & Teisberg, E.O. (2006). *Redefining Health Care: Creating Value-Based Competition on Results*. Harvard Business Review Press.

Ries, E. (2011). *The Lean Startup: How Constant Innovation Creates Radically Successful Businesses*. Penguin.

Rother, M. (2009).*Toyota Kata: Managing People for Improvement, Adaptiveness and Superior Results*. McGraw-Hill Education.

Sadun, R. (2017). *Good Management = Good Clinical Outcomes*. NEJM Catalyst.

Schein, E. H. (2013). *Humble Inquiry: The Gentle Art of Asking Instead of Telling*. Berrett-Koehler.

Shewart, W. A. (1939). *Statistical Method from the Viewpoint of Quality Control*. Graduate School of the Department of Agriculture.

Skarzynski, D., Kruger, D., Katsogridakis, Y. L., & Burns, R. R. (2018). *Reducing Length of Stay in the ED*. NEJM Catalyst.

Sluka, J., Shilton, D., & J.S., T. (2018). Improving governance through principles. *Healthcare Executive* (July / August).

Somlo, D. R. M., Repenning, N. P., & Mangi, A. A. (2018). Improving patient flow with dynamic work design. NEJM Catalyst.

Taylor, F. W. (1911). *The Principles of Scientific Management*. Harper & Brother.

The Shingo Institute. (2021). *The Shingo Model Version 14.7*. The Shingo Institute, Utah State University.

Toussaint, J., & Berry, L. (2013). The promise of lean in healthcare. *Mayo Clinic Proceedings 88*(1), 74–82.

Toussaint, J. S. (2015). Hospitals can't improve without better management systems. *Harvard Business Review*, *4*, 2–5. https://hbr.org/2015/10/hospitals-cant-improve-without-better-management-systems

Toussaint, J. S. (2016). *How Health Care Systems Can Effectively Manage Process*. NEJM Catalyst.

Toussaint, J. S., & Barnas, K. (2020). *Becoming the Change: Leadership Behavior Strategies for Continuous Improvement in Healthcare*. McGraw Hill.

Toussaint, J. S., & Ehrlich, S. P. (2017). *Five Changes Great Leaders Make to Develop an Improvement Culture*. NEJM Catalyst.

Womack, J. P., & Jones, D. T. (1996). *Lean Thinking*. New York: Free Press.

Kim Barnas is a recognized authority in creating fully integrated management systems in hospitals around the world. She is the current chief executive of Catalysis, a former hospital president, author of *Beyond Heroes: A Lean Management System for Healthcare* (winner of the 2014 Shingo Prize for Research) and co-author of *Becoming the Change: Leadership Behavior Strategies for Continuous Improvement in Healthcare*.

Chapter 13

Learning How to Apply Lean

Elaine Mead, Cameron Stark, and Maimie Thompson

Contents

Aims

The aims of this chapter are to:

- Reflect on the learning from the chapter authors.
- Note the importance of taking organisational context into account in planning and delivering change.
- Confirm the importance of respect for staff, involvement of patients, and clarity on organisational values.
- Discuss the attributes that organisations can consider if they wish to engage with strategic partners in Lean implementation.
- Reflect on the importance of shared learning.

Introduction

The authors of this book provide an insight into the use of Lean in healthcare in the 2020s. Their collective work reflects the breadth and range of implementation of Lean around the globe in the

DOI: 10.4324/9780429346958-13

last decade. The contributions emphasise that while systems of healthcare delivery and funding vary by country, there are shared challenges that cross international and political boundaries. The range of organisations reporting in this volume, and the many other organisations using Lean around the world, reflect the widespread acceptance that quality improvement is a rigorous methodology, based on replicable experiments and for which there is evidence of positive change in real healthcare organisations.

Lean is based on respect for staff (Graban, 2017). It values their expertise and insights and links them with the patients who use their services to create solutions to long-standing problems. Obtaining the benefits of Lean at scale requires appropriate organisational support and aligned management purpose (Mead et al., 2017).

The contributors are united in recognising that there is no quick and easy solution to making changes, and no single route to guaranteed sustainability. Instead, the case examples demonstrate that achieving positive change requires long-term effort and application of techniques, process by process, specialty by specialty, organisation by organisation, with careful attention to the local context.

While a good understanding of Lean tools remains important, the chapters that include detailed descriptions of the tools and techniques also reflect the nuances of application in different settings and the importance of system leadership. Many authors emphasise the importance of clarity of purpose and a desire to change organisational culture as a basis for a successful Lean journey (Barnas & Adams, 2014; Gabow & Goodman, 2014; Plsek, 2014; Toussaint & Adams, 2015). Imposing a methodology without preparing the conditions carries the risk of a continued cycle of short-term gains and predictable long-term disappointment.

The authors presenting here have practised, and supported practice, for many years. Notably, they have all arrived at similar conclusions: that successful implementation takes leadership, purpose, and continued practice over time. Improvements can be achieved by applying Lean at the team or department level, but to achieve system-level change, an organisation must be focused and committed to a common approach to make the wheels of change turn effectively. Making and maintaining gains is difficult in most organisations, but improvement science offers a systematic approach to achieving this. Through a Lean management system, intentionally applied, the authors describe how it is possible to secure and build on the incremental changes that are made by individual teams.

The skill and effort of the individuals, teams, and organisations deserve celebration. This volume seeks to illustrate some of the gains they have achieved. Many other organisations are making similar improvements to the health and care of the unique populations that they serve. The learning from the work described in this book, and work presented in papers and conferences worldwide can give heart to organisations that want to set out on an improvement journey, or which are already on that pathway but want to learn from the experience of others.

The Foundations of Lean Application in Healthcare

The use of the Lean tools and techniques such as 5S, error proofing, visual controls, and standard work is fundamental to the success described by the authors in this book (Stark & Hookway, 2019). These form the basis for the change in practice, and many organisations invest heavily in training in tools and techniques in the early stages of a Lean implementation. The use of tools and techniques can increase understanding and capability, encourage engagement, and create excitement. The approach to Lean can become more sophisticated over time but these early efforts act as the opportunity for practice for every member of the organisation.

Starting with enthusiastic leaders working on real problems increases the credibility of the method. Sponsorship from executives demonstrates the commitment to this way of working and encourages engagement at all levels. One of the most effective supports for organisational change is local stories of success. These need to come from staff, patients, and their families who have participated and benefited from the changes. Sharing the results of an improvement initiative driven by local staff based on real-time data that has resolved a long-standing problem can have an enormous impact. The staff who work on these projects and see the benefits for both staff and patients, often become enthusiastic advocates of Lean methods. This unsolicited endorsement has a positive effect and is less likely to be dismissed than an organisational newsletter attached to an 'all users' e-mail. The effect of personal communication from project team to project team should not be underestimated and contributes to the rapid and effective rollout.

Several contributors described event-focused work on Lean. Events, such as Rapid Process Improvement Workshops (RPIWs) or shorter events can be highly effective if supported and effectively directed. The events allow groups of staff to come together with other stakeholders to assess, reflect, and improve on a process or pathway. These events sometimes happen spontaneously with little pre-existing organisational knowledge because a local leader attends a course, watches a lecture, or reads a relevant textbook. This can work well, but to produce and maintain gains, organisational buy-in can make an enormous difference. Without this engagement and endorsement, it can be difficult for even the most enthusiastic team to maintain service improvements over time if the wider culture does not align with their approach.

In event-focused work, an early and thorough understanding of the importance of scope is critical. This requires adequate work to understand the problem, which must include staff views, objective evidence, and the perspectives and experience of the people who use the service. It is also important to be realistic about what can be achieved in any one event. Many workshop-based initiatives fail through poorly defined aims, but others run into trouble because their scope is too wide. As several examples in this book demonstrate, however, improvement workshops can be linked together to deliver across a wider Value Stream, but careful preparation is required to allow this to work in practice.

Some organisations use external coaches to support their staff for at least the first few events they run. Others decide to focus on training their own staff through a combination of courses and on-the-job learning. These are not mutually exclusive options, and training may be delivered on-site by external coaches who then support early events. Whether external coaches are used or not, early events produce enormous learning. The overall experience reported by the contributors suggests that most organisations will want to become self-sufficient over time, although as this book demonstrates, there is much to be gained from collaboration and peer review.

Agreeing on the Need for Change

In healthcare, informal networks are often faster and more effective than any formal communication channel. It is important to be cognisant of this and the need for an introduction and clear explanation of the need for change. Regardless of the approach, it will be important to first describe the need to change and to develop a compelling and genuinely engaging statement that is clear to all.

The challenges for healthcare services described in Chapter 1, and in many of the contributions, can make it feel obvious that change must happen. Many staff feel under pressure and worry about the service they can deliver. It is common for patients to experience waits and errors are unfortunately frequent in healthcare. Surprisingly, agreement on these problems does not always produce an impetus for change: the source of the problem can feel distant; it may be seen as the responsibility of other teams, other departments, or other services to fix; hospital services may regard it as a community service problem, and community services may feel secondary services need to make improvements, and health services may see social services as failing in their duties. Obtaining acceptance of a collective problem with an agreed direction of travel and shared responsibility can be difficult.

Some challenges feel too big for individual services to influence. Ageing populations and the increase in long-term conditions are societal challenges in many parts of the world. Services can have some influence on preventative activity and early intervention to reduce harm, but there is nothing they can do about population ageing itself. Similarly, publicly funded services depend on government decisions, and therefore political processes and public views on funding. Private services are often limited by insurance company decisions, political views, and available public programmes. All these issues are outside local control. If these external factors are seen as the only possible sources of improvement, service providers can feel unable to act. In the context of services subject to competition, this view can be catastrophic and for publicly funded services, it can result in stagnation.

Organisational decisions and messaging on quality improvement do not remove these external factors, but they can help to return some degree of control. Services can focus on variables they can influence, including their own processes and performance. Identification of a quality improvement method and support for learning and use of this approach can be powerful. Executive groups can support by achieving clarity on priorities. Staff in individual services can build on this, but leaders have an essential role in supporting methods and purposes. This will include agreement on underlying organisational values, which will help to guide staff actions. It can also help to avert some of the concerns that staff may have if they have pre-existing views that Lean approaches are not compatible with healthcare. A statement of values and evidence that executives, managers, and improvement coaches are following these can go a long way to reassuring staff and patient groups about the fit between Lean and healthcare.

Developing Support for Lean in Healthcare

There can be tacit or explicit resistance to the implementation of a structured methodology of quality improvement in a healthcare organisation. Often this arises from understandable scepticism in an organisation that has previous cycles of management or funder-driven initiatives. Experience is that these have often come and gone leaving little trace other than an organisational memory of failed implementations. In the light of this, there is often a powerful desire to ignore the approach and hope that it blows over.

In other instances, staff are concerned that approaches developed in industry will be inappropriate for use in health and social care. They may be anxious that limits will be imposed on their professional decision making, or worried that they will be expected to undertake unreasonable amounts of work, to the detriment of their professional performance and their personal wellbeing. For people with a good working knowledge of Lean, it is tempting to dismiss these concerns as misguided and ill-informed. This view runs into the challenge that some of these problems have arisen in poorly implemented Lean applications in healthcare, so the worries have some basis in fact. Instant dismissal of such concerns risks leading to staff feeling undervalued and ignored and becoming still more convinced that the approach is wrong for healthcare.

Fortunately, there is now a significant body of research and practice by organisations, like Virginia Mason, Catalysis, and Stanford University, demonstrating that Lean can work well in practice. The case studies in this book add to the available information. The contributions in this volume, together with the published research, can give confidence about the value of the method. The authors have also made it clear, however, that organisational context is important, and there are well-researched examples of failures in Lean application (Bateman et al., 2018).

This means that rather than blanket reassurances, it is important to take time to understand concerns. Published guidelines and accruing research evidence on most medical topics already create limits on medical practice. Lean is largely focused on processes, however, so most Lean work does not affect the underlying clinical decision-making: it seeks to deliver value to patients by reducing waste. This is hard to argue against but concerns sometimes come down to views on definitions of 'value'. Staff often prove to be worried that transactional elements of healthcare – time to explain things to a patient, to discuss treatment options, to provide preventative care – will be deemed inefficient, and that time for this will be squeezed in a bid for efficiency. Concerns about Taylorism often emerge, accompanied by worries about 'time and motion' studies.

There is overwhelming evidence that patients value time with professionals and see it as value (Bidmon et al., 2020; Joffe et al., 2003). Work to increase understanding, gain concordance, and reduce relapse is not only valued, but they are also likely to reduce system pressures. No reputable Lean work is likely to remove any of these types of work. Showing that staff are listened to, and that their expertise is respected, will often be reassuring. Reassurance will help some staff to feel more confident about Lean, but many will need to see the approach first-hand and to talk to other staff and patients who have taken part in similar work. As discussed below, this is a good reason to prioritise high-profile pieces of work that can then be shared across the organisation.

There can also be worries that outside experts will apply unproven theories to the staff members' areas of expertise. Senior clinical staff, including doctors, sometimes see no role for them in the analysis of the process. Their training and experience have not always helped them to think about health services as a series of enormously complex and intersecting processes. It is common for specialist staff to be unaware of why delays and problems occur, and to have truly little knowledge of processes in other departments. Work in imaging departments, booking services, laboratory services, and ambulance services, may have an enormous impact on their own work, and vice versa, without them being aware of it. Supporting people to take the time to meet with other services, to see what they do and how their processes interact with their own can be time well spent. Crucially it can let people see how processes that appear reasonable can work against systems in other parts of a patient journey to produce confusion, error, and delay.

Service managers are not immune to concerns about change. Senior positions within healthcare organisations are often held by individuals who have not had the opportunity to work in a different way (Mann, 2015). It can cause anxiety if their favoured style of management is challenged by a new approach. The move to be humbler rather than heroic leaders, described in several of the chapters, is vital for the success of any improvement programme. Many current leaders, however, have been selected because of their ability to make decisions and to be seen to solve problems. Delegating authority and focusing on change methods can feel alien.

Cultivating curiosity about how things happen in practice, regardless of the stated policy, is an important part of leaders' work in the new healthcare models. Managers all want their service to be successful, to support staff, and to provide what is needed by patients. If they have developed as leaders in a different system, they will need support to cultivate an environment within which ideas are grown and shared, and then tested. Creating the conditions in which ideas for improvement can arise from anywhere in the organisation rather than being centrally decided by distant experts. Supporting managers to undertake that journey alongside service providers who are given permission to make changes is an exciting opportunity to gain experience together and respect each other's unique roles and positions, on the most personal of levels. Training and coaching must be available for managers at least as much as any other staff group.

Often a few staff members prove to be more worried about change of any kind. This can be an unspoken internal position, or it can relate to concerns about personal impact. This is more difficult to work with, particularly if these staff members are very senior in the organisation and are used to having the last word. It can also be challenging if the staff member cannot explain, or prefers not to explain, the reason for their concerns. Explicit discussion of the reasons for change and the pressures on healthcare can often help, as can documenting the problems experienced by patients. Bringing in the patient voice to explain the difficulties in navigating systems and the impact of delays and confusion can be valuable. All of these show the need for change. For the very few people who oppose any change at all, their concerns and sometimes frank opposition need to be recognised and discussed openly, but as with any individual in a large organisation, their concerns are not a reason to stop work but a potential barrier to be understood and managed. As evidence of positive impact in the organisation emerges, many staff with initial concerns will change their position and sometimes become enthusiasts of the work.

A Sense of Place in Lean

Each healthcare system will feel that it is unique, and no service will be the same as another. The local context – location, population, funding, language and culture, national and local history – will affect how it sees itself and how it is viewed by others. By building on this unique history and sense of place and by embracing the local characteristics and appetite for change, the healthcare organisation can encourage the embedding of quality improvement. Healthcare organisations are often the biggest employers in a local area and have a special relationship with the local population as can be seen from public concerns and campaigns when services change. Good local delivery needs close working with key partners like local authorities, universities, and other training institutions.

These chapters exude a sense of pride. The efforts of many thousands of individuals across numerous organisations have been captured as illustrations of the implementation of Lean in healthcare. Pride comes from a recognition of success as a direct result of personal effort, to deliver an important aim. Being associated with something successful that has a benefit to others is a positive experience and creates a sense of belonging and camaraderie which lasts longer than any improvement event. Staff will go still further if they find that their personal passion for service improvement is shared by their colleagues and by their organisation. Producing a culture that allows the use of the creativity and innovation of staff is an important part of supporting an effective improvement approach (Breckenridge et al., 2019).

Being part of a high-performing healthcare organisation creates an impetus and desire to be part of something good. It helps to attract good people to already good services, and the impact can be positive on recruitment and retention. People will also respond well to an organisation that works hard to demonstrate their value, and the pride within an organisation can manifest in a genuine sense of family.

Leaders often underestimate the importance of thanks. Simple, personal, and authentic gestures of thanks are hugely memorable for staff and the positive experience will be shared around an organisation more quickly than any staff ceremony. Being available to value staff and being an active supporter of their improvement journeys is an important leadership behaviour which should be practised and enjoyed. There is more to learn from being where the work happens than in any long performance meeting. This active engagement of managers with service delivery is one of the actions that can lead to a sense of place, a feeling of 'how things are done here'.

Encouraging publication, presentations, and visitors is another exciting way to develop pride in the work of an organisation as well as sharing ideas and learning together. The application of the initiative of others, and sharing your work in turn with others, and the recognition that something that you have done may be important to another health system, in another country, is an invaluable opportunity to develop a sense of pride. This volume is part of that process of sharing and spreading experience in the application of Lean in healthcare.

Spreading Improvement Across an Organisation

Undertaking quality improvement and producing measurable benefits for patients feels empowering and exciting. Spreading this across organisations to produce scale and spread is challenging, but essential. Much improvement work is undertaken on local processes in areas separated from other parts of the healthcare system. Mental health initiatives for example may remain within this sector, rather than influencing the wider healthcare system. Several chapters describe successful sector or area-specific initiatives which have been successful. Spreading the benefits requires intentional effort and service leaders can help to make these wider connections. Creating networks of improvers across an organisation allows the language, expertise, and ideas to be shared and encouraged. Bringing in trusted colleagues as outside eyes can be a highly effective way of creating excitement and sharing knowledge across an organisation, and independent of role or position.

Many organisations invest heavily in opportunities for leaders to understand the basics of Lean methodology but are not always supportive of the practice of these skills. The development of a network across an organisation of these leaders to create safe spaces to participate in workshops, coach at huddles, and develop their own fresh style of leadership can be encouraged.

Creating regular monthly reports of improvement to the wider organisation is another opportunity for senior leaders and executives to model their commitment to the approach, coming together to celebrate the work that has been undertaken by staff. This can be extended to the Board of the organisation: there is a powerful impact from hearing the voices and the enthusiasm of teams who have made real changes.

Aligning a management system and paying attention to flow across departments also pays dividends. Several chapters discuss the role of clarity in values, aims, and 'true north'. True north is the idea that the organisation agrees to use as the compass to guide its development (Akao, 2004). Clarity on this enables staff at all levels to make decisions and to be confident that they are in line with the organisation's aims and priorities. The management system approaches linked to metrics described in the contributions in the book help to draw these ideas together and embed these approaches to the delivery and maintenance of gains in the wider organisation.

Engaging Strategic Partners in Lean Implementation

Many of the chapters describe the involvement of external training partners with experience of Lean application in healthcare, referred to here as 'strategic partners'. As noted earlier, this can be valuable for training and early improvement events, but it can also provide a long-term support and coaching relationship. For organisations that chose to link to external organisations, it is important to think of potential partners as more than training providers and to assess how their methods and approach fit with that of the host organisation.

Some healthcare services want to try out individual methods, train a small group of staff or deliver one or two isolated events. Others are looking to deliver more widespread applications of Lean or to move to a Lean management system. This spectrum implies quite diverse needs and a different set of demands on a strategic partner. Offering training to one group of staff, delivering training in individual methods, or facilitating one or two events may be comfortably accommodated by many providers, but wholesale change across a major organisation or individual coaching of a chief executive may need a distinct set of skills that may require a larger team or a different approach.

One of the challenges for organisations considering a Lean implementation may be that they do not yet know how widely they want to use Lean methods. This affects the type of strategic partner that may be sought. Some strategic partners focus on large-scale organisational change and like to work with an organisation over years. Others may be happy to offer small-scale support for events or training but may be less able to scale up over time, requiring a change of contractor.

When looking for wider or long-term involvement, a key early task is for any strategic partner to take stock of the current attitudes and applications of quality improvement in the organisation they are supporting. This is important as the work must begin in an environment that is ready for, and open to change. A diagnostic evaluation of 'readiness' which includes in-depth conversations with a cross-section of staff is key to the success of co-producing a plan which is both true to Lean values and bespoke to the organisation. This also provides an opportunity for the two parties to ensure that their interests are aligned. Either the host organisation or the strategic partner may decide that there is not a good fit. This should not be taken as a failure on an insult: it is better for both parties to move on to work with people who better fit with their aspirations and plans in the case of the host organisation, and with their experience, expertise, and approach in the case of the strategic partner.

When considering engaging a strategic partner, there is a range of useful questions to consider. None of the questions implies that one answer is correct: what works for one host organisation will not necessarily be right for another.

ISSUES TO CONSIDER WHEN CONTRACTING WITH A STRATEGIC PARTNER

What is the experience of this partner? Are they a generic provider that offers Lean training and advice to all industries, or a healthcare specialist?

What is the size of their organisation? Are they an individual consultant, part of a small firm or larger network, or a major organisation with many associates?

Is the main contractor likely to be constant over time? Will there be one or more named people who work with the organisation or is there likely to be a range of people over time?

What is the experience of previous clients? Speaking to clients can give a good feel for the approach of the strategic partner, assuming the situations are similar.

What is their relative focus on Lean methods, improvement events, and management systems? Some providers may have more interest and experience in one area, others on more or all of these.

Will there be a staff legacy? Does the partner support creation of an in-house improvement capacity or is their focus on direct provision of improvement support?

Are there ongoing licence fees? If you use training materials from the partner, what are the cost implications?

Do they offer executive coaching? As the accounts in the book make clear, the senior leadership group in an organisation plays a key role in Lean. The leadership group or chief executive may want individual or group support during the change.

Conclusions

The accounts in this volume provide descriptions of the positive impact and dexterity of the Lean approach when applied to healthcare. When taken together, the work reported by these authors demonstrates how leadership, combined with the use of quality improvement methods and staff who are supported to apply their expert knowledge to the improvement of their own services, can produce large and lasting changes.

This book contributes to connecting leaders, practitioners, and healthcare staff to allow them to learn together and share their experience. Previous generations of Lean teachers in healthcare came from industry. There remains an important need for healthcare to learn from industrial applications of Lean and for staff with industrial backgrounds to be able to share their knowledge and experience. There is also a generational change as there are now also leaders and coaches who have learnt Lean from staff who have only ever applied it in healthcare. Continuing cross-fertilisation of Lean methods and expertise across industry remains valuable but inevitably some degree of specialisation will continue.

Future healthcare leaders will have lived experience of the challenges and benefits of implementing a Lean approach at scale. They will recognise that their job is never done and, although recognising that perfection can never be reached, will strive to master the continuous implementation through the development of their teams. Graduates from Lean healthcare programmes are already being appointed into more senior positions of influence within organisations, and that will help to embed the methodology for the future.

The most effective healthcare organisations are supported by clinicians at the most senior level who remain fully engaged and confident to cede power to carers to change clinical practice. This does not always sit easily with previous training and power relationships and it is important to acknowledge the efforts of senior clinical staff in learning to look at systems as well as individual clinical care. The enormous value of the enthusiasm of junior doctors, nurses, and allied healthcare professionals in training for this approach should not be underestimated. It will be important in the future to have these approaches endorsed and taught by institutions that recognise the value of continuous change.

These chapters emphasise the importance of leadership behaviours to the success of any Lean improvement approach. Much communication is now electronic, with increasing use of blogs, vox pops, and social media to share personalised messages quickly and effectively. However, many of these authors talk about the importance of the visibility of leadership. This refers to the real-life and personal opportunity for staff to interact with leaders who show curiosity and genuine interest in improvement work. Whether that is as chief executive, or team leader, there are important messages that must be communicated. Leaders act as connectors and communicators and can add vital value to improvement efforts by making the purpose of change clear, and by demonstrating consistent organisational values. Creating a psychologically safe environment where improvement can flourish and staff can make small experiments to test their ideas for change is the role of leaders at all levels across an organisation. By modelling this, senior managers allow staff to highlight their experience, build connections, and develop the openness and sharing that is required for success.

The authors in this book also explain that the large-scale application of Lean is challenging, and that dogged application is required over time. Adequate attention to organisational context, local culture, and the role of senior clinical staff is needed. Several authors also noted the need to support managers. It is easy to assume that by virtue of their position, managers and clinical team leaders will be able to adapt to new working methods. This is not always the case and people who trained in one type of management system may find alterations challenging. Good support and coaching for this group pay dividends, as illustrated by the gains made by teams reporting in this book.

Quality Improvement methods offer benefits to organisations, and Lean has been used successfully in different organisations and settings. The accounts in this book emphasise the importance of context, but also show the commonalities in implementation. Individual methods can be used with benefit, but to deliver scale and service-wide impact, linking approaches across an organisation by investment, coaching, and sharing of success is required. This book contributes to this and acts as a base on which to build future sharing of learning and success.

Learning Points

- The chapter authors describe success with the use of Lean in different settings, and at different scales.
- Lean can be used at the team level, across Value Streams and service groups, and organisation wide.
- Embedding respect for staff in Lean implementations is essential. Patient experience of services and ideas for improvement are also invaluable resources for change.
- Change can be difficult and careful analysis of problems and identification of barriers to change may be needed. There is not a one size fits all response to concerns, and all concerns must be taken seriously, considered, and resolved.
- The senior leadership team of an organisation plays an essential role in creating the conditions for change and in modelling the required behaviours.
- Using a Lean management system can take time but can help to produce and maintain organisation-wide gains.

Bibliography

Akao, Y. (2004). *Hoshin Kanri. Policy Deployment for Successful TQM*. CRC Press.

Barnas, K., & Adams, E. (2014). *Beyond Heroes: A Lean Management System for Healthcare*. ThedaCare Center for Healthcare Value.

Bateman, N., Radnor, Z., & Glennon, R. (2018). Editorial: The landscape of Lean across public services. *Public Money & Management*, 38(1), 1–4. https://doi.org/10.1080/09540962.2018.1389482

Bidmon, S., Elshiewy, O., Terlutter, R., & Bortug, Y. (2020). What patients value in physicians: analyzing drivers of patient satisfaction using physician-rating website data. *Journal of Medical Internet Research*, 22(2), e13830. https://doi.org/10.2196/13830

Breckenridge, J. P., Gray, N., Toma, M., Ashmore, S., Glassborow, R., Stark, C., & Renfrew, M. J. (2019). Motivating Change: a grounded theory of how to achieve large-scale, sustained change, co-created with improvement organisations across the UK. *BMJ Open Quality*, *8*(2), e000553. https://doi.org/10.1136/bmjoq-2018-000553

Gabow, P. A., & Goodman, P. L. (2014). *The Lean Prescription*. Productivity Press.

Graban, M. (2017). *Lean Hospitals: Improving Quality, Patient Safety, and Employee Engagement* (3rd ed.). CRC Press.

Joffe, S., Manocchia, M., Weeks, J. C., & Cleary, P. D. (2003). What do patients value in their hospital care? An empirical perspective on autonomy centred bioethics. *Journal of Medical Ethics*, *29*(2), 103–108. http://www.jstor.org/stable/27719024

Mann, D. (2015). *Creating a Lean Culture: Tools to Sustain Lean Conversions*. CRC Press.

Mead, E., Stark, C., & Thompson, M. (2017). Creating and leading a quality improvement culture at scale. *Management in Healthcare*, *2*(2), 115–124.

Plsek, P. (2014). *Accelerating Health Care Transformation with Lean and Innovation: The Virginia Mason Experience*. CRC Press.

Stark, C., & Hookway, G. (2019). *Applying Lean in Health and Social Care Services*. Routledge.

Toussaint, J. S., & Adams, E. (2015). *Management on the Mend*. ThedaCare Center for Healthcare Value.

Elaine Mead is an executive director of Improvement, Care and Compassion, IC&C, an organisation committed to supporting leaders on their improvement journey across the UK and Europe. She has worked as Executive Sensei for National Health Service (NHS) Improvement in England and is a Leadership Faculty member of the Institute of Health Improvement. Elaine is a founding member of the Catalysis European CEO Forum and continues to connect and support colleagues from across Europe, from her base in Scotland. She is a certified Lean Leader from Tees, Esk and Wear Valley NHS Foundation Trust having had a close association with the Virginia Mason Institute. Elaine is also a Fellow of, and tutor for, the Institute of Quality and Safety (ISQua). Prior to establishing IC&C Elaine was chief executive for NHS Highland for eight years where she led the development of the Highland Quality Approach to improve the quality of care based on increasing value. She has over 30 years of experience of working in the NHS including as a clinician and in executive roles.

Cameron Stark, MB ChB, MPH, MSc (Dist), MRCPsych, FFPH, is an Honorary Reader and Part-time Lecturer at the University of the Highlands and Islands (UHI) Outer Hebrides. Stark leads the UHI postgraduate module on the application of Lean in healthcare. After graduating from the University of Glasgow, he trained in psychiatry and public health and worked as an NHS Public Health Doctor for over 30 years. Stark was the quality improvement science lead for NHS Highland and trained as a Lean leader with Tees, Esk and Wear Valley NHS Foundation Trust. He has published over 60 papers in peer-reviewed journals and has written or edited 5 previous textbooks.

Maimie Thompson is an engagement and communication specialist currently working in healthcare planning and the use of digital technologies in the public sector. She has contributed to a range of publications including as a co-author of a chapter for the *International Handbook on Integrated Care* (second edition) about Scotland. Maimie is a certified Lean leader and a former recipient of NHS Scotland's manager of the year award for her work on unscheduled care.

Index

Printed in the United States
by Baker & Taylor Publisher Services